Fire & E

Fire & Blood
The Burning of Washington & the Battle of New Orleans, 1814, Through the Eyes of a Young British Soldier

George R. Gleig

Fire & Blood: The Burning of Washington & the Battle of New Orleans, 1814, Through the Eyes of a Young British Soldier
by George R. Gleig

Originally published in 1827 under the title:
The Campaigns of the British Army at Washington and New Orleans

Published by Leonaur Ltd

Copyright in this form © 2007 Leonaur Ltd

ISBN: 978-1-84677-163-7 (hardcover)
ISBN: 978-1-84677-161-3 (softcover)

http://www.leonaur.com

Publisher's Notes

In the interests of authenticity, the spellings, grammar and place names used have been retained from the original editions.

The opinions of the authors represent a view of events in which he was a participant related from his own perspective, as such the text is relevant as an historical document.

The views expressed in this book are not necessarily those of the publisher.

Contents

Publisher's Note	7
A Young Soldier Without a War	11
The Battlefields of Southern France	20
The March to the Ships	28
Ocean & Island	35
Towards the West Indies	43
Bermuda	53
Landing in America	62
Marches & Skirmishes	71
The Battle of Bladensburg	81
The Burning of Washington	91
Fighting Outside the Capital	101
Afloat Again	111
Attack on Baltimore	121
Back to the Ships	131
To Sea Again	140
We Battle an American Privateer	149
Jamaica	159
To New Orleans	167
Marching Towards the Attack	180
Hand to Hand Fighting	189
Piquets & Raiders	202
Before the Breastworks	209
Storm & Slaughter	215
Defeat & Retreat	225
The Seige of Mobile	235
Peace	239
To England	245
An Overview	248

Publisher's Note

In the course of this comprehensive account of his experiences during the campaigns for Washington and New Orleans, George R. Gleig reveals very little about himself.

George Robert Gleig was born 20th April, 1796, in Stirling, Scotland, to clergyman George Gleig, later Bishop of Brechin, and his wife Janet. George Robert Gleig became not only a soldier but also a writer of military history who chronicled his own experiences and 'ghost wrote' the accounts of others, and, like his father, a noted clergyman.

In 1813, a month after Wellington won the battle of Vittoria, Gleig, a student of divinity, gave up a scholarship to Balliol College to join Wellington's army as an Ensign in the 85th Regiment of Foot (Bucks. Volunteers). After the battle of Toulouse he was sent to the war against the United States, where he fought in five engagements—Bladensburg, Baltimore, Washington, New Orleans and Mobile—and was wounded three times. He resumed his scholarship at Oxford in 1816.

Gleig married in 1819, while at Oxford, and, with a B.A. and M.A., he took holy orders in 1820. He held several posts as curate and then became Rector of Ivychurch. He began writing articles on his Peninsular War experiences for Blackwood's Magazine and these were collected into a book entitled *The Subaltern* (1825). In 1827 he published an account of his experiences in the USA—the book you are now holding. By 1832 Gleig was Chaplain to the Chelsea Hospital (the Chelsea Pensioners)

In 1829 he was invited to meet Wellington, and became his regular house-guest. Gleig enjoyed an excellent relationship with the Duke, but nevertheless Wellington still issued a public reprimand to Gleig in 1840 over his proposals for the education of NCOs and private soldiers.

Gleig was appointed Chaplain-General of the Forces in 1844, and resigned the post in 1875; from 1846 to 1857 he was Inspector-General of Military Schools.

He was a well-known author, mainly on military subjects and was a frequent contributor to reviews and magazines. In addition to books already mentioned he also wrote *The Adventures Of A Light Dragoon*, published by Leonaur, and lives of Warren Hastings, Robert Clive, Wellington and other military commanders, Chelsea Pensioners, etc.

He died at Stratfield Turgis, Hampshire in 1888.

The Leonaur Editors

Introduction

The following Narrative contains, it is believed, the only connected and authentic account, which has yet been given, of the expedition directed against Washington and New Orleans, towards the close of the late American war. It has been compiled, not from memory alone, but from a journal kept by the author whilst engaged in the enterprise; and as the adventures of each were faithfully noted down as they occurred, and such remarks made upon passing events as suggested themselves to his mind at the moment, the public may rely with confidence upon general correctness of the details.

The issues of the expedition were not, indeed, of the most gratifying nature, but it is hoped that a plain relation of the proceedings of those to whom it was intrusted, will not, on that account, prove uninteresting; whilst nothing can be more evident than that the portion of our history which it embraces ought not to be overlooked because it is little conducive to the encouragement of national vanity. It was chiefly, indeed, upon this account, as well as with a view to redeem from an oblivion which they hardly merit, the actions and sufferings of a few brave men, that the Narrative now submitted to the public was written.

George R. Gleig

Chapter 1
A Young Soldier Without a War

A revolution must occur in the condition and sentiments of mankind more decided than we have any reason to expect that the lapse of ages will produce, before the mighty events which distinguished the spring of 1814 shall be spoken of in other terms than those of unqualified admiration. It was then that Europe, which during so many years had groaned beneath the miseries of war, found herself at once, and to her remotest recesses, blessed with the prospect of a sure and permanent peace. Princes, who had dwelt in exile till the very hope of restoration to power began to depart from them, beheld themselves unexpectedly replaced on the thrones of their ancestors; dynasties, which the will of one man had erected, disappeared with the same abruptness with which they had arisen; and the influence of changes which a quarter of a century of rapine and conquest had produced in the arrangements of general society, ceased, as if by magic, to be felt, or at least to be acknowledged. It seemed, indeed, as if all which had been passing during the last twenty or thirty years, had passed not in reality, but in a dream; so perfectly unlooked for were the issues of a struggle, to which, whatever light we may regard it, the history of the whole world presents no parallel.

At the period above alluded to, it was the writer's fortune to form one of a body of persons in whom the unexpected cessation of hostilities may be supposed to have excited sensations more powerful and more mixed than those to which the common occurrences of life are accustomed to give birth. He was then attached to that portion of the Peninsular army to which the siege of Bayonne had been intrusted; and on the 28th of April beheld, in common with his comrades, the tri-coloured flag, which, for upwards of two months, had waved defiance from the battlements, give place to the ancient *drapeau blanc* of the Bourbons. That such a spectacle could be regarded by any British soldier without stirring up in him strong feelings of national pride and exultation, is not to be imagined. I believe, indeed, that there was not a man in our ranks, however humble his station, to whose bosom these feelings were a stranger.

But the excitation of the moment having passed away, other and no less powerful feelings succeeded; and they were painful, or the reverse, according as they ran in one or other of the channels into which the situations and prospects of individuals not unnaturally guided them. By such as had been long absent from their homes, the idea of enjoying once more the society of friends and relatives, was hailed with a degree of delight too engrossing to afford room for the occurrence of any other anticipations; to those who had either no homes to look to, or had quitted them only a short time ago, the thoughts of revisiting England came mixed with other thoughts, little gratifying, because at variance with all their dreams of advancement and renown.

For my own part I candidly confess, that though I had just cause to look forward to a return to the bosom of my family with as much satisfaction as most men, the restoration of peace excited in me sensations of a very equivocal nature.

At the age of eighteen, and still enthusiastically attached to my profession, neither the prospect of a reduction to half-pay, nor the expectation of a long continuance in a subaltern situation, were to me productive of any pleasurable emotions; and hence, though I entered heartily into all the arrangements by which those about me strove to evince their gratification at the glorious termination of the war, it must be acknowledged that I did so, without experiencing much of the satisfaction with the semblance of which my outward behaviour might be marked.

Such being my own feelings, and the feelings of the great majority of those immediately around me, it was but natural that we should turn our views to the only remaining quarter of the globe in which the flame of war still continued to burn. Though at peace with France, England, we remembered; was not yet at peace with the United States; and reasoning, not as statesmen but as soldiers, we concluded that she was not now likely to make peace with that nation till she should be able to do so upon her own terms. Having such an army on foot, what line of policy could appear so natural or so judicious as that she should employ, if not the whole, at all events a large proportion of it, in chastising an enemy, than whom none had ever proved more vindictive or more ungenerous? Our view of the matter accordingly was, that some fifteen or twenty thousand men would be forthwith embarked on board of ship and transported to the other side of the Atlantic; that the war would there be carried on with a vigour conformable to the dignity and resources of the country which waged it; and that no mention of peace would be made till our general should be in a situation to dictate its conditions in the enemy's capital.

Whether any design of the kind was ever seriously entertained, or whether men merely asserted as a truth what they earnestly desired to be such, I know not; but the white flag had hardly been hoisted on the citadel of Bayonne, when a rumour became prevalent that an extensive encampment of troops, destined for the American war, was actually forming in the vicinity of Bordeaux. A variety of causes led me to anticipate that the corps to which I was attached would certainly be employed upon that service. In the progress of the war which had been just brought to a conclusion, we had not suffered so severely as many other corps; and though not excelling in numbers, it is but justice to affirm that a more effective or better organized battalion could not be found in the whole army. We were all, moreover, from our commanding officer down to the youngest ensign, anxious to gather a few more laurels, even in America; and we had good reason to believe that those in power were not indisposed to gratify our inclinations. Under these circumstances we clung with fondness to the hope that our martial career had not yet come to a close; and employed the space which intervened between the eventful 28th of April and the 8th of the following month, chiefly in forming guesses as to the point of attack towards which it was likely that we should be turned.

Though there was peace between the French and British nations, the form of hostilities was so far kept up between the garrison of Bayonne and the army encamped around it, that it was only by an especial treaty that the former were allowed to send out parties for the purpose of collecting forage and provisions from the adjacent country. The foraging parties, however, being permitted to proceed in any direction most convenient to themselves, the supplies of corn and grass, which had heretofore proved barely sufficient for our own horses and cattle, soon began to fail, and it was found necessary to move more than one brigade to a distance from the city. Among others, the brigade of which my regiment formed a part, received orders on the 7th of May to fall back on the road towards Passages. These orders we obeyed on the following morning; and after an agreeable march of fifteen or sixteen miles, pitched our tents in a thick wood, about halfway between the village of Bedart and the town of St. Jean de Luz. In this position we remained for nearly a week, our expectations of employment on the other side of the Atlantic becoming daily less and less sanguine, till at length all doubts on the subject were put an end to by the sudden arrival of a dispatch, which commanded us to set out with as little delay as possible towards Bordeaux.

It was on the evening of the 14th that the route was received, and on the following morning, at daybreak, we commenced our march. The country through which we moved had nothing in it, unconnected with past events, calculated in any extraordinary degree to attract attention. Behind us, indeed, rose the Pyrenees in all their grandeur, forming, on that side, a noble boundary to the prospect; and on our left was the sea, a boundary different it is true in kind, though certainly not less magnificent. But, excepting at these two extremities, there was nothing in the landscape on which the eye loved particularly to rest, because the country, though pretty enough, has none of that exquisite richness and luxuriance which we had been led to expect as characteristic of the South of France. The houses, too, being all in a ruinous and dilapidated condition, reminded us more forcibly of the scenes of violence and outrage which had been lately acted among them, than of those ideas of rural contentment and innocence which various tales and melodramas had taught us to associate in our own minds with thoughts of the land of the vine.

Regarded, however, in connexion with past events, the scene was indeed most interesting; though to a stranger fresh from England—a man, we will suppose, of retired and peaceful habits, I can readily imagine that it would have been productive of much pain; for on each side of the road, in whatever direction we cast our eyes, and as far as the powers of vision extended, we beheld cottages unroofed and in ruins, chateaux stripped of their doors and windows, gardens laid waste, the walls demolished, and the fruit-trees cut down; whole plantations levelled, and vineyards trodden under foot. Here and there, likewise, a redoubt or breastwork presented itself; whilst caps, broken firelocks, pieces of clothing, and accoutrements scattered about in profusion, marked the spots where the strife had been most determined, and where many a fine fellow had met his fate. Our journey lay over a field of battle, through the entire extent of which the houses were not only thoroughly gutted (to use a vulgar but most expressive phrase), but for the most part were riddled with cannon-shot. Round some of the largest, indeed, there was not a wall nor a tree which did not present evident proofs of its having been converted into a temporary place of defence, whilst the deep ruts in what had once been lawns and flower-gardens, showed that all their beauty had not protected them from being destroyed by the rude passage of heavy artillery.

Immediately beyond the village of Bedart such spectacles were particularly frequent. It was here, it may be remembered, that in the preceding month of December there had been fighting for four successive days; and the number of little hillocks now within our view; from under most of which legs and arms were beginning to show themselves, as well as the other objects which I have attempted to describe, sufficiently attested the obstinacy with which that fighting had been maintained.

In the bosom of a man of peace it is very conceivable that all this would have excited feelings exceedingly painful; in ours, such feelings were overborne by others of a very different nature. If we gazed with peculiar interest upon one hovel more than upon another, it was because some of us had there maintained ourselves; if we endeavoured to count the number of shot-holes in any wall, or the breaks in any hedge, it was because we had stood behind it when "the iron hail" fell thick and fast around us. Our thoughts, in short, had more of exultation in them than of sorrow; for though now and then, when the name of a fallen comrade was mentioned, it was accompanied with a "poor fellow" the conversation soon returned again to the exploits and hair-breadth escapes of the survivors. On the whole, therefore, our march was one of deep interest and high excitement, feelings which did not entirely evaporate when we halted, about two hours after noon, at the village of Anglet.

We found this village in the condition in which it was to be expected that a place of so much importance during the progress of the late siege would be found, in other words, completely metamorphosed into a chain of petty posts. Being distant from the outworks of Bayonne not more than a mile and a half, and standing upon the great road by which all the supplies for the left of the British army were brought up, no means, as may be supposed, had been neglected, which art or nature could supply, towards rendering it as secure against a sudden excursion of the garrison as might be.

About one hundred yards in front of it felled trees were laid across the road, with their branches turned towards the town, forming what soldiers, in the language of their profession, term an abattis. Forty or fifty yards in rear of this a ditch was dug, and a breastwork thrown up, from behind which a party might do great execution upon any body of men struggling to force their way over that impediment.

On each side of the highway again, where the ground rises into little eminences, redoubts and batteries were erected, so as to command the whole with a heavy flanking fire; while every house and hovel lying at all within the line of expected operations was loop-holed, and otherwise put in a posture of defence. But upon the fortification of the church a more than ordinary degree of care seemed to have been bestowed.

As it stood upon a little eminence in the middle of the hamlet, it was no hard matter to convert it into a tolerably regular fortress, which might serve the double purpose of a magazine for warlike stores and a post of defence against the enemy. With this view the churchyard was surrounded by a row of stout palings, called in military phraseology stockades, from certain openings in which the muzzles of half a dozen pieces of light artillery protruded. The walls of the edifice itself were, moreover, strengthened by an embankment of earth to the height of perhaps four or five feet from the ground, above which narrow openings were made, in order to give to its garrison an opportunity of levelling their muskets; while on the top of the tower a small howitzer was mounted, from which either shot or shell could be thrown with effect into any of the lanes or passes near. It is probably needless to add that the interior arrangements of this house of God had undergone a change as striking as that which affected its exterior. Barrels of gunpowder, with piles of balls of all sizes and dimensions, now occupied the spaces where worshippers had often crowded; and the very altar was heaped up with spunges, wadding, and other implements necessary in case of an attack.

I have been thus minute in my description of Anglet, because what has been said of it will apply more or less exactly to every village, hamlet, or cluster of cottages, within the compass of what were called the lines. It is true that neither here nor elsewhere, excepting at one particular point, and that on the opposite side of the river, were any serious intentions entertained of broaching or storming the place; and that the sole object of these preparations was to keep the enemy within his works, and to cut him off from all communication with the surrounding country. But to effect even this end, the utmost vigilance and precaution were necessary, not only because the number of troops employed on the service was hardly adequate to discharge it, but because the garrison hemmed in was well known to be at once numerous and enterprising. The reader may accordingly judge what appearance a country presented which, to the extent of fifteen or twenty miles round, was thus treated; where every house was fortified, every road blocked up, every eminence mined with fieldworks, and every place swarming with armed men. Nor was its aspect less striking by night than by day. Gaze where he might, the eye of the spectator then rested upon some portion of one huge circle of fires, by the glare of which the white tents or rudely constructed huts of the besiegers were from time to time made visible.

While things continued thus, the condition of the peaceful inhabitant of this district could hardly fail to be one of extreme discomfort. Of these the greater number had indeed fled on the advance of the British army, leaving their houses and effects a prey to the conquerors; but there were some who, having probably no place of refuge to retire to, remained in their homes, and threw themselves upon our mercy for protection.

It is not requisite that I should now inform the reader of the strict discipline which Lord Wellington preserved in every division of his army; his first step, on entering France, had been to inform the people that against them no violence was intended; and the assurance thus given, was in no instance, at least wantonly, violated. But, however orderly the conduct of an invading force may be, their very presence must occasion a thousand inconveniences to those upon whom they are quartered; not the least distressing of which is, perhaps, the feeling of degradation which the consciousness of being in the power of armed foreigners can hardly fail to produce. Then there is the total destruction of all domestic comfort, which the occupation of a man's house by large bodies of soldiers produces; the liability to which the females, in particular, are exposed to insult from the common troopers; and the dread of vengeance from any delinquent on whom their complaints may have brought down chastisement, all these things must and do create a degree of misery, of which the inhabitants of Great Britain may thank God that they know nothing except by name. In the vicinity of Bayonne, moreover, the country people lived in daily and nightly expectation of finding themselves involved in all the horrors and dangers of a battle. Sorties were continually looked for, and however these might terminate, the non-combatants felt that they must be equally the sufferers. Nay, it was no uncommon ground of complaint among them, that even the total defeat of our forces would bring with it no relief, because, by remaining to receive us, they had disobeyed the proclamations of Marshal Soult, and were consequently liable to punishment as traitors.

CHAPTER 2
The Battlefields of Southern France

A soon as the bustle of encamping was over, and my time absolutely at my own disposal, I took advantage of an offered passport, and proceeded into Bayonne. It will be readily believed that I entered this city with feelings very different from those of a common traveller. Having lain before it as a besieger for upwards of two months, its shops, its trade, its public buildings and places of amusement were to me objects of, comparatively speaking, little interest or curiosity. Its fortifications and means of defence were, in truth, what I was principally anxious to examine. Hitherto I could judge of them only from outward appearances and vague reports; and now that an opportunity offered of so doing with greater accuracy, I confess that my inclination prompted me to embrace that opportunity, rather than to hunt for pictures which I could not value, or fatigue my imagination by endeavouring to discover fine specimens of architecture amidst heavy and ill-built churches.

It is not my intention to attempt any scientific or technical review of the works which a very natural curiosity tempted me to examine; partly because I confess myself little competent to the task and partly because, were the contrary the case, I am inclined to believe that such a review would not prove very interesting to the public in general. Enough is done if I endeavour to impress my reader with as many of the feelings which I then experienced, as may be done by detailing them; and, at the same time, enable him to form some general idea of a place before whose walls no trifling quantity of British blood has been spilt.

The city of Bayonne stands, as everybody knows, upon the Adour, about six or eight miles from the point where that river falls into the sea. On the southern or Spanish bank, where the whole of the city, properly so called, is built, the country, to the distance of two or three miles from the walls, is perfectly flat and the soil sandy, and apparently not very productive. On the bank the ground rises rather abruptly from the brink of the stream, sloping upwards likewise from the sea, till you arrive at the pinnacle upon which the citadel is erected, and which hangs immediately over the town. Thus, though the Adour in fact separates the city from the suburbs and citadel, yet as the ramparts of the former extend to the water's edge on both sides, and as those of the latter continue the sweep from points immediately opposite, the general appearance presented is that of one considerable town, with a broad river flowing through the middle of it.

It will be seen, even from this short and imperfect sketch, that its situation gives to Bayonne, considered as a military post, a superiority over most cities; inasmuch as it affords peculiar facilities towards rendering it a place of great strength. On one side there is a plain, always accounted by engineers the most convenient for the construction of fortifications; on the other an eminence, lofty enough to command the surrounding country, and at the same time sufficiently level at the summit to receive the walls of a fortress, powerful at once from its position and regularity. But the great strength of Bayonne arose at this juncture not so much from its original defences as from the numerous outworks which had been lately added to it. It was along the course of the Adour, as the reader will probably recollect, or rather between the Adour and the Nieve, that Soult formed his famous intrenched camp. The right of this chain of stupendous works rested upon the city, the importance of which was consequently much increased; and as the capture of it would have occasioned not only the loss of a town, but the turning of the whole position, no pains were spared in rendering it as nearly impregnable as possible. That I may convey some notion to the minds of others of the nature of these works, I will describe the aspect which they presented to myself, as I rode from Anglet towards the city.

When I had proceeded about a mile and a half beyond our advanced posts, I found myself in front of the first line of defence. This consisted of a battery mounting three eighteen-pounders, upon the road, flanked by other batteries, one on each side; all so placed as that whichsoever of them should be attacked, it might be defended by a cross-fire from the rest. These were of course additionally strengthened by ditches and felled trees; but they were open in the rear; and though very formidable to an assailing party, yet, when taken, could have been of small service to the conquerors, being themselves exposed to the fire of the second line. The situation of the second line, again, was similar in every respect to that of the first, being, like it, open in the rear, and placed under the guns of the town. Thus, after having forced two powerful lines of defence, the besiegers would find themselves almost as far as ever from the attainment of their object, being then only arrived at the point where the labours of a siege could commence.

But the maintenance of Bayonne must at all times depend upon keeping possession of the citadel. The city lying upon a plain, and the castle standing upon an eminence immediately above it, it is clear that, were the latter taken, the former must either surrender or be speedily reduced to ruins. It is true that, by destroying the bridge which connects them, all communication between the two places would be cut off; but the distance from the one to the other being not more than half-musket shot, and the guns of the fort pointing directly down upon the streets and of the city, any attempt to hold out could cause only the destruction of the town, and the unavenged slaughter of its garrison. Of the truth of this the French were as much aware as their enemies, nor did they neglect any means which an accurate knowledge of engineering could point out, for the defence of what they justly considered as the key of the entire position. In addition to its own very regular and well-constructed fortifications, two strong redoubts were thrown up, on two sides of the fort, upon the only spots of ground calculated for the purpose; both of which, I was informed by my guide, were undermined and loaded with gunpowder, ready to be sprung as soon as they should fill into our hands. They had judged, and judged correctly, that if ever the place should be invested, it would be that the trenches would be opened and the breaching batteries erected; and they made every preparation to meet the danger which great prudence and military skill could suggest.

Bayonne, though a populous place, does not cover so much ground as a stranger would be led to suppose. Like most walled towns, its streets, with the exception of one or two, are in general narrow, and the houses lofty: but it is compact, and, on the whole, clean, and neatly built. The number of inhabitants I should be inclined to estimate at somewhere about thirty thousand, exclusive of the garrison, which at this time amounted to fourteen or fifteen thousand men; but as most of the families appear to live in the style of those in the old town of Edinburgh, that is to say, several under the same roof, though each in a separate story or flat, it is not difficult to conceive how they contrive to find sufficient room, within a compass apparently so narrow. Of its commerce and manufactures I can say little, except that I should not imagine either to be extensive. I am led to form this opinion, partly from having seen no shipping at the wharfs, and partly because the Adour, though here both wide and deep, is rendered unnavigable to vessels of any size, by a shallow or bar at its mouth. There was, indeed, a sloop of war close to the town, but how it got there I am at a loss to conceive, unless it were built upon the river, and kept as an additional protection against a surprise from the water. The shops are, however, good, particularly those where jewellery is sold; an article in the setting and adorning of which the French, if they do not excel us in really substantial value, undoubtedly surpass us in elegance.

When I had taken as complete a survey of the town as I felt disposed to take, I crossed the bridge with the intention of inspecting the interior of the citadel. Here, however, I was disappointed, no strangers being admitted within its gates; but as there was no objection made to my reconnoitring it from without, I proceeded towards the point where our trenches had been dug, and where it had been designed to breach and storm the place. To this I was urged by two motives, partly from the desire of obtaining the best view possible of the fort, and partly that I might examine the ground upon which the desperate affair of the 14th of April took place. The reader cannot have forgotten, that some hours before daylight on the morning of that day, a vigorous and well-arranged sortie was made by the garrison, and that it was not without hard fighting and a severe loss on both sides that the attack was finally repulsed.

Mounting the heights, I soon arrived at St. Etienne, a little village nearly on a level with the citadel, and not more than a quarter of a mile from its walls. From this point I could satisfy my curiosity to the full, and as the account may not, perhaps, be uninteresting, I shall describe, as well as I am able, the scene which here met my eyes.

The ridge of little hills upon which the fort and village are built, though it rises by gentle gradation from the sea, towards the spot where I now stood, is nevertheless intersected and broken here and there by deep glens or ravines. Two of these glens, one to the right, the other to the left, chance to occur immediately under the ramparts of the fortress, supplying, in some measure, the purposes of a ditch, and leaving a sort of table or elevated neck of land between them, the extremity of which is occupied by the village. On this neck of land the besieged had constructed one of the redoubts to which I alluded as having been lately thrown up; whilst on another table, at the opposite side of the left ravine, which winds round in the direction of the wall, as nearly as if it were the work of art, stands the other redoubt. Beyond this, again, there is a perpendicular precipice, the hills there abruptly ending; so that on two sides the walls of the fort skirt the extremity of a bare rock. It was along the outer ridges of these ravines, and through the churchyard of St. Etienne, that our trenches were drawn, the village itself being the most advanced British post; and it was along these ridges, and in the street of this village, that the action of the 14th of April was fought.

It is not my business, neither indeed is it my intention, to relate here the particulars of that affair. The French, having contrived, in a dark night, to elude the vigilance of our sentinels, came upon the piquets unperceived, and took them completely by surprise. The battle was maintained on both sides with great determination, and had it not been for the unfortunate capture of Sir John Hope and the fall of General Hay, the assailants would have had little cause to rejoice at the result: for though the loss of the English was certainly great, that of the French was at least not inferior. Yet the business was an unfortunate one to both parties, since, before it took place, Buonaparte had already abdicated, and the preliminaries of peace were already signed between the two nations.

I found the village, in which the fighting had been most obstinately maintained, in the condition of most villages where such dramas have been acted. The street had been barricaded, but the barricade was almost entirely torn down; the houses, trees, and church, like those we had passed upon the march, were covered with the marks of cannon and musket balls, whilst quantities of round and grape shot, of musket and pistol bullets, broken bayonets, swords, etc., lay scattered about in every direction. Nor were these the only evidences of strife discernible. In many places—on the pavement of the street, in the churchyard, but above all, on the floor of the church itself,—the traces of blood were still distinctly visible. Beside the remains of the barricade there stood a solitary six-pounder, which had been taken and re-taken nine times during the struggle; and a sprinkling of what looked like a mixture of blood and brains still adhering to its carriage and breech, showed that it had never been given up without the most desperate resistance. The mounds, too, under which the dead were buried, presented a peculiarly striking appearance; for the field of action having been narrow, those that fell, fell in heaps together, and being buried in the same way, one was led to form an idea of greater slaughter than if double the number of graves had been distinguishable in a more extended space.

Having now accomplished my wishes as far as I could, and beginning to feel somewhat fatigued with strolling about, I adjourned to an hotel in the city, from whence, in the evening, I went to the play. The house was poor and the performance miserable, consequently there was no great inducement to sit out the whole of the piece. After witnessing an act or two, therefore, I returned to the inn, where I slept, and at an early hour next morning rejoined my regiment, already under arms and making preparations for the continuance of the march.

As it would have been considerably out of our way to go round by the floating bridge, permission was applied for and granted, to pass directly through Bayonne. With bayonets fixed, band playing, and colours flying, we accordingly marched along the streets of that city; a large proportion of the garrison being drawn up to receive us, and the windows crowded with spectators, male and female, eager to behold the troops from whom not long ago they had probably expected a visit of a very different nature. The scene was certainly remarkable enough, and the transition from animosity to good-will as singular as it was sudden; nor do I imagine that it would be easy to define the sensations of either party, on being thus strangely brought in contact with the other. The females, indeed, waved their handkerchiefs, whilst we bowed and kissed our hands; but I thought I could discover something like a suppressed scowl upon the countenances of the military. Certain it is, that in whatever light the new state of affairs might be regarded by the great bulk of the nation, with the army it was by no means popular; and at this period they appeared to consider the passage of British troops through their lines as the triumphal entrance of a victorious enemy.

As soon as we had cleared the entrenchments of Bayonne, and got beyond the limits of the allied camps, we found ours in a country more peaceful and more picturesque than any we had yet traversed. There were here no signs of war or marks of violence. The cottages were covered with honeysuckle and roses, the gardens were blooming in the most perfect order; the corn was growing in great plenty and richness, and the vines were clustering round their poles like the hops in the gardens of Kent. It is impossible to describe the feeling of absolute refreshment which such a sight stirred up in men who, for so long a time, had looked upon nothing but ruin and devastation. It is true that with respect to grandeur, or even beauty, the scenery through which we now travelled was not to be compared with the sublime passes of the Pyrenees, or with many spots which we had beheld; but in truth, a hamlet uninjured and tenanted by its own rude peasantry, a field of Indian corn exhibiting no wasteful track of foragers, nay, a single cottage with its flowers and evergreens budding around it, was at this a more welcome object to our eyes than the wildest mountains or most romantic valleys displaying no habitations except white tents and no inhabitants except soldiers. For my own part I felt as if I had once more returned into the bosom of civilized and domestic life, after having been for many months a wanderer and a savage.

The road along which we proceeded had been made by Napoleon, and was remarkably good. It was sheltered, on each side, from the rays of the sun, by groves of cork-trees mingled with fir; by which means, though the day was overpoweringly hot, we did not suffer so much as we should otherwise have done. Our march was, therefore, exceedingly agreeable, and we came in, about noon, very little fatigued, to the village of Ondres, where the tents were pitched, and we remained till the morrow.

Chapter 3
The March to the Ships

The dawn was just beginning to appear, when the bugles sounded, and the tents were struck. For the first few leagues, our route to-day resembled that of yesterday, in almost every particular. There was the same appearance of peaceful quiet, the same delightful intermingling of woods, corn-fields, vineyards, and pasture; but we had not proceeded far, when a marked difference was perceptible; every step we trod, the soil became more and more sandy, the cultivation less frequent, and the wood more abundant, till at last we found ourselves marching through the heart of an immense forest of pines. We had diverged, it appeared, from the main road, which carries the traveller through a rich and open country, and were pursuing another through the middle of those deserts and savannahs which lie towards the coast; a district known by the name of Les Landes. There was something, if not beautiful, at least new and striking in the scenery now around us. Wherever the eye turned, it was met by one wide waste of gloomy pine-trees; diversified, here and there, by the unexpected appearance of a modest hamlet, which looked as if it were the abode of some newly arrived settlers in a country hitherto devoid of human habitations.

Were I to continue the detail of a long march through these barren regions, I should soon fatigue, without amusing my reader: I shall, therefore, content myself with observing, that day after day the same dreary prospect presented itself, varied by the occasional occurrence of huge uncultivated plains, which apparently chequer the forest, at certain intervals, with spots of stunted and unprofitable pasturage; upon these there were usually flocks of sheep grazing, in the mode of watching which, the peasants fully evinced the truth of the old proverb, that necessity is the mother of invention. I do not know whether the practice to which I allude be generally known, but as it struck me as very remarkable, I shall offer no apology for relating it.

The whole of this district, as well where it is wooded, as where it is bare, is perfectly flat, containing scarcely a knoll or eminence any sort, as far as the eye can reach. In addition to this, the vast plains where the sheep are fed, many of which extend two or three leagues in every direction, produce not so much as a fir-tree, by climbing which, a man might see to any of its extremities: and the consequence is, that the shepherds are constantly in danger of losing their sheep, as one loses sight of a vessel at sea, in the distance. To remedy this evil, they have fallen upon a plan not more simple than ingenious; they all walk on stilts, exactly similar to those with which our school-boys amuse themselves; the only difference lying here, that whereas the school-boys' stilts are with us seldom raised above ten or twelve inches from the ground, those of the French peasants are elevated to the height of six or eight feet.

When we first caught a glimpse of these figures, it was in the dusk of the morning, and for awhile we were willing to persuade ourselves that the haze had deceived us, by seeming to enlarge bodies beyond their real dimensions. But when we looked at the trees, we saw them in their own proper size, nor could we suppose that the atmosphere would have an effect upon one object, which it had not upon another; yet there appeared to be no other way of accounting for the phenomenon, unless indeed this wild country were the parent of a race of giants, for the men whom we saw resembled moving towers rather than mortals. I need not observe that our astonishment was very great; nor, in was it much diminished when, on a nearer approach, we discovered the truth, and witnessed the agility with which they moved, and the ease with which, aided by the poles which each carried in his hand, they would stoop to the ground, pick up the article, and stand upright again. But if we admired the skill of one or two individuals, our admiration rose to a still higher pitch when we saw crowds of them together, all equally skilful; till they informed us that the thing was not an amusement, but universally practised for the purpose I have stated.

Besides this, I know of nothing in the customs of this isolated people at all worthy of notice, unless, indeed, it be their method of supplying themselves with lights. Being completely cut off from the rest of the world, it is not in their power, except when once or twice a-year they travel to the nearest towns with their wool, to purchase candles; and as they have no notion how these can be made, they substitute in their room a lamp, fed with the turpentine extracted from the fir-trees. The whole process is simple and primitive: to obtain the turpentine they out a hole in the tree, and fasten a dish in it to catch the sap as it oozes through; and as soon as the dish is filled, they put a wick of cotton into the midst of the liquor, and burn it as we do a lamp. The light is not indeed of the most brilliant nature, but it is at least better than none; and as they have fir-trees in abundance within their reach, there is no danger of their oil being quickly exhausted.

In this manner was an entire week expended, each succeeding day introducing us to a repetition of the same adventures, and a renewal of the same scenery, which had amused us during the day before; nor was it till the morning of the twenty-third that we at last began to emerge from the forests, and to find ourselves once again in a more open country. At first, however, it cannot be said that, with respect to beauty, the change was greatly for the better. Upon the borders of the deserts there is a little village called Le Barp, where we spent the night of the twenty-second; from whence, till you arrive at a place called Belle-Vue, the country is exactly in that state which land assumes when nature has begun to lose ground, and art to gain it—when the wild simplicity of the one is destroyed, and the rich luxuriance of the other has not yet been superinduced. So far, therefore, we proceeded, regretting, rather than rejoicing, that we had quitted the woods; but no sooner had we attained that point, than there burst upon us, all on a sudden, a prospect as gloriously fertile as ever delighted the eyes of a weary traveller.

Instead of boundless forests of pine, the whole face of the country was now covered with vineyards, interspersed, in the most exquisite and tasteful manner, with corn-fields and meadows of the richest pasturage. Nor was there any deficiency of timber; a well-wooded chateau, with its lawn and plantations, here and there presenting itself, while quiet hamlets and solitary cottages, scattered in great abundance over the scene, gave to it an appearance of life and prosperity exceedingly bewitching. Had there been but the addition of a fine river flowing through the midst of it, and had the ground been somewhat more broken into hill and dale, I should have pronounced it the most enchanting prospect of the kind I had ever beheld; but, unfortunately, both these were wanting. Though the effect of a first view, therefore, was striking and delightful, and though to the last we could not help acknowledging the richness of the land and its high state of cultivation, its beauty soon began to pall. The fact is, that an immense plain, however adorned by the labour of man, is not an object upon which it is pleasing to gaze for any length of time; the eye becomes wearied with the extent of its own stretch, and as there is no boundary but the horizon, the imagination is left to picture a continuance of the same plain, till it becomes as tired of fancying as the eye is of looking. Besides, we were not long in discovering that the vineyards were unworthy to be compared, in point of luxuriant appearance, with those of Spain and the more southern regions of France. In this neighbourhood the vine is not permitted to grow to a greater height than or four feet from the ground; whereas in Spain, and on the borders, it climbs, like the hop-plant in England, to the top of high poles, and hangs over from one row to another, in the most graceful festoons. In spite of these objections, however, no one could do otherwise than admit that the change we had experienced was agreeable, and we continued to move on with greater alacrity, till it was evident, from the increasing number of seats and villas, that we were rapidly approaching the vicinity of Bordeaux.

Nor was it long before the towers and buildings of that magnificent city began to be discernible in the distance. Prompted by I know not what impulse, we almost involuntarily quickened our pace at the sight, and in a short time reached the suburbs, which like those of most French towns, are composed of low houses, inhabited by the poorest and meanest of the people. Here we halted for a few minutes to refresh the men, when having again resumed the line of march, we advanced under a triumphal arch, originally erected in honour of Napoleon, but now inscribed with the name of the Duke d'Angouleme, and ornamented with garlands of flowers. Passing under this, we proceeded along one or two handsome streets, till we reached the Military Hospital, a large and commodious structure fitted up for the reception of several thousands of sick, where it was arranged that we should spend the night.

The city of Bordeaux has been too often described, and is too well known to my countrymen, in general, to render any particular account of it at all necessary from me; and were the case otherwise, I confess that my opportunities of examining it were not sufficient to authorize my entering upon such an attempt. The whole extent of our sojourn was only during the remainder of that day (and it was past noon before we got in) and the ensuing night; a space of time which admitted of no more than a hurried stroll through some of the principal streets, and a hasty visit to such public buildings as are considered most worthy of attention. The palace of the Duke d'Angouleme, the Military Hospital, the Theatre, and the Cathedral, are all remarkably fine of their kind; whilst the public gardens, the Exchange, and fashionable promenades, are inferior only to those of Paris itself.

I have said that our sojourn in Bordeaux was limited to the short space of a few hours. We could have wished indeed to prolong it, but to wish was needless, for at an early hour next morning we were again in motion, and proceeded to an extensive common, near the village of Macau, about three leagues from Bordeaux, where we found a considerable force already assembled. Judging from the number of tents upon the heath, I conceive that there could not be fewer than eight or ten thousand men in that camp, the whole of whom, we naturally concluded, were destined for the same service with ourselves. The sight was at once pleasing and encouraging, because there could be no doubt that such a force, ably commanded, would carry everything before it.

In this situation we continued, without the occurrence of any incident deserving of record, till the 27th, when an order arrived for the officers to dispose of their horses without delay. This was necessarily done at an enormous loss; and on the morning of the 28th, we set forward towards the point of embarkation. But, alas! in the numbers allotted for the trans-Atlantic war, we found ourselves grievously disappointed, since, instead of the whole division, only two regiments, neither of them surpassingly numerous, were directed to move; it was not our business, however, to question the wisdom of any measure adopted by our superiors; and we accordingly marched on in as high spirits as if we had been followed by the entire Peninsular army.

The remainder of our journey occupied two days, nor do I often remember to have spent a similar space of time with greater satisfaction; our route lay through some of the most fertile districts in France, passing Chateau Margaux, famous for its wine, with other places not inferior to it either in richness of soil or in beauty of prospect. The weather was delightful, and the grapes, though not yet ripe, were hanging in heavy bunches from the vines, giving promise of much wealth to come; the hay season had commenced, and numerous groups of happy-looking peasants were busy in every field; in short, it was a march upon which I shall never look back without pleasure.

The close of the first day's progress brought us to a village called La Moe, beautifully situated within view of the majestic waters of the Garonne. Here, for the first time since we quitted Bayonne, were we quartered upon the inhabitants—a measure which the loss of our tents rendered necessary. They received us with so much frankness, and treated us with so much civility, I had almost said kindness, that it was not without a feeling of something like regret that we parted from them. The second day carried us to Pauliac, an inconsiderable town upon the banks of the same river, where we found boats ready to convey us to the shipping, which lay at anchor to receive us.

To embark the troops in these boats, and to huddle them on board two dirty little transports, occupied some time, and the provoking part of the business was, that all this trouble was to be gone through again. The men-of-war in which we were to cross the Atlantic, could not come up so high for want of water; and on this account it was that transports were sent as passage-boats to carry us to them. But the wind was foul, and blew so strong that the masters would not venture to hoist a sail; so we were obliged to endure the misery of a crowd in a small vessel for two nights and a day; nor was it till past noon on the 31st, that the regiment to which I was attached found itself finally settled in His Majesty's ship *Diadem* of 64 guns.

CHAPTER 4
Ocean & Island

The land army, destined for the invasion of the United States, which took shipping at this period in the Garonne, consisted but of three battalions of infantry, the 4th, 44th, and 85th regiments; the two former mustering each about eight hundred bayonets, the last not more than six hundred. In addition to these, there were two officers of engineers, a brigade of artillery, a detachment of sappers and miners, a party of artillery drivers, with a due proportion of officers belonging to the Medical and Commissariat departments. The whole together could not be computed at more than two thousand five hundred men, if indeed it amounted to so great a number; and was placed under the command of Major-General Ross, a very gallant and experienced officer.

The fleet, again, consisted of the *Royal Oak*, of 74 guns, bearing the flag of Rear-Admiral Malcolm; the *Diadem* and *Dictator*, two sixty-fours, armed *en flute*; the *Pomone*, *Menelaus*, *Trave*, *Weser*, and *Thames*, frigates, the three last armed in the same manner as the *Diadem* and *Dictator*; the *Meteor* and *Devastation*, bomb-vessels; together with one or two gun-brigs, making in all a squadron of eleven or twelve ships of war, with several store ships and transports.

On board the *Royal Oak* were embarked the General, with his staff, and the artillery; the *Trave* and *Weser* were filled with the 4th; the 44th were divided between the *Dictator* and the *Thames*, in the first of which ships were also the engineers; the 85th occupied the *Diadem*; and the rest were scattered through the fleet, partly in the men-of-war and partly in the transports.

As soon as the troops, with all their baggage, were finally settled in the vessels allotted for their accommodation, the signal was made to weigh; but the wind being adverse, and the navigation of the Garonne far from simple, it could not be obeyed with safety. Every thing, therefore, remained quiet till the evening of the 2nd of June, when the gale moderating a little, the anchors were raised and the sails hoisted. The tide was beginning to ebb when this was done, favoured by which the ships drifted gradually on their course; but before long, the breeze shifting, blew directly in their sterns, when they stood gallantly to sea, clearing the river before dark; and, as there was no lull during the whole of the night, by daybreak the coast of France was not to be discerned. All was now one wide waste of waters, as far as the eye could reach, bounded on every side by the distant horizon; a scene which, though at first it must strike with awe and wonder a person unaccustomed to it, soon becomes insipid, and even wearisome, from its constant sameness.

The fair wind which carried us out of the Garonne continuing to blow without any interruption till the 19th of June, it was that day calculated, by consulting the log and taking observations, that the Azores, or Western Islands, could not be very distant. Nor, as it turned out, were these calculations incorrect; for, on ascending the deck next morning, the first object that met our eyes was the high land of St Michael's rising, like a collection of blue clouds, out of the water. With such a prospect before us our consternation may be guessed at, when we found ourselves deserted by the breeze which had hitherto so uniformly favoured us, and lying as motionless as logs, under the influence of a dead calm.

But the complaints to which we had begun to give utterance, were speedily changed again into rejoicings, for before mid-day the breeze once more freshened, and we approached every moment nearer and nearer to the object of our wishes. As soon, too, as we contrived to double the projecting headland which had attracted our attention in the morning, our course became productive of much interest and pleasure. We had neared the shore considerably, and were moving at a rate sufficiently rapid to prevent further repining, and at the same time slow enough to permit a distinct and calm survey of the beach, with the numerous villages, seats, and convents that adorned it.

The island of St. Michael is mountainous, even to the very edge of the water, but the heights, though lofty, do not present a rugged or barren appearance. Here and there, indeed, bare rocks push themselves into notice, but in general the ascent is easy, and the hills are covered to the tops with groves of orange-trees and beautiful green pasturage. Like other Portuguese settlements, this island abounds in religious houses, the founders of many of which do not appear to have been deficient in taste when they pitched upon situations for building. There was one of these in particular that struck me: it stood upon a sort of platform or terrace, about half-way between the sea and the summit of the mountain; above it were hanging woods, whether natural or artificial I cannot say, broken in upon here and there by projecting rocks; and round it were plantations of orange-trees loaded with fruit, and interspersed with myrtles and other odoriferous shrubs. Being greatly pleased with the mansion and the surrounding scenery, I naturally inquired from the pilot (for one had already come off to us) as to its use, and the quality of Its owner; and from him I learnt that it was a convent, I forget of what order,—a piece of intelligence which was soon confirmed by the sound of bells distinctly audible as we passed.

In this manner we continued to coast along, being seldom at a greater distance than four or five miles from the land, till we came opposite to a small town called Villa Franca. Here, as the wind threatened to die away, several others and myself agreed to go onshore: a boat was accordingly lowered, and we pushed off from the ship; but the operation of landing did not prove to be altogether so simple as we had expected. An immense reef of rocks, some under water, others barely above it, but none distinguishable till we had almost run against them, opposed our progress; and it was not without considerable difficulty, and the assistance of the country people, who made signals to us from the beach, that we contrived to discover a narrow channel leading up to the strand.

Having at length so far attained our wishes as to tread once more upon firm ground, the next thing to be done was to find out some inn, or house of public entertainment, where we might pass the night, a measure which the increasing darkness rendered necessary. In this, however, we were disappointed, the town of Villa Franca boasting of no such convenience on any scale. But we were not on that account obliged to bivouac; for the Alcalde, or mayor of the place, politely insisted upon our accompanying him home, and entertained us with great hospitality; nor, in truth, had we any cause to regret the unsuccessful issue of our inquiries, since, in addition to the good cheer with which we were presented, our host, being an intelligent person, did not fail to render himself an agreeable companion; and what contributed in no slight degree to the facility of our intercourse was, that though he assured us he had never quitted St. Michael's in his life, he spoke English with the fluency of a native. Among other pieces of information we learnt from him that the reef which impeded our progress towards the land, had formerly been an island. It appeared, he affirmed, one morning, in the most sudden and extraordinary manner, as if it had been thrown up by an earthquake during the night, and having continued so long above water as to embolden a single family of fishers to settle upon it, it disappeared again as suddenly as it had come, leaving no trace of its existence except the rocks which we had found so troublesome. Whether there be truth in this story, I cannot pretend to determine; and yet I see no reason to doubt the word of a man of respectability, who could have no motive whatever for deceiving us. But this was not all that we learnt from him respecting the reef. He declared that previous to the appearance of the island, the water in that very spot was unfathomable; and it was not till after it had sunk, that a single rock stood in the way to prevent the largest ship of war from anchoring within a stone's throw of the beach.

Finding our new acquaintance so civil and obliging, we naturally informed him of our intention to proceed next morning to Ponto del Gada, the principal town in St. Michael's, and requested his assistance in procuring some mode of conveyance; but we were startled by the intelligence that nothing of the kind could be had, and that there were not even horses or mules to be hired at any place nearer than the very town whither we were going. This was rather an alarming piece of news, for our boat had left us, the weather was too hot for walking, and the distance to be travelled full fifteen miles. Had we been prudent enough to detain our boat, the matter would have been easily managed, because we might have sailed round to the point where the fleet was to anchor; but this was no longer in our power, and being rather unwilling to pursue our journey on foot, we were altogether at a loss upon what course to determine. Whilst we thus hesitated, the Alcalde suggested that if we would condescend to ride upon asses, he thought he could obtain a sufficient number for our party; a proposal with which we gladly closed, prudently determining that any mode of being carried was better than walking. Leaving the arrangement of this affair, therefore, to our obliging friend, we retired to rest upon clean comfortable mattresses spread for us on the floor; and on waking in the morning, we found that he had not been negligent in the charge assigned to him. Our party consisted of five officers, with five servants, for whose accommodation we found ten asses at the door, each attended by its driver, who wielded a long pole tipped with an iron spike, for the purpose of goading the animal whenever it should become lazy.

It was not without a good deal of laughing that the cavalcade, after bidding adieu to the hospitable Mayor, began to move forward. Our asses, of no larger size than ordinary English donkeys, were uncaparisoned, at least with bridles; and the saddles were neither more nor less than the pack-saddles upon which goods are transported to market. For our own comfort, therefore, we were obliged to sit a la femelle, and having no command over the heads of our steeds, we were content to be guided by the hallooing and punching of the drivers. In spite, however, of these inconveniences, if so they may be called, I shall never cease to congratulate myself on having been of the party, because the ride proved to be one of the most agreeable I remember at any time to have taken.

The road from Villa Franca to Ponto del Gada quits the water's edge, and turns, for a little way, inland, carrying you through a region as romantic and beautiful as can well be imagined. There are here no level plains, no smooth paths over which a landau or tilbury might glide, but, on the contrary, a rugged and stony track, sometimes leading down the face of steep hills, sometimes scaling heights which at the distance of a mile appear to be almost perpendicular, and sometimes winding along the side of a cliff, and by the edge of a fearful precipice. Except when you reach the summit of a mountain, the road is in general shaded by the richest underwood, hanging over it from above; but the whole aspect of the country is decidedly that of a volcanic production: the rocks seem to have been cast up and torn asunder by some prodigious violence, and hurled, by a force which nothing but a volcano could possess, into the most grotesque and irregular shapes. It is no uncommon thing to pass under a huge crag, leaning almost horizontally over the road, and bedded in the earth by a foundation apparently so slight, as to appear liable to fall every moment, precipitating the enormous mass upon the luckless wretch beneath. Nay, the very colour of the stones, and the quantity of what bears every resemblance to vitrification, scattered about, all tend to induce the, belief that the main island owes its formation to the same cause which doubtless produced the smaller one that has now disappeared.

It is not, however, to be inferred from the above description that St. Michael's is nothing but a barren rock; far from it. There is, indeed, in this direction at least, a fair proportion of that commodity; but tracts of cultivated ground are not therefore wanting. I should not certainly suppose that the soil was remarkably rich in any part of the island; but it produces the fig, the orange-tree, and a grape from which the inhabitants make very tolerable wine; and there is excellent pasture for sheep, and a competent supply of grain. But that in which the Azores, and St. Michael's among the number, particularly excel, is the extreme salubrity of the climate. Lying in nearly the same degree of latitude with Lisbon, the intense heat which oppresses in that city is here alleviated by refreshing sea-breezes; by which means, though I believe there is no occasion at any season to complain of cold, it is only in the very height of the dog-days, if then, that a person, not actually engaged in violent exercise, is justified in complaining of sultriness.

The trade of St. Michael's, as far as I could learn, is confined exclusively to fruit: the fig and the orange are the staple commodities; and being both very abundant, they are, of course, proportionably cheap. Into the praise of a St. Michael's orange it is unnecessary for me to enter, because it is generally allowed to be the best with which the English market is supplied; but of the excellence of the St. Michael's fig, I am not sure that my countrymen in general are so much aware. It might be, that not having seen a fig for a considerable lapse of time, my appetite was peculiarly sharpened towards its good qualities, but it struck me that I never before tasted any so highly flavoured or so delicate. Besides these, they sell to vessels putting in, as we did, for water, some of the wine made in this and the neighbouring islands; but the quantity thus disposed of must be too inconsiderable to entitle it to be classed among the articles of merchandise.

I find, however, that I am entering upon subjects in which I am but little versed, and digressing from my narrative. Let me return, then, to self, that beloved idol of all travellers, and state that, after we had ridden about six miles, the road, which had hitherto conducted us along a narrow glen, where the vision was intercepted on both sides, now carried us to the summit of a lofty mountain, from whence we enjoyed the satisfaction of an extensive prospect, both of the sea and of the interior. Looking towards the former, we beheld our own fleet bearing down majestically upon Ponto del Gada, and fast approaching the anchorage. Turning our eyes inland again, we were delighted with a view of mountain and valley, rock and culture, wood and pasturage, intermingled in the most exquisite degree of irregularity; but what principally attracted our attention was a thick dark smoke rising slowly from the summit of a high hill that bounded the prospect. Our curiosity being excited by this phenomenon, we inquired from our guides into its cause, and were informed that the mountain in question was a volcano, and that at its base and along its sides were hot springs of water, of a temperature sufficient to boil an egg in three minutes. This piece of intelligence confirmed me in my former opinion relative to the operative cause in the production of these islands; though, indeed, had such evidence been wanting, I should have equally concluded, either that they were thrown up, in their present form, from the bottom of the sea, or at least that they were torn asunder from one another by the force of fire. It must be confessed, however, that mine is the opinion of one who has devoted little of his attention to geology; but I would by all means advise the disciples of Werner to come hither, if they desire further helps in the prosecution of that very interesting and practically useful study.

Chapter 5
Towards the West Indies

Descending the mountain, on which we had paused for a few minutes to feast our eyes and satisfy our curiosity, we arrived at a small hamlet, or rather a group of two or three hovels, as romantically situated as it is possible for the imagination of man to conceive. They stood at the further end of a sort of recess, formed by the hills, which are here broken into a circular valley, cut off, to all appearance, from the rest of the habitable world; behind them rose a towering crag, as perpendicular as the drop of a plummet, from the top of which a little rivulet came tumbling down, giving to the scene an appearance of the most delightful coolness, and amusing the ear with the unceasing roar of a waterfall. From the very face of the cliff, where there seemed to be scarcely soil enough to nourish a thistle, numerous shrubs and dwarf trees protruded themselves; whilst above it, and on every side of the area, the hills were covered with wood, interrupted now and then by the bald forehead of a blackened rock. In front of the hamlet again, there was an opening sufficient to admit the most delicious glimpse of the ocean; and through this the stream, after boiling for awhile in a little basin, which it has excavated for itself out of what resembles the foundation of the cliff, makes its way, brawling over a clear pebbly bottom, till it joins the sea.

This paragon of valleys burst upon us as such scenes, to be witnessed with advantage, ought to do, without the slightest warning or expectation. The road by which we approached it, being completely shut in with wood, and winding considerably to aid the descent, brought us out nearly at the gorge of the vale, so as to throw the hamlet, the cliff, and the waterfall into the background; and as the whole was of such extent as to be taken in at one glance, the effect was striking beyond anything of the kind I ever witnessed. It is but natural to suppose that we had no desire to hurry through such a glen as this; and seeded not the additional motive which the weariness of our donkeys afforded, to persuade us to a temporary halt. Giving the animals, therefore, to the care of their owners, we dismounted, and went into some of the cabins, the inhabitants of which appeared to be as simple as the situation of their abodes had prepared us to expect. The men were all goatherds, and the women seemed to be as idle as their countrywomen in Portugal, sitting at the doors of their houses, surrounded by groups of half-naked and filthy-looking children. If it be fair to judge from their dress and the furniture of their hovels, they were miserably poor, though perfectly contented; they did not ask us for money, but astonished, I suppose, at the glaring colour of our coats, they were very inquisitive to know who we were and whence we had come. The English, the French, and the Portuguese seemed to be the only three nations of whose existence they had any knowledge; and having been assured, in answer to their first question, that we were not French, they immediately added, "Then you must be English." They did not appear, however, to be without some degree of cunning, for as long as we paused in replying to their query, they were silent; but no sooner had we answered in the negative than they launched forth into the most violent invectives against the French; convincing us that the animosity of the mother-country towards its barbarous invaders was not more implacable than that of the colonies.

Having loitered away half an hour in this romantic spot, and distributed a few dollars among its inhabitants, we remounted our steeds and continued our journey. The remainder of the ride carried us through scenery very similar to what we had already passed; the only difference was, that the nearer we approached to Ponto del Gada the more frequent became the spots of cultivation, the width and smoothness of the road improving in proportion; till at last, when we had attained the brow of an eminence, from whence the town with its port and bay were distinguishable, we looked down upon an extensive valley, richly covered with fields of standing corn. Quickening our pace, we soon entered the capital of St. Michael's, and were conducted by the drivers to a good hotel, kept by an Englishwoman of the name of Currie, where we found every accommodation which we could desire, at a very moderate expense.

As we had started at an early hour from Villa Franca, the clocks were just striking ten when we alighted at Mrs. Currie's hotel; consequently, there was a long day yet before us, in which we might see everything that was to be seen in the place. Having discharged our muleteers, therefore, who seemed overjoyed at the receipt of one dollar a-piece, swallowed a hasty breakfast, and made ourselves somewhat comfortable, we lost no time in setting out upon a stroll of examination and discovery.

Ponto del Gada is, on the whole, rather a neat town, containing from twelve to fourteen thousand inhabitants; but being built, especially in the outskirts, without much regard to compactness, it covers more ground than many places of double the amount in population. It stands upon a little bay, formed by two projecting headlands, and can boast of a tolerable harbour excellent roadstead. In its immediate vicinity the country a more uniformly level than any I had yet observed; the vale extending to the distance of four or five miles on every side, had ending in an amphitheatre of low green hills, which resemble appearance, the downs as they are seen from Eastbourne in Sussex. The whole of this flat is in a state of high cultivation, being cleared, perhaps too completely, of wood, and portioned off into different fields and parks by hedges and stone walls. Judging from the appearance of the crops, I should conceive that the soil was here of some depth, as well as fertility, the whole valley being covered with wheat, barley, and Indian corn. And in truth, if the aspect of the country beyond the downs, where rocks tower one above another in rude and barren grandeur, furnish a legitimate criterion by which to determine respecting the general fertility of the island, I should be almost tempted to believe that the whole industry of its people has been expended upon this spot, simply because it was the only one capable of rewarding it. I was assured, however, by the natives, that such is not the case; and that, in the interior, and towards the opposite coast, the rugged magnificence of mountain scenery gives place to a more profitable though less picturesque Champaign.

The principal streets of Ponto del Gada are paved, and kept once cool and clean by a. constant sprinkling of water, which is the business of two or three men stationed at pumps within obtain distance of one another, to scatter over them. Of the by-streets little can be said in praise, they being, like those of other Portuguese towns, composed of mean cottages, unpaved, and extremely dirty. There is, however, an air of elegance given to the town, particularly when looked at from a distance, by the intermixture of orange-groves among the houses; the largest of these, wherever they happen to stand, being, in general, surrounded by extensive gardens, all of which are abundantly stocked with that graceful and odoriferous plant. Add to this the number of towers and spires with which its numerous churches and convents are supplied, and the first aspect of the whole may be conceived to be extremely striking and imposing.

As soon as we had taken a hurried survey of the streets, the next object of attention was the religious houses. In these there was but little to admire, the architecture being of the plainest kind, and even the chapels as much wanting in ornament as can be imagined. There were, indeed, in most of them some trifling attempts at carved work and gilding upon the roof, a little stained glass, neither rich nor ancient, in the windows, and a few tawdry pictures suspended above the altars; but the general appearance was decidedly that of buildings which did not even aim at beauty or grandeur. The monks we found a good-natured, obliging set of men, very willing to give us any information in their power; by one of whom we were fortunate enough to be conducted through a convent of Augustine friars. Into their mode of living it is not to be supposed that we could obtain much insight. It seemed, however, to be less indolent than that of some convents which we had visited in the old country, and approached proportionably nearer to a college life among ourselves; though it must be admitted that the fellows and undergraduates of Oxford and Cambridge have a better notion of both comfort and elegance than the Augustine friars of St. Michael's. Of the nuns we of course saw nothing, excepting through the grates. We found them full of curiosity, and eager to know as much as they could learn of the world from which they were excluded; but quite as fond of flirting as any set of young ladies at a boarding-school. It was amusing to observe their mode of begging, for all the nuns in this part of the world are licensed beggars. The younger and fairer members of the sisterhood came to the grate first; chatted, sung, and presented us with artificial flowers, and then retiring, made way for the old and the ugly, who requested a little money for the good of our souls and their bodies. To solicitations thus expressed it was impossible to turn a deaf ear, and the consequence was, that we soon discovered it to be quite as expensive an amusement to flirt with a nun, as with any other belle in London or elsewhere.

Besides the churches and convents, amounting in all to not fewer than nine, there is a fort erected for the protection of the harbour, which we likewise endeavoured to see, but were prevented by the sentinel at the gate, who refused us admittance. The disappointment, however, was not great, as it was easy to perceive, from its outward appearance, that the fort could possess few points worthy of observation; and, indeed, we attributed the reluctance evinced in admitting strangers to its utter uselessness as a place of defence.

To describe all this occupies but a small portion of time; but to see it was the laborious employment of an entire day. Wearied out at length with my exertions, and not feeling much rewarded, at least for the latter part of my trouble, I returned in the evening to the hotel, where, as the ships were still at anchor, taking on board water and fresh provisions, I ventured to spend the night.

Having thus discovered that there was little in the works of art, and a great deal in those of nature, throughout St. Michael's, to interest the traveller, a friend and myself determined to set off next morning on a visit to the volcano. With this design we ordered asses, for asses are the only animals for hire, to be in readiness by daybreak; and finding them in waiting at the time appointed, we took a guide with us and pushed forward in the direction of the dark smoke. The mountain with its crater being distinctly visible from Ponto del Gada, we took it for granted the distance between the two places could not exceed twelve or fourteen miles; but, on inquiring of our guide, we learned that the nearest road would carry us at least twenty-seven miles from the town. This was at once a startling and unpleasant piece of intelligence, affecting our arrangements in no trifling degree. To proceed was dangerous, because, mounted as we were, to go and return in one day was impossible; and, if we remained so far from the shipping during the night, the fleet might sail v before we should be able to get back. On the other hand, to give up our design, and quit a country where a volcano was to be seen, without seeing it, appeared rather a mortifying prospect. After weighing for a few minutes the chances on both sides, I shall not say with the utmost impartiality, curiosity finally prevailed over apprehension; and, in order to prevent any further repentance and consequent change of mind, we put our donkeys into a gallop, and hurried on as fast as they could carry us. But the speed of the asses and our own venturous determination proved, after all, equally unavailing; for, on gaining the summit of the downs, and looking back upon the fleet, we beheld, to our great sorrow, the signal for sailing displayed at the topmasts of all the ships. Mortified at our disappointment, and at the same time rejoicing that we had got no farther on our journey, we were compelled to turn our asses' heads, and to retrace our steps towards Ponto del Gada, where we found everything in the bustle and confusion of a re-embarkation. The beach was covered with sailors, soldiers, bullocks, and casks of fresh water, hurrying, and being hurried, indiscriminately into the boats which had arrived to take them off. The townspeople were running about upon the strand, some offering their skiffs to convey the officers on board the ships, some helping to swing the bullocks into the barges, and others shouting and hallooing apparently from the disinterested love of noise. In short, it was a scene of great liveliness and bustle, perhaps rather too much so to be agreeable.

Seeing this universal eagerness to reach the fleet, we, like the rest, threw ourselves into the first boat we could approach, and in a short time found ourselves on board our own ship. But here a very tantalizing piece of intelligence awaited us, for we learnt that, in spite of all this show of preparation, the Admiral had not begun to weigh anchor; and that no intention of moving was entertained, at soonest, before the morrow. The opportunity, however, was lost; it could not be recovered, and we were obliged to submit as cheerfully as we could, though it was impossible to help regretting, what had at first been a source of consolation, the circumstance of our having caught a view of the signal at the time we did. But, as the event proved, all had turned out for the best; for on the day following the signal was again repeated; and by way of giving additional weight to it, the Admiral began to shake loose his topsails. Nor did it prove, like that of yesterday, a false alarm. By mid-day, the victualling and watering being complete, the fleet immediately began to get under weigh; and, as the wind blew fair and fresh, before dark the mountains of St. Michael's could be seen only like a thin vapour in the sky. Next morning nothing but the old prospect of air and water met the gaze, as we stood our course, at a rapid rate, towards Bermuda.

The voyage from St. Michael's to Bermuda occupied the space of almost an entire month, the first having been lost sight of on the 27th of June, and it being the 24th of July before the low shores of the last could be discerned. It was, however, a passage of more interest and productive of more variety than that from Bordeaux to the Azores. We had now arrived within the influence of the tropical climate, and were not unfrequently amused with water-spouts, and other phenomena peculiar to warm regions. The flying-fish, likewise, and its pursuer, the dolphin, afforded at least something to look at; whilst many idle hours were whiled away in attempts to catch or strike the latter with harpoons.

In these we were not always unsuccessful, consequently we enjoyed several opportunities of watching the change of colour which that fish undergoes whilst it is dying; and though the description generally given of it is certainly indebted in some degree to the imagination of voyagers, I must confess that the transitions from blue to purple, and from purple to green, with all their intermediate shades, are extremely beautiful. When the fish is in the water, it is by no means remarkable for brilliancy of hue, and as soon as it is dead it returns to its original colour—a dingy sea-green; but whilst it is floundering and flapping upon the deck, it is impossible to say what is its real appearance, so many and so different are the hues which it assumes. Nor did we escape without the occasional occurrence of a less agreeable species of variety; I mean squalls, thunder-storms, and whirlwinds. As we approached Bermuda, indeed, these became too frequent to excite any interest beyond an earnest desire that they would cease: but while we were yet a good way off, and the incident rare, they were witnessed with more of admiration than terror.

Besides these amusements with which nature supplied us,

we were not backward in endeavouring to amuse ourselves. Being now pretty well accustomed to the atmosphere of a ship, we began to consider ourselves at home, and to give balls and other public entertainments through the fleet. One of these I shall take leave to describe, because I am sure it must interest from its novelty. On the 19th of July, at an early hour in the morning, a signal was made from the *Royal Oak*, that the Admiral would be happy to see the officers of the fleet on board his ship that evening. Boats were accordingly sent off from the different vessels, loaded with visitors; and on mounting the gangway, a stage, with a green curtain before it, was discovered upon the quarter-deck. The whole of the deck, from the poop to the mainmast, was hung round with flags, so as to form a moderate-sized theatre; and the carronades were removed from their port-holes, in order to make room for the company. Lamps were suspended from all parts of the rigging and shrouds, casting a brilliant light upon this singular playhouse; and the crew, arrayed in their best attire, crowded the booms, yards, and fore part of the deck; whilst the space from the mainmast to the foot of the stage was set with benches for the more genteel part of the audience.

At seven o'clock the curtain drew up, and discovered a scene painted with such taste as would not have disgraced any theatre in London. The play was the *Apprentice*, with the *Mayor of Garret* as an afterpiece, performed by the officers of the ship and of the artillery, and went off in high style, applauded, as it deserved to be applauded, with the loudest acclamations. The quarter-deck of a British line-of-battle ship has often enough been a stage for the exhibition of bloody tragedies; but to witness a comedy and a farce upon that stage, and in the middle of the Atlantic Ocean, was delightful from its very singularity. When the performance came to an end, the stage was knocked down, the seats removed, and everything cleared for dancing. The music was excellent, being composed of the band of the *Royal Oak*; and the ball was opened by Admiral Malcolm and the Honourable Mrs. Mullens, in a country dance, followed by as many couples as the space would permit; the greater number of officers dancing, as necessity required, with one another. In this amusement every person, from the Admiral and General, down to the youngest ensign and midshipman, joined, laying aside for the time all restraint or form of discipline; and having kept it up with great spirit till considerably beyond midnight, a blue light was hoisted as a signal for the different boats to come off for the strangers, and each returned to his own ship highly gratified with the evening's entertainment.

Chapter 6
Bermuda

By employing ourselves in this manner, and by keeping up what is emphatically called a good heart, we contrived to pass out time agreeably enough. As often as the weather would permit, and the fleet lay well together, we made parties of pleasure to the different ships; when the wind was too high, and the fleet too much scattered for such proceedings, we remained at home, and amused ourselves in the best way we could. Some of the captains, and ours among the number, were possessed of very tolerable libraries, the doors of which they politely threw open for the benefit of their military guests; and thus, by reading, fishing, and boating, we were enabled to make head, with some success, against the encroachments of ennui. It must be confessed, however, that in spite of strenuous efforts to the contrary, that determined enemy of all idle persons was beginning to gain ground upon us, when, about mid-day on the 24th of July, a cry of land was heard from the mast-head. All eyes were immediately turned in the direction to which the sailor pointed, and as wind blew fair and moderately fresh, no great length of time before the same object was distinguishable from the deck. A signal was immediately hoisted for a pilot, who lost no time in coming off to us; and before dark we were at anchor opposite to the tanks in Bermuda.

The appearance of Bermuda is altogether as different from that of St. Michael's as one thing can be from another. Whilst the last, with its lofty mountains and bold shores, can be seen at the distance of many leagues, a ship must be within a few miles of the first before the slightest symptom of land is discernible. On this account it is that mariners find greater difficulty in making Bermuda than perhaps any other island or continent in the known world; the most experienced seaman frequently sailing past it, and not a few suffering shipwreck every year upon its numerous shoals and rocks. For not only is the land itself low, and thus apt to be run against by vessels which may have approached in stormy weather too near to put about, but for many miles round, reefs of sunken rocks stretch out into the sea in every direction; insomuch, that even the approach to the principal anchorage is no more than a narrow channel between two reefs, in many places scarcely exceeding a mile or a mile and a half in width. The navigation, even in calm weather, is therefore attended with considerable danger; the idea of which is greatly heightened by the remarkable clearness of the water and the peculiar brightness of the rocks. In some places this is so much the case, that the bottom may be seen at the depth of six or seven fathoms; whilst the aspect of the reefs which lie on each side, as you steer towards the anchorage, is such, as almost to persuade you, contrary to the evidence of reason, that a man might leap upon them from a boat without incurring the danger of being wet above the knees. Yet these very reefs are seldom covered with less than six, and sometimes with fourteen and fifteen feet of water.

Low as they are, the shores of Bermuda are nevertheless extremely beautiful. They are covered with cedar, a tree which here, at least, seldom exceeds the height of twenty feet, and from which, before the sun has risen and after he has set, the land breeze comes loaded with the most delicious perfume. Under the wood there grows a rich short turf, apparently struggling to spread itself over the chalky rocks, of which the entire island, or rather islands, seem to be composed; and, as the houses of the better orders are chiefly built within reach of the cool air from the water, they, with their little lawns and gardens, produce a lively and pleasing effect.

As darkness had come on before the ship could be properly moored, no boats were permitted to leave her that night; but at an early hour next morning I embraced the first opportunity of going on shore. To reach St. George's, the capital of the colony, you are obliged to row for several miles up a narrow frith called the ferry, immediately on entering which the scenery becomes in the highest degree picturesque. Though still retaining its character of low, the ground on each side looks as if it were broken into little swells, the whole of them beautifully shaded with groves of cedar, and many of them crowned with country-houses as white as the drifted snow. But the fact is, that this appearance of hill and dale is owing to the prodigious number of islands which compose the cluster; there being in all, according to vulgar report, not fewer than three hundred and sixty-five, of which the largest exceeds not seven or eight miles in diameter. Yet it is only when you follow what at first you are inclined to mistake for a creek or the mouth of a river, that you discover the absence of valleys from between these hills; and even then you are more apt to fancy yourself upon the bosom of a lake studded with islets, than steering amid spots of earth which stand, each of them distinct, in the middle of the Atlantic Ocean.

In the town of St. George's there is nothing to be seen at all worthy of record. It consists of about fifty or sixty houses, the glare from which, as they are all built of the chalk stone, is extremely dazzling to the eyes. It is called the capital, because here the court-house stands and the magisterial sittings are held; but in point of size, and, as far as I could learn, in every other respect, it is greatly inferior to Hamilton, another town at the opposite extremity of the cluster, which I did not visit. A little way from St. George's, and on the summit of a bare rock, stand the barracks, fitted up for the accommodation of a thousand men; and about a mile and a half beyond them are the tanks, well worth the notice of travellers. The object of this work is to catch and preserve the rain—a measure which the total deficiency of fresh springs throughout the colony renders absolutely necessary. There are, indeed, wells dug upon the beach, but the water in these is nothing more than sea-water, filtered and rendered brackish in making its way through the sand, and by no means fit to be used, at least in any quantity. To supply this deficiency, the bad effects of which were experienced in the unhealthiness of many of the crews upon the American station, Government was induced to build these tanks; consequently the water contained in them is the property of the king, and none but king's ships, with the troops in garrison, are permitted, except in extreme cases, to be supplied from thence.

The climate of Bermuda has been extolled by many, and among the rest by Mr. Moore in his odes and epistles, as salubrious and delightful. It is possible that he, and the rest of its eulogists, may have visited these islands at a season of the year different from that in which I visited them, but to me the heat was beyond measure oppressive. Lying, as they do, under the influence of a vertical sun, and abounding in all directions with cliffs of white chalk, it is obvious that the constant reflection of the sun's rays thereby occasioned must be quite overpowering. If these panegyrists mean to say, that as long as you contrive to keep in the shade, and take care not to stir abroad till after sunset, you will find the Bermudas deserving of their title of summer-islands, then I will agree with them; but I believe there is no man who ever walked the street of St. George's at noon, or any other spot where the sun-beams could reach him, that did not consider the heat as anything rather than temperate.

But whatever may be thought of the climate, there can, I think, be but one opinion as to the soil. It is generally admitted that there is no more unproductive spot of earth upon the face of the deep than Bermuda. The only animals which appear to thrive are the goat and the duck; the cedar and a few calabash-trees are the only wood, and, except the most common kinds of vegetables, such as cabbages, onions, and sweet potatoes; I know of hardly another thing brought to perfection, even in the gardens. The fruits which a stranger may meet with are no doubt delicious, since among them he will find the shaddock and the pine-apple; but for these, as well as for almost all their other comforts and luxuries, the Bermudians are indebted to the continent of America or to the West Indies. Whether this be owing to the natural sterility of the soil, or to the extreme indolence of the inhabitants, I cannot pretend to decide; though I should be inclined to suspect that both were, in some degree, to blame; but its consequences are felt by all visitors, in a very sensible manner, every article of living being here sold for thrice its intrinsic value. That provisions should be dear in this country cannot surprise, when it is considered that this small colony is the general depot and place of resort for repairs and stores to a large proportion of the British navy, scattered along the coast of America; but, surely, if the natives were a little more industrious, they might afford to sell their goods at a cheaper rate, and at the same time secure an equal, if not a greater profit. But their indolence is beyond all conception, and can be attributed only to, what I believe is its real cause, the facility with which they acquire fortunes, from men who are necessitated to give whatever they demand for the most trifling article. The poorest and meanest freeman upon the island never dreams of applying his own hand, or even his own head, to the cultivation of the ground; and being abundantly supplied with negro slaves, they leave everything, even the care of providing necessaries for themselves, to the industry of that ill-used race. I may perhaps be considered as expressing myself with too much severity towards the Bermudians, but, in truth, I repeat only what I was told by some of themselves; nor did I, from my own personal observation, discover any cause to question the veracity of my informers.

In the praise bestowed by Mr. Moore upon the beauty of these regions, I do, however, most cordially join. There is something bewitchingly pretty, for pretty is perhaps the most appropriate epithet to be used, in every one of the many views which you may obtain from different points. The low and elegant cedar, the green short turf, the frequent recurrence of the white and dazzling rock, the continual rise and fall of the numerous small islands, but above all, the constant intermingling of land and water, seem more like a drawing of fairy land than a reality. There is nothing grand, nothing imposing, or calculated to excite any feeling bordering upon the awful, throughout the whole; but it is soft, gentle, and exquisitely pleasing.

Having spent the day at St. George's, I returned on board to sleep; and on the morrow removed, with my baggage, to a transport then lying at anchor within the ferry, which was thenceforth to be my head-quarters. Thither my friend Grey also removed, and as our ship was well stored, and its commander civil and accommodating, we had no reason to complain of any suffering consequent upon our change of residence.

It will be readily believed that a very small portion of our time was now wasted on board ship; for economy's sake we usually slept there, because at the inn the charge for beds, as well as for everything else, was enormous; but all the hours of daylight were devoted to rowing round the different islands, and climbing the different eminences, from whence the most extensive prospects were to be obtained. Among other curiosities, we were informed of two caves in one of the little isles, distant about four or five miles from the place where we lay. Being assured that they were highly deserving of notice, we determined to visit them; and setting off one evening for that purpose, we reached the spot which had been pointed out to us a little before dark. We fastened the boat to the stump of a tree, and were proceeding towards the caves, when a fine manly voice, singing one of the Irish melodies, attracted our attention. Being rather curious to discover who, in this extramundane place, had learnt to sing with so much taste, we followed the direction of the sound, till we came upon a party sitting under the shade of a tent, and, like ourselves, enjoying the cool of the evening; on perceiving us, some of them came forward, and the satisfaction was mutual when we recognised one another as old acquaintances. They urged us to relinquish our design, and to partake of their good cheer, with which, as the hour was late, we had small reluctance in complying; and it was agreed, that instead of going on without proper guides, and at so unseasonable a time, we should breakfast together at the same spot in the morning, and proceed in a body to examine the caverns. Here, therefore, we remained till the moon had risen, when we returned to our boat, and sailed back to the ship.

Next morning everything was prepared for the expedition, but a heavy squall coming on, prevented us from setting out as early as we had intended; as soon, however, as this blew over, we took to our boat, and reached the place of rendezvous in time to share the remains of a good breakfast which our friends had prepared for themselves and us. When our meal was finished, we supplied ourselves with torches from some dry branches of the calabash-tree, and, headed by a guide, moved towards the mouth of the nearest and largest of the two caves. We descended into this by a ladder of sixteen steps, and arrived upon a broad ledge of rock, where we halted for a few minutes to light the torches, and accustom our vision to the gloom; when, both of these ends being attained, we advanced a few paces into the cave, and a sight of the most indescribable sublimity burst upon us. The appearance was that of a huge Gothic cathedral, having its roof supported upon pillars of spar, moulded into the most regular shapes, and fluted and carved after the most exact models of architecture. The roof itself was indeed too lofty to be discerned, nor could the eye penetrate to anything like an extremity, all beyond a certain extent being wrapped in the most profound darkness; but the flashes of light which at intervals streamed out, as the glare of the torches fell upon pieces of spar as clear as crystal, and the deep echo of our own voices as we spoke, inspired us with a feeling of awe bordering upon superstition. It is in such a situation as this, that the poverty of the mightiest monument of human art becomes conspicuous. The most magnificent churches and abbeys, with their sculptured pillars and vaulted ceilings, were thought of as mean in comparison of what was now before us; indeed, I for one could not help imagining that these very churches and abbeys had been built in humble imitation of this, which looked like a temple reared by some beings more powerful than men. It seemed a shrine worthy of the genii of old, while yet they were in the zenith of their glory, ere they had been driven from their thrones and oracles of darkness by the light of Christianity.

As we moved onward we found the sides of the cave gradually narrow upon us, and the roof become lower and lower. There was, however, a continuance of the same fane-like appearance to the last, though growing more and more contracted; till, finally, we were compelled to advance one by one, and to stoop in order to prevent our heads from coming into contact with the rock. We had proceeded as far as it was possible to proceed with any degree of comfort, and were informed by the guide that we were upwards of three hundred yards from the entrance, when we found it expedient to wheel about, and to return to the open air. But the effect of so sudden a change from darkness to light was exceedingly disagreeable; insomuch that we hastened into the smaller cave, as well for the purpose of deferring the moment of suffering as to continue our search after the sublime.

The entrance to this cavern is extremely dangerous, and not to be ventured upon without either a trusty guide or a thorough knowledge of the ground. After descending a ladder, not quite so deep as that which leads into the larger cave, we arrived at the brink of a fearful chasm, across which a flat stone, about two feet in width, was laid, connecting the edges by a bridge four or five feet in length. To what depth the chasm may reach, the guide could not inform us; but that it is considerable we discovered by dropping a large stone, which we could hear for some time as it dashed against the projecting edges of the rock, and at length splashed with a tremendous echo into water. The man maintained that the sea beat under the foundation of the island as far as the spot where we now stood, and his story was rendered at least probable by the number of pools of salt water which we met with in the interior of the cave.

After having visited the larger cavern, this certainly appeared to disadvantage; though in truth it is in its dimensions only that the one can be pronounced inferior to the other. The spar is equally clear and proportionably as abundant in both: the pillars are quite as regularly formed, and the lesser has an advantage over its rival in two or three broken columns, which give to it the semblance of a temple in ruins. There is also in this cave a strange propinquity of salt and fresh water pools, the situation of two of which struck me as peculiarly curious. They were divided from each other by a piece of rock not much thicker than a man's hand; and yet the water from the one tasted as if it had been taken from the German Ocean, whilst that from the other was as fresh and pleasant as possible.

We had by this time fully gratified our curiosity, and once more ascended to the world of sunshine, the splendour of which was at first almost insupportable. By degrees, however, our eyes became accustomed to the change and recovered their original tone, when we separated, each party returning to its respective ship in high good humour with the day's employment.

But to dine quietly on board was no longer endurable. A tent was accordingly carried on shore, and having sought out the most shady and agreeable nook within a moderate distance of the vessel, our dinner was brought thither, and we spent the evening, as we had done the morning, among the works of nature. Here we remained till a late hour, talking over the adventures of the day, and occasionally attempting a blind peep into futurity, till our friend the moon having risen, we again pulled on board by her light, and lay down to dream of sparry domes and enchanted temples.

Chapter 7
Landing in America

Some apology is due to the reader, whose attention has been thus long withdrawn from other and more important matters, to follow the adventures of an humble individual like myself. The fault, however, of which I have been guilty may be at once repaired, when I inform him that on our arrival at Bermuda we found Sir Alexander Cochrane, in the *Tonnant*, of eighty guns, waiting to receive us, and to take the command of the whole fleet.

The secret of our destination likewise, which up to that moment had been kept, transpired almost as soon as we cast anchor off the island; and it was publicly rumoured that our next point of debarkation would be somewhere on the shores of the Bay of Chesapeake. Nor are these the only interesting public occurrences of which no notice has as yet been taken.

On the 4th of June our little army was reinforced by the arrival of the 21st Fusiliers, a fine battalion, mustering nine hundred bayonets, under the command of Colonel Patterson. On the evening of the 29th a squadron of four frigates and several transports appeared in the offing, which by midday on the day following were all at anchor in the roads. They proved to be from the Mediterranean, having the 21st, 29th, and 62nd Regiments on board, of which the two latter were proceeding to join Sir George Prevost's army in Canada, whilst the former attached itself to that under the command of General Ross. By this very acceptable reinforcement, our numbers were increased to upwards of three thousand effective men, and a greater confidence in themselves, as well as a better grounded hope of success in whatever they might undertake, was at the same time given to the troops.

Having already dwelt sufficiently upon my own personal adventures at Bermuda, I shall not waste time by a particular detail of the various preparations which during this interval were making throughout the fleet. Stores of provisions, fresh water, ammunition, clothing, &c., were provided, and magazines for the future supply of the expedition established; when, on the 3rd of August, all things being complete, the ships once more got under weigh, and stood towards America.

During the whole of this day the wind was light and unsteady, consequently little progress was made, nor did the white rocks of Bermuda disappear till darkness concealed them; but towards morning a fresher and more favourable breeze springing up, the rest of the voyage was performed in reasonable time, and without the occurrence of any incident worthy of notice. The heat, indeed, became more and more oppressive every day, and the irksomeness of renewed confinement was more sensibly experienced from the long holiday which we had enjoyed on shore; but, in other respects, everything returned to its former state, till towards evening on the 14th, when a signal was made by the Admiral that land was in sight. As yet, however, there was no appearance of it from the deck of our transport, nor for a full half-hour could our anxious gaze be rewarded by the slightest trace of what it sought; but at the end of that time the low sandy point of Cape Charles began to show itself, and we rejoiced in the prospect of a speedy release from the ennui of a seafaring life.

The coast of America, at least in this quarter, is universally low and uninteresting; insomuch, that for some time before the land itself can be discerned, forests of pines appear to rise, as it were, out of the water. It is also dangerous from the numerous shoals and sandbanks which run out in many places to a considerable extent into the sea, and which are so formidable that no master of a vessel, unless he chance to be particularly well acquainted with the navigation, will venture to approach after dark. The fleet was accordingly anchored within a few miles of the shore, but no sooner had the day begun to break than the sails were again hoisted, and the ships, steering under the influence of a leading wind, between the Capes Charles and Henry, stood in gallant style up the Chesapeake.

This noble bay is far too wide, and the land on each side too flat, to permit any but an indistinct glimpse of the shore from the deck of a vessel which keeps well towards the middle. On the present occasion we could distinguish nothing, on either hand, except the tops of trees, with occasionally a windmill or a lighthouse; but the view of our own fleet was in truth so magnificent as to prevent any murmuring on that account. Immediately on entering, we were joined by Admiral Cockburn with three line-of-battle ships, several frigates, and a few sloops of war and gun-brigs, by which means the squadron could now muster above twenty vessels entitled to display the pendant, besides an equal if not a greater number of victuallers and transports.

Nor were we strengthened by this addition in the naval part of the expedition alone. On board these ships was embarked a powerful reinforcement for the army, consisting of a battalion of seven hundred marines, a hundred negroes lately armed and disciplined, and a division of marine artillery, so that we could now calculate on landing a corps of at least four thousand men. The spectacle was therefore as agreeable and imposing as might be; because we could not help remembering that this magnificent fleet was sailing in an enemy's bay, and that it was filled with troops for the invasion of that enemy's country. Thus, like a snowball, we had gathered as we went on, and from having set out a mere handful of soldiers, were now become an army, formidable as well from its numbers as its discipline.

The shoals and sandbanks which abound on the outside of the bay, continue to encumber the navigation after it is entered, and the fleet was in consequence compelled to anchor every night. This proceeding unavoidably occasioned much delay. The first day's sail carried us only to the mouth of the James river, and the second to the mouth of the Potomac; but, on both occasions, we brought up at too great a distance from the beach to permit perfect or distinct view of either of these rivers. Opposite to the latter, indeed, we remained for a night and a considerable part of the following day, and the sky being remarkably clear, we saw something more of it than we had been able to see of the other river. It appeared to be a fine piece of water making its way through the centre of huge forests, and, though the current is in reality strong, flowing on without any apparent motion. But it would have been impossible to trace its course, even had we been nearer to the shore, above a few miles, on account of its numerous windings, the first of which, overshadowed as it is with wood, shuts it out from further observation. By continuing here so long, we had begun to conjecture that a landing somewhere on the banks of this river was in contemplation. In this, however, we were deceived, for about one o'clock the fleet was again under sail, and moving towards the Patuxent, a river which empties itself into the bay, several miles above the Potomac.

It was singular enough, that the ships had scarcely begun to lift their anchors, when the sky, which had hitherto continued clear and serene, became suddenly darkened and overcast with heavy clouds: and the water, which before had been as smooth and bright as a mirror, began to rise in black waves tipped with foam, though there was not a breath of air to fill the sails. Hurricanes are, I believe, not unfrequent in this part of the world, and it was expected that these changes in the sea and sky foreboded the arrival of one; but they passed by without producing any violent results, and when we brought up, which was done in the evening, the clouds had dispersed, and the water was again like a glassy lake.

The 18th of August had now arrived, and as yet we had advanced no farther than to the mouth of the Patuxent. There we lay, as we had done the day before, anxiously expecting a breeze; till about noon, the wind beginning to blow fair, the fleet entered the river and made its way slowly and majestically against the stream. The voyage soon became picturesque and interesting in the highest degree. Fields of Indian corn, with meadows of the most luxuriant pasture, stretched along the margin of the stream on either hand; whilst the neat wooden houses of the settlers, all of them painted white, and surrounded with orchards and gardens, presented a striking contrast to the boundless forests which formed a background to the scene. Of the prodigious extent and gloomy appearance of these forests, it is impossible for any language to convey an adequate conception. There is nothing, at least nothing which I have seen, in the Old World, at all resembling or to be compared with them; and hemming in, as they do, on every side, the tiny spots of cultivation, they certainly convey no very enlarged idea of the power of human industry. The cleared fields on the banks of the Patuxent, for example, could in no direction measure above half a mile across,—in many places their breadth fell short of that, from the river to the woods; and then all was one vast forest, through which no eye could penetrate, nor any traveller venture to seek his way. We were, as may be imagined, greatly taken by scenery so novel; and we continued to gaze upon it with the liveliest interest, till our attention was drawn away to other and more important matters.

We had not proceeded many miles from the river's mouth when a telegraph from the Admiral gave orders for the troops to be in readiness to land at a moment's notice. Everything was forthwith put in a state of forwardness; provisions for three days, that is to say, three pounds of pork, with two pounds and a half of biscuit, were cooked and given to the men; the cartouch-boxes were supplied with fresh ammunition, and the arms and accoutrements handed out. The fleet, however, continued to move on, without showing any inclination to bring to; till at length, having ascended to the distance of ten leagues from the bay, the ships of the line began to take the ground;

and in a little while after, even the frigates could proceed no farther. But by this time the sun had set, and darkness was coming on; consequently, there was no possibility, for that day, of getting the troops on shore without much confusion, if not danger. All therefore remained quiet for the night, with this exception, that the soldiers were removed from the large ships into such as drew least water; which running up as high as prudence would permit, under convoy of the gun-brigs and sloops of war, there cast anchor.

As soon as the dawn began to appear, on the morning of the 19th, there was a general stir throughout the fleet. A gun-brig had already taken her station within a hundred and fifty yards of a village called St. Benedict's, on the left bank of the river, where it was determined that the disembarkation should be effected. Her broadside was turned towards the shore, and her loaded with grape and round shot, were pointed at the beach, to cover the landing of the boats; and being moored and aft with spring-cables, she was altogether as manageable as if she had been under sail. The rest of the ships were several miles lower down the stream, some of them being aground the distance of four leagues from this point; but the boats were quickly hoisted out from every one of them, and the river as covered in a trice with a well-manned and warlike flotilla. The disembarkation was conducted with the greatest regularity and dispatch. Though the stream ran strong against them, and some of them were obliged to row fourteen or fifteen miles backwards and forwards, so strenuously did the sailors exert themselves, that by three o'clock in the afternoon the whole army was landed, and occupied a strong position about two miles above the village.

From what I have stated respecting the gun-brig, it will be seen that all things were in readiness to meet and repel opposition, should such be offered. Her broadside being pointed directly towards the village, whilst it hindered the enemy from bringing down troops in that direction, gave to our people an opportunity of forming, and being able to meet, in good order, whatever force might be posted to check their advance up the country. Had a few pieces of artillery been mounted, indeed, upon the high ground, afterwards taken possession of by us, some execution might have been done upon the boats as they drew towards the beach; but even that would have been trifling, because, unless they had had leisure to heat their shot, no artillery, in the open country could have long stood before the fire of even a gun-brig, armed as this was for the occasion with long thirty-two pounders. Each boat-load of soldiers, likewise, drew up the moment they stepped on shore, forming line without any regard to companies or battalions; whilst parties were instantly dispatched to reconnoitre, and to take possession of every house, as well as to line every hedge, in front of the shore where their comrades were arriving. But these preparations, though no more than common prudence required, were unnecessary; since there was not only no opposition to the landing, but, apparently, no enemy within many miles of the place.

So much time was unavoidably expended in establishing the different regiments on the ground allotted to them, in bringing up the hospital and commissariat stores, and arranging the materiel, that when all things were ready, the day appeared too far spent to permit an advance into a country, of the nature and military situation of which we were of course ignorant. The afternoon was accordingly devoted to a proper distribution of the force; which was divided into three brigades, in the following order:—

The first, or light brigade, consisted of the 85th, the light infantry companies of the 4th, 21st, and 44th regiments, with the party of disciplined negroes, and a company of marines, amounting in all to about eleven hundred men; to the command of which Colonel Thornton, of the 85th regiment, was appointed.

The second brigade, composed of the 4th and 44th regiments, which mustered together fourteen hundred and sixty bayonets, was intrusted to the care of Colonel Brooke, of the

44th; and the third, made up of the 21st, and the battalion of marines, and equalling in number the second brigade, was commanded by Colonel Patterson, of the 21st. The whole of the infantry may, therefore, be estimated at four thousand and twenty men. Besides these, there were landed about a hundred artillery-men, and an equal number of drivers; but for want of horses to drag them, no more than one six-pounder and two small three-pounder guns were brought on shore. Except those belonging to the General and staff-officers, there was not a single horse in the whole army. To have taken on shore a large park of artillery would have been, under such circumstances, absolute folly, indeed, the pieces which were actually landed, proved in the end of very little service, and were drawn by seamen sent from the different ships for the purpose. The sailors, thus employed, may be rated at a hundred, and those occupied in carrying stores, ammunition, and other necessaries, at a hundred more; and thus, by adding these, together with fifty sappers and miners, to the above amount, the whole number of men landed at St. Benedict's may be computed at four thousand five hundred.

This little army was posted upon a height which rises at the distance of two miles from the river. In front was a valley, cultivated for some way, and intersected with orchards; at the further extremity of which the advanced piquets took their ground; pushing forward a chain of sentinels to the very skirts of the forest. The right of the position was protected by a farm-house with its enclosure and outbuildings, and the left rested upon the edge of the hill, or rather mound, which there abruptly ended. On the brow of the hill, and about the centre of the line were placed the cannon, ready loaded, and having lighted fusees beside them; whilst the infantry bivouacked immediately under the ridge, or rather upon the slope of the hill which looked towards the shipping, in order to prevent their disposition from being seen by the enemy; should they come down to attack. But as we were now in a country where we could not calculate upon being safe in rear, any more than in front, the chain of piquets was carried round both flanks, and so arranged, that no attempt could be made to get between the army and the fleet, without due notice, and time given to oppose and prevent it. Everything, in short, was arranged with the utmost skill, and every chance of surprise provided against; but the night passed in quiet, nor was an opportunity afforded of evincing the utility of the very soldier-like dispositions which had been made.

Chapter 8
Marches & Skirmishes

Next morning the troops, as is customary during a state of active warfare, were under arms an hour before daylight, and remained in position till after the sun had risen. It was then confidently expected that the column would be put in motion, though in what direction it was to proceed, or what was the object of the descent, none but the General himself appeared to know. A rumour, indeed, prevailed, that a flotilla of gun-boats upon the Patuxent, commanded by the American Commodore Barney, was the point of attack; and that while the land force advanced up the river to prevent their retreat, armed boats from the fleet were to engage them in front. That such was in reality the primary object of the landing, I have every reason to believe, though circumstances afterwards occurred to bring about a change in the plan of operations. Into these, however, I shall not now enter, because they are in no way, connected with the present stage of my narrative, but shall merely observe, that in their expectations of an immediate advance the troops were disappointed. Whether it was that the arrangements had not been completed, or that intelligence respecting the state of the country and the enemy's preparations was wanting, I do not know; but the regiments returned to the ground which they had occupied during the night, and everything resumed the same face which it had worn on the evening before.

In this state affairs continued till four o'clock in the afternoon, when the General suddenly made his appearance in the camp, the bugles sounded, and the regiments formed in order for marching. Nor did many minutes elapse before the word was given, and the army began to move, taking the direction of Nottingham, a town situated on the river, where it was understood that the flotilla lay at anchor. The march was conducted with the same caution and good order that had marked the choice of ground for encamping and the disposition of the troops in position. The advanced-guard, consisting of three companies of infantry, led the way. These, however, were preceded by a section of twenty men, moving before them at the distance of a hundred yards; and even these twenty were but the followers of two files, sent forward to prevent surprise, and to give warning of the approach of the enemy. Parallel with the head of the three companies marched the flank patrols; parties of forty or fifty men, which, extending in files from each side of the road, swept the woods and fields to the distance of nearly half a mile. After the advanced guard, leaving an interval of a hundred or a hundred and fifty yards, came the light brigade; which, as well as the advance, sent out flankers to secure itself against ambuscades. Next to it, again, marched the second brigade, moving steadily on, and leaving the skirmishing and reconnoitring to those in front; then came the artillery, consisting, as I have already stated, of one six and two three-pounder guns, drawn by seamen; and last of all came the third brigade, leaving a detachment at the same distance from the rear of the column, as the advanced guard was from its front.

In moving through an enemy's country, the journeys of an army will, except under particular circumstances, be regulated by the nature of the ground over which it passes: thus, though eight, ten, or even twelve miles may be considered as a short day's march, yet if at the end of that space an advantageous position occur (that is, a piece of ground well defended by natural or accidental barriers, and at the same time calculated for the operations of that species of force of which the army may be composed), it would be the height of imprudence to push forward, merely because a greater extent of country might be traversed without fatiguing the troops. On the other hand, should an army have proceeded eighteen, twenty, or even twenty-five miles, without the occurrence of any such position, nothing except the prospect of losing a large proportion of his men from weariness ought to induce a general to stop, until he has reached some spot at least more tenable than the rest. Our march to-day was, upon this principle, extremely short, the troops halting when they had arrived at a rising ground distant not more than six miles from the point whence they set out; and having stationed the piquets, planted the sentinels, and made such other arrangements as the case required, fires were lighted, and the men were suffered to lie down.

It may seem strange, but it is nevertheless true, that during this short march of six miles a greater number of soldiers dropped out of the ranks, and fell behind from fatigue, than I recollect to have seen in any march in the Peninsula of thrice its duration. The fact is that the men, from having been so long cooped up in ships, and unused to carry their baggage and arms, were become relaxed and enervated to a degree altogether unnatural; and this, added to the extreme sultriness of the day, which exceeded anything we had yet experienced, quite overpowered them. The load which they carried, likewise, was far from trifling, since, independent of their arms and sixty rounds of ball-cartridge, each man bore upon his back a knapsack, containing shirts, shoes, stockings, &c., a blanket, a haversack, with provisions for three days, and a canteen or wooden keg filled with water. Under these circumstances, the occurrence of the position was extremely fortunate, since not only would the speedy failure of light have compelled a halt, whether the ground chanced to be favourable or the reverse, but even before darkness had come on scarcely two-thirds of the soldiers would have been found in their places.

The ground upon which we bivouacked, though not remarkable for its strength, was precisely such as might tempt a

General to halt, who found his men weary and in danger of being benighted. It was a gentle eminence, fronted by an open and cultivated country, and crowned with two or three houses, having barns and walled gardens attached to them. Neither flank could be said to rest upon any point peculiarly well defended, but they were not exposed; because, by extending or condensing the line, almost any one of these houses might be converted into a protecting redoubt. The outposts, again, were so far arranged differently from those of yesterday, that, instead of covering only the front and the two extremities, they extended completely round the encampment, enclosing the entire army within a connected chain of sentinels; and precluding the possibility of even a single individual making his way within the lines unperceived.

These precautions were, however, like those of the preceding day, unnecessary; no enemy making his appearance, even to reconnoitre: and yet it cannot be said that the night was passed in uninterrupted quiet, for the troops had scarcely lain down when they were disturbed by a tremendous storm of thunder and lightning, accompanied by a heavy fall of rain. The effect of the lightning, as it glanced for a moment upon the bivouac, and displayed the firelocks piled in regular order, and the men stretched like so many corpses beside them, was extremely fine. The effect of the rain, however, was not so agreeable, for, being perfectly destitute of shelter, we were speedily wet to the skin; and the remainder of our resting-time was rendered thereby the reverse of comfortable. But the feeling of fretfulness, natural on such an occasion, lasted no longer than till the day dawned, and the line of march was again formed; when their former good-humour returning, and seasoned in some degree by the fatigues of yesterday, the troops moved on in excellent order and in the highest spirits.

The route to-day was different, in many respects, from that of yesterday. In the first place, we had now got beyond the stretch of cultivation, and were proceeding through forests of immeasurable extent; this, of itself, gave a very different aspect to all around, because hitherto we had seen houses and fields of corn on each side of the road, and now we could discover nothing but wild savannahs, apparently untenanted by a single human being. In the next place, we learnt from some of the country people, who had been impressed as guides into our service, that numerous detached bodies of riflemen lay in ambush among the thickets; and the very expectation of having something to do, created a degree of excitement which, till now, we had not experienced. In consequence of that information, the flank patrols were strengthened and commanded to extend to a greater distance; the advanced guard marched at a greater interval from the head of the column, and the whole army moved forward with more caution and circumspection than had hitherto been used.

In the course of this day's march a little adventure occurred to myself, which, in the illiberality of my heart, I could not but regard as strikingly characteristic of the character of the people to whom we were now opposed, and which, as at the time it had something in it truly comical, I cannot resist the inclination of repeating, though aware that its title to drollery must in a great measure be lost in the relation. Having been informed that in a certain part of the forest a company of riflemen had passed the night, I took with me a party of soldiers, and proceeded in the direction pointed out, with the hope of surprising them. On reaching the place, I found that they had retired, but I thought I could perceive something like the glitter of arms a little farther towards the middle of the wood. Sending several files of soldiers in different directions, I contrived to surround the spot, and then moving forward, I beheld two men dressed in black coats, and armed with bright firelocks and bayonets, sitting under a tree; as soon as they observed me, they started up and took to their heels, but being hemmed in on all sides, they quickly perceived that to escape was impossible, and accordingly stood still. I hastened towards them, and having arrived within a few paces of where they stood, I heard the one say to the other, with a look of the most perfect simplicity, "Stop, John, till the gentlemen pass." There was something so ludicrous in this speech, and in the cast of countenance which accompanied it, that I could not help laughing aloud; nor was my mirth diminished by their attempts to persuade me that they were quiet country people, come out for no other purpose than to shoot squirrels. When I desired to know whether they carried bayonets to charge the squirrels, as well as muskets to shoot them, they were rather at a loss for a reply; but they grumbled exceedingly when they found themselves prisoners, and conducted as such to the column.

But to return to the principal narrative. The army had now advanced within a few miles of Nottingham, and the men were beginning to look forward with some anxiety to a halt; whilst as yet nothing beyond the capture of a few stragglers had occurred to confirm the rumours which, in the morning, and during the whole of the march, had occasioned so much more circumspection than appeared to be requisite. The day was likewise far spent, and, as was to be expected, the ranks were beginning to be less carefully preserved, when a smart firing in the wood upon the right of the road gave new life and energy to the soldiers. It was now confidently expected that the enemy would make a stand. The column closed its order, ready to wheel into line in a moment, and everything was on the qui vive: but it proved to be no more than a reencounter between a party of American riflemen and the flank patrol. After firing a few shots, the enemy gave way, and our main body, which had continued to move on during the skirmish, came in without the slightest opposition to the town of Nottingham.

We found this place (a town or large village, capable of containing from a thousand to fifteen hundred inhabitants) completely deserted. Not an individual was to be seen in the streets, or remained in the houses; whilst the appearance of the furniture, &c., in some places the very bread left in the ovens, showed that it had been evacuated in great haste, and immediately before our arrival. The town itself stands upon the banks of the Patuxent, and consists of four short streets, two running parallel with the river, and two others crossing them at right angles, The houses are not such as indicate the existence of much wealth or grandeur among the owners, being in general built of wood, and little superior to cottages; but around the village are others of a far better description, which convey the idea of good substantial farm-houses, a species of mansion very common in the United States. For several miles in every direction the country was in a high state of cultivation; though, instead of the maize and wheat which we had hitherto seen, the fields were covered with an abundant and luxuriant crop of tobacco. This plant seems, indeed, to be at all times the staple commodity of that district; for, besides what was growing and unripe, we found numerous barns filled with the remains of last year's crop; the whole of which was, of course, seized in the name of His Majesty King George the Third. But in the main object of our pursuit we were disappointed. The flotilla, which had been stationed opposite to Nottingham, retired, on our approach, higher up the stream; and we were consequently in the situation of a huntsman who sees his hounds at fault, and has every reason to apprehend that his game will escape.

In this posture the army continued during the night, having its right defended by the river, and its left extending considerably beyond the town, and secured, as usual, by a connected chain of outposts; nor was it put in motion, as had been done the day before, as soon as there was sufficient light to distinguish objects. There seemed, indeed, to be something like hesitation as to the course to be pursued,—whether to follow the gun-boats, or to return to the shipping; but, at last, the former proceeding was resolved upon, and the column set forward about eight o'clock, in the direction of Marlborough, another village, about ten miles beyond Nottingham. The road by which we travelled, as well to-day as during the whole of the excursion, was remarkably good; in some places rather heavy, from being cut through a sandy soil, but in general hard, dusty, and, to use an expressive phrase, having a sound bottom. Running, as it did for the most part, through the heart of thick forests, it was also well sheltered from the rays of the sun; a circumstance which, in a climate like this, is of no slight importance. To-day, our whole journey was of this description, nor did we reach a single cultivated spot till we approached the vicinity of Marlborough; when we found ourselves in a country not more fertile than beautiful. The ground, which had been hitherto perfectly flat, was now broken into the most graceful swells, generally cleared of wood to within a short space of the summits, and then crowned with hoar and venerable forests. The village itself lies in a valley formed by two green hills; the distance from the base of one hill to the base of the other may be about two miles, the whole of which was laid out in fields of corn, hay, and tobacco; whilst the slopes themselves were covered with sheep, for whose support they furnished ample means. But Marlborough is not, like an English village, compact, and consisting of one or two lanes the houses are scattered over the plain, and along the sides of the hills, at considerable intervals from one another, and are all surrounded by orchards and gardens, abounding in peaches and other fruits of the most delicious flavour. To add to the beauty of the place, a small rivulet makes its way through the bottom, and winding round the foot of one of these ridges, falls into the Patuxent, which flows at its back.

During our progress to-day the same caution was observed which had been practised yesterday. Nor was it altogether unnecessary, several bodies of the enemy's horse occasionally showing themselves, and what appeared to be the rear-guard of a column of infantry evacuating Marlborough, as our advance entered.

There was, however, little or no skirmishing, and we were allowed to remain in the village all night without molestation. But if we were not harassed, we were at least startled on the march by several heavy explosions. The cause of these we were at first unable to discover; but we soon learnt that they were occasioned by the blowing up of the very squadron of which we were in pursuit, and which Commodore Barney, perceiving the impossibility of preserving, prudently destroyed, in order to prevent its falling into our hands.

In Marlborough we remained not only during the night, but till past noon on the following day. The hesitation which had caused the loss of a few hours at Nottingham again interfered, and produced a delay which might have been attended with serious consequences. At length, however, orders were given to form, and we quitted Marlborough about two in the afternoon, taking the road to Washington. During this day's march there was more skirmishing than had yet occurred. We had scarcely got above three miles from the village, when the advanced guard fell in with a party of riflemen, who maintained a sharp contest before they gave way. The column, however, continued to move on without molestation, till arriving at a point where two roads meet, the one leading to Washington, the other to Alexandria, a strong body of troops, with some artillery, were observed upon the slope of a height opposite. The capture of Washington was now the avowed object of our invasion; but the General, like an experienced officer, was desirous of keeping his enemy in the dark as to his plan of operations. Whilst the advanced guard, therefore, reinforced by two additional companies, marched directly forward to dislodge the party from the heights, the rest of the army wheeled to the left, taking the road which leads, not to Washington, but to Alexandria. These movements were not lost upon the enemy, who, observing by the dust in what direction the main body had filed off, immediately began to retreat, without waiting for the approach of the detachment sent against ahem. As they ascended the hill, however, they made a show of halting and forming a line. Our men moved steadily on in column, covered by one company in extended order along the front; but the enemy, having merely thrown a few round shot with great precision among the skirmishers, broke once again into marching order, and were quickly hid by the rising ground. As soon as they had disappeared, the advance halted; and having remained for about an hour on a little hill to watch their motions, turned to the left, and followed the rest of the army, which they found advantageously posted at a place called Woodyard.

Chapter 9
The Battle of Bladensburg

I had almost forgotten to state that, from the first moment of our landing, the want of cavalry, so useful in obtaining information and reconnoitring the open country, was very sensibly felt. To remedy this evil, as far as it could by such means be remedied, orders had been issued to catch and bring in all the horses that were found in the fields or stables of any houses along the road; and these orders being punctually obeyed, there were now fifty or sixty in the camp. Upon these some of the artillery-drivers were mounted, and the command of the troop being given to an officer of experience, it was found of great service during the remainder of the march.

The advanced guard having joined the main body, the whole army, with the exception of a party which had been sent to the rear to bring up a convoy of provisions, was now bivouacked upon a rising ground, well defended by hedge-rows and thickets. The night, however, was not spent in as much quietness as usual. It was late before the troops got to their ground, consequently the piquets, for want of light, could not be posted in their customary good order, neither had there been time to examine the country in the neighbourhood of the position. The outposts were, therefore, kept in a state of constant anxiety by the frequent appearance of small parties of the enemy, who hovered about, probably with the design of cutting off stragglers, or perhaps of surprising, if they could, some of the piquets themselves. But whatever their intentions might be, the vigilance of the sentries contrived to render them abortive; nor did anything occur during the night productive of serious alarm; and the following day, being joined by the convoy which came up in safety, the column was again in motion, hastening across the country into the highroad, which had been deserted for no other purpose than to mislead the Americans.

Having started on the 24th at an early hour, our march was for some time both cool and agreeable. The road—if road it could be called—wound for the first five miles through the heart of an immense forest, and being, in every sense of the word, a by-path, was completely overshadowed by projecting branches of trees, so closely interwoven, as to prevent a single sunbeam from making its way, even at noon, within the arch. We continued to move on, therefore, long after the sun had risen, without being sensible that there was not a cloud in the sky to screen us from his influence; whilst a heavy moisture continually emitted from the grass and weeds on both sides of us, produced a coolness which, had it been less confined, would have proved extremely pleasant. So far, then, we proceeded without experiencing any other inconvenience than what was produced by the damp and fetid atmosphere which we breathed; but no sooner had we begun to emerge from the woods and to enter the open country, than an overpowering change was perceived. The sun, from which we had been hitherto defended, now beat upon us in full force; and the dust rising in thick masses from under our feet, without a breath of air to disperse it, flew directly into our faces, occasioning the greatest inconvenience both to the eyes and respiration. I have stated this at length, because I do not recollect a period of my military life during which I suffered more severely from heat and fatigue; and as a journey of a few miles, under such circumstances, tells more than one of thrice the distance in a cool day and along a firm wintry road, it is not surprising that before many hours had elapsed numbers of men began to fall behind from absolute inability to keep up.

Yet, in spite of all this, there was that in to-day's march which rendered it infinitely more interesting than any we had performed since the landing. We had learnt, from various quarters, that the enemy was concentrating his forces for the purpose of hazarding a battle in defence of his capital. The truth of these rumours we had no cause to doubt, confirmed as they were by what we had ourselves witnessed only the evening before; indeed the aspect of various fields on each side of the high road (which we had now regained), where smoking ashes, bundles of straw, and remnants of broken victuals were scattered about, indicated that considerable bodies of troops had passed the night in this neighbourhood. The appearance of the road itself, likewise, imprinted as it was with fresh marks of many feet and hoofs, proved that these troops could be no great way before us; whilst our very proximity to Washington, being now distant from it not more than ten or twelve miles, all tended to assure us that we should at least see an American army before dark.

It was now that we experienced the great usefulness of our badly mounted troopers, or as they were called by the private soldiers, our Cossacks. The country, from being extremely close, had become open on every side to a considerable extent, although thick groves, instead of hedges, frequently separated one field from another. This was exactly the ground on which cavalry could act with advantage; because they might lie in ambush behind these groves, totally unperceived, and when an opportunity offered, charge the column, before it had time to prepare for their reception. There were one or two places, indeed, where such events were confidently anticipated; whole rows of paling having been pulled up from the side of the road, and open spaces left, through which several squadrons of horse might gallop; and the consequence was that every man held his breath in expectation, and prepared himself to form square in a moment. It was here that the mounted drivers became peculiarly useful. They were divided into small parties of six or eight, and sent out in different directions to reconnoitre, two of them generally taking post at every suspicious corner, that one might give notice to the column, whilst the other watched the motions of an enemy.

It so happened that these precautions were unnecessary, for whatever might be the strength of the Americans in cavalry, their General did not think fit to employ it in harassing our march. But the very knowledge that every danger was provided against, and that they could not be attacked without having time to make ready, gave to the soldiers a degree of steady confidence which they would otherwise have wanted; and the want of which, had the case been different, might have been productive of disorder at a moment when good order was of vital importance.

We had now proceeded about nine miles, during the last four of which the sun's rays had beat continually upon us, and we had inhaled almost as great a quantity of dust as of air. Numbers of men had already fallen to the rear, and many more could with difficulty keep up; consequently, if we pushed on much farther without resting, the chances were that at least one half of the army would be left behind. To prevent this from happening, and to give time for the stragglers to overtake the column, a halt was determined upon, and being led forward to a spot of ground well wooded, and watered by a stream which crossed the road, the troops were ordered to refresh themselves. Perhaps no halt ever arrived more seasonably than this, or bid fair to be productive of more beneficial effects; yet so oppressive was the heat, that we had not resumed our march above an hour, when the banks by the way side were again covered with stragglers; some of the finest and stoutest men in the army being literally unable to go on.

The hour of noon was approaching, when a heavy cloud of dust, apparently not more than two or three miles distant, attracted our attention. From whence it originated there was little difficulty in guessing, nor did many minutes expire before surmise was changed into certainty: for on turning a sudden angle in the road, and passing a small plantation, which obstructed the vision towards the left, the British and American armies became visible to one another. The position occupied by the latter was one of great strength and commanding attitude. They were drawn up in three lines upon the brow of a hill, having their front and left flank covered by a branch of the Potomac, and their right resting upon a thick wood and a deep ravine. This river, which may be about the breadth of the Isis at Oxford, flowed between the heights occupied by the American forces and the little town of Bladensburg. Across it was thrown a narrow bridge, extending from the chief street in that town to the continuation of the road, which passed through the very centre of their position; and its right bank (the bank above which they were drawn up) was covered with a narrow stripe of willows and larch trees, whilst the left was altogether bare, low, and exposed. Such was the general aspect of their position as at the first glance it presented itself; of which I must endeavour to give a more detailed account, that my description of the battle may be in some degree intelligible.

I have said that the right bank of the Potomac was covered with a narrow stripe of willow and larch trees. Here the Americans had stationed strong bodies of riflemen, who, in skirmishing order, covered the whole front of their army. Behind this plantation, again, the fields were open and clear, intersected, at certain distances, by rows of high and strong palings. About the middle of the ascent, and in the rear of one of these rows, stood the first line, composed entirely of infantry; at a proper interval from this, and in a similar situation, stood the second line; while the third, or reserve, was posted within the skirts of a wood, which crowned the heights. The artillery, again, of which they had twenty pieces in the field, was thus arranged on the high road, and commanding the bridge, stood two heavy guns; and four more, two on each side of the road, swept partly in the same direction, and partly down the whole of the slope into the streets of Bladensburg. The rest were scattered, with no great judgment, along the second line of infantry, occupying different spaces between the right of one regiment and the left of another; whilst the cavalry showed itself in one mass, within a stubble field, near the extreme left of the position. Such was the nature of the ground which they occupied, and the formidable posture in which they waited our approach; amounting, by their own account, to nine thousand men, a number exactly doubling that of the force which was to attack them.

In the mean time, our column continued to advance in the same order which it had hitherto preserved. The road, having conducted us for about two miles in a direction parallel with the river, and of consequence with the enemy's line, suddenly turned, and led directly towards the town of Bladensburg. Being of course ignorant whether this town might not be filled with American troops, the main body paused here till the advanced guard should reconnoitre. The result proved that no opposition was intended in that quarter, and that the whole of the enemy's army had been withdrawn to the opposite side of the stream, whereupon the column was again put in motion, and in a short time arrived in the streets of Bladensburg, and within range of the American artillery. Immediately on our reaching this point, several of their guns opened upon us, and kept up a quick and well-directed cannonade, from which, as we were again commanded to halt, the men were directed to shelter themselves as much as possible behind the houses. The object of this halt, it was conjectured, was to give the General an opportunity of examining the American line, and of trying the depth of the river; because at present there appeared to be but one practicable mode of attack, by crossing the bridge, and taking the enemy directly in front. To do so, however, exposed as the bridge was, must be attended with bloody consequences, nor could the delay of a few minutes produce any mischief which the discovery of a ford would not amply compensate.

But in this conjecture we were altogether mistaken; for without allowing time to the column to close its ranks, or to be joined by such of the many stragglers as were now hurrying, as fast as weariness would permit, to regain their places, the order to halt was countermanded, and the word given to attack; and we immediately pushed on at double quick time, towards the head of the bridge. While we were moving along the street, a continued fire was kept up, with some execution, from those guns which stood to the left of the road; but it was not till the bridge was covered with our people that the two-gun battery upon the road itself began to play.—Then, indeed, it also opened, and with tremendous effect; for at the first discharge almost an entire company was swept down; but whether it was that the guns had been previously laid with measured exactness, or that the nerves of the gunners became afterwards unsteady, the succeeding discharges were much less fatal. The riflemen likewise began to gall us from the wooded bank with a running fire of musketry; and it was not without trampling upon many of their dead and dying comrades that the light brigade established itself on the opposite side of the stream.

When once there, however, everything else appeared easy. Wheeling off to the right and left of the road, they dashed into the thicket, and quickly cleared it of the American skirmishers; who, falling back with precipitation upon the first line, threw it into disorder before it had fired a shot. The consequence was, that our troops had scarcely shown themselves when the whole of that line gave way, and fled in the greatest confusion, leaving the two guns upon the road in possession of the victors.

But here it must be confessed that the light brigade was guilty of imprudence. Instead of pausing till the rest of the army came up, the soldiers lightened themselves by throwing away their knapsacks and haversacks; and extending their ranks so as to show an equal front with the enemy, pushed on to the attack of the second line. The Americans, however, saw their weakness, and stood firm, and having the whole of their artillery, with the exception of the pieces captured on the road, and the greater part of their infantry in this line, they first checked the ardour of the assailants by a heavy fire, and then, in their turn, advanced to recover the ground which was lost. Against this charge the extended order of the British troops would not permit them to offer an effectual resistance, and they were accordingly borne back to the very thicket upon the river's brink; where they maintained themselves with determined obstinacy, repelling all attempts to drive them through it; and frequently following, to within a short distance of the cannon's mouth, such parts of the enemy's line as gave way.

In this state the action continued till the second brigade had likewise crossed, and formed upon the right bank of the river; when the 44th regiment moving to the right, and driving in the skirmishers, debouched upon the left flank of the Americans, and completely turned it. In that quarter, therefore, the battle was won; because the raw militia-men, who were stationed there as being the least assailable point, when once broken could not be rallied. But on their right the enemy still kept their ground with much resolution; nor was it till the arrival of the 4th regiment, and the advance of the British forces in firm array to the charge, that they began to waver. Then, indeed, seeing their left in full flight, and the 44th getting in their rear, they lost all order, and dispersed, leaving clouds of riflemen to cover their retreat; and hastened to conceal themselves in the woods, where it would have been madness to follow them. The rout was now general throughout the line. The reserve, which ought to have supported the main body, fled as soon as those in its front began to give way; and the cavalry, instead of charging the British troops, now scattered in pursuit, turned their horses' heads and galloped off, leaving them in undisputed possession of the field, and of ten out of the twenty pieces of artillery.

This battle, by which the fate of the American capital was decided, began about one o'clock in the afternoon, and lasted till four. The loss on the part of the English was severe, since, out of two-thirds of the army, which were engaged, upwards of five hundred men were killed and wounded; and what rendered it doubly severe was, that among these were numbered several officers of rank and distinction. Colonel Thornton, who commanded the light brigade, Lieutenant-Colonel Wood, commanding the 85th regiment, and Major Brown, who led the advanced guard, were all severely wounded; and General Ross himself had a horse shot under him.

On the side of the Americans the slaughter was not so great. Being in possession of a strong position, they were of course less exposed in defending, than the others in storming it; and had they conducted themselves with coolness and resolution, it is not conceivable how the battle could have been won. But the fact is, that, with the exception of a party of sailors from the gun-boats, under the command of Commodore Barney, no troops could behave worse than they did. The skirmishers were driven in as soon as attacked, the first line gave way without offering the slightest resistance, and the left of the main body was broken within half an hour after it was seriously engaged. Of the sailors, however, it would be injustice not to speak in the terms which their conduct merits. They were employed as gunners, and not only did they serve their guns with a quickness and precision which astonished their assailants, but they stood till some of them were actually bayoneted, with fuses in their hands; nor was it till their leader was wounded and taken, and they saw themselves deserted on all sides by the soldiers, that they quitted the field. With respect to the British army, again, no line of distinction can be drawn. All did their duty, and none more gallantly than the rest; and though the brunt of the affair fell upon the light brigade, this was owing chiefly to the circumstance of its being at the head of the column, and perhaps also, in some degree, to its own rash impetuosity. The artillery, indeed, could do little; being unable to show itself in presence of a force so superior; but the six-pounder was nevertheless brought into action, and a corps of rockets proved of striking utility.

Our troops being worn down from fatigue, and of course as ignorant of the country as the Americans were the reverse, the pursuit could not be continued to any distance. Neither was it attended with much slaughter. Diving into the recesses of the forests, and covering themselves with riflemen, the enemy were quickly beyond our reach; and having no cavalry to scour even the high road, ten of the lightest of their guns were carried off in the flight. The defeat, however, was absolute, and the army which had been collected for the defence of Washington was scattered beyond the possibility of, at least, an immediate reunion; and as the distance from Bladensburg to that city does not exceed four miles, there appeared to be no further obstacle in the way to prevent its immediate capture.

Chapter 10
The Burning of Washington

An opportunity so favourable was not endangered by any needless delay. While the two brigades which had been engaged remained upon the field to recover their order, the third, which had formed the reserve, and was consequently unbroken, took the lead, and pushed forward at a rapid rate towards Washington.

As it was not the intention of the British Government to attempt permanent conquests in this part of America, and as the General was well aware that, with a handful of men, he could not pretend to establish himself, for any length of time, in an enemy's capital, he determined to lay it under contribution, and to return quietly to the shipping. Nor was there anything unworthy of the character of a British officer in this determination. By all the customs of war, whatever public property may chance to be in a captured town, becomes, confessedly, the just spoil of the conqueror; and in thus proposing to accept a certain sum of money in lieu of that property, he was showing mercy rather than severity to the vanquished. It is true that if they chose to reject his terms he and his army would be deprived of their booty, because without some more convenient mode of transporting it than we possessed, even the portable part of the property itself could not be removed. But, on the other hand, there was no difficulty in destroying it; and thus, though we should gain nothing, the American Government would lose probably to a much greater amount than if they had agreed to purchase its preservation by the money demanded.

Such being the intention of General Ross, he did not march the troops immediately into the city, but halted them upon a plain in its immediate vicinity, whilst a flag of truce was sent forward with terms. But whatever his proposal might have been, it was not so much as heard; for scarcely had the party bearing the flag entered the street, when it was fired upon from the windows of one of the houses, and the horse of the General himself, who accompanied it, killed. The indignation excited by this act throughout all ranks and classes of men in the army, was such as the nature of the case could not fail to occasion. Every thought of accommodation was instantly laid aside; the troops advanced forthwith into the town, and having first put to the sword all who were found in the house from which the shots were fired, and reduced it to ashes, they proceeded without a moment's delay to burn and destroy everything in the most distant degree connected with Government.

In this general devastation were included the Senate-house, the President's palace, an extensive dock-yard and arsenal, barracks for two or three thousand men, several large storehouses filled with naval and military stores, some hundreds of cannon of different descriptions, and nearly twenty thousand stand of small-arms. There were also two or three public ropewalks which shared the same fate, a fine frigate pierced for sixty guns, and just ready to be launched, several gun brigs and armed schooners, with a variety of gun-boats and small craft. The powder-magazines were set on fire, and exploded with a tremendous crash, throwing down many houses in their vicinity, partly by pieces of the walls striking them, and partly by the concussion of the air; whilst quantities of shot, shell, and hand-grenades, which could not otherwise be rendered useless, were cast into the river. In destroying the cannon a method was adopted which I had never before witnessed, and which, as it was both effectual and expeditious, I cannot avoid relating. One gun of rather a small calibre was pitched upon as the executioner of the rest, and being loaded with ball and turned to the muzzles of the others, it was fired, and thus beat out their breechings. Many, however, not being mounted, could not be thus dealt with; these were spiked, and having their trunnions knocked off, were afterwards cast into the bed of the river.

All this was as it should be, and had the arm of vengeance been extended no further, there would not have been room given for so much as a whisper of disapprobation. But unfortunately it did not stop here; a noble library, several printing-offices, and all the national archives were likewise committed to the flames, which, though no doubt the property of Government, might better have been spared. It is not, however, my intention to join the outcry which was raised at the time against what the Americans and their admirers were pleased to term a line of conduct at once barbarous and unprofitable. On the contrary, I conceive that too much praise cannot be given to the forbearance and humanity of the British troops, who, irritated as they had every right to be, spared, as far as possible, all private property, neither plundering nor destroying a single house in the place, except that from which the General's horse had been killed.

Whilst the third brigade was thus employed, the rest of the army, having recalled its stragglers, and removed the wounded into Bladensburg, began its march towards Washington. Though the battle came to a close by four o'clock, the sun had set before the different regiments were in a condition to move, consequently this short journey was performed in the dark. The work of destruction had also begun in the city before they quitted their ground; and the blazing of houses, ships, and stores, the report of exploding magazines, and the crash of falling roofs, informed them, as they proceeded, of what was going forward. It would be difficult to conceive a finer spectacle than that which presented itself as they approached the town. The sky was brilliantly illumined by the different conflagrations; and a dark red light was thrown upon the road, sufficient to permit each man to view distinctly his comrade's face. Except the burning of St. Sebastian's, I do not recollect to have witnessed at any period of my life a scene more striking or more sublime.

Having advanced as far as the plain, where the reserve had previously paused, the first and second brigades halted; and forming into close column, passed the night in bivouac. At first this was agreeable enough, because the air was mild, and weariness made up for what was wanting in comfort. But towards morning a violent storm of rain, accompanied with thunder and lightning, came on, which disturbed the rest of all who were exposed to it. Yet in spite of the inconvenience arising from the shower, I cannot say that I felt disposed to grumble at the interruption, for it appeared that what I had before considered as superlatively sublime, still wanted this to render it complete. The flashes of lightning vied in brilliancy with the flames which burst from the roofs of burning houses, whilst the thunder drowned for a time the noise of crumbling walls, and was only interrupted by the occasional roar of cannon, and of large depots of gunpowder, as they one by one exploded.

I need scarcely observe, that the consternation of the inhabitants was complete, and that to them this was a night of terror. So confident had they been of the success of their troops, that few of them had dreamt of quitting their houses or abandoning the city; nor was it till the fugitives from the battle began to rush in, filling every place as they came with dismay, that the President himself thought of providing for his safety. That gentleman, as I was credibly informed, had gone forth in the morning with the army, and had continued among his troops till the British forces began to make their appearance. Whether the sight of his enemies cooled his courage or not I cannot say, but according to my informant, no sooner was the glittering of our arms discernible, than he began to discover that his presence was more wanted in the senate than in the field; and having ridden through the ranks, and exhorted every man to do his duty, he hurried back to his own house, that he might prepare a feast for the entertainment of his officers, when they should return victorious. For the truth of these details I will not be answerable; but this much I know, that the feast was actually prepared, though, instead of being devoured by American officers, it went to satisfy the less delicate appetites of a party of English soldiers. When the detachment sent out to destroy Mr. Maddison's house, entered his dining parlour, they found a dinner-table spread, and covers laid for forty guests. Several kinds of wine in handsome cut-glass decanters were cooling on the sideboard; plate-holders stood by the fireplace, filled with dishes and plates; knives, forks, and spoons, were arranged for immediate use; everything in short was ready for the entertainment of a ceremonious party. Such were the arrangements in the dining-room, whilst in the kitchen were others answerable to them in every respect. Spits loaded with joints of various sorts turned before the fire; pots, saucepans, and other culinary utensils stood upon the grate; and all the other requisites for an elegant and substantial repast were in the exact state which indicated that they had been lately and precipitately abandoned.

The reader will easily believe that these preparations were beheld, by a party of hungry soldiers, with no indifferent eye. An elegant dinner, even though considerably over-dressed, was a luxury to which few of them, at least for some time back, had been accustomed; and which, after the dangers and fatigues of the day, appeared peculiarly inviting. They sat down to it, therefore, not indeed in the most orderly manner, but with countenances which would not have disgraced a party of aldermen at a civic feast; and having satisfied their appetites with fewer complaints than would have probably escaped their rival gourmands, and partaken pretty freely of the wines, they finished by setting fire to the house which had so liberally entertained them.

I have said that to the inhabitants of Washington this was a night of terror and dismay. From whatever cause the confidence arose, certain it is that they expected anything rather than the arrival among them of a British army; and their consternation was proportionate to their previous feeling of security, when an event, so little anticipated, actually came to pass. The first impulse naturally prompted them to fly, and the streets were speedily crowded with soldiers and senators, men, women, and children, horses, carriages, and carts loaded with household furniture, all hastening towards a wooden bridge which crosses the Potomac. The confusion thus occasioned was terrible, and the crowd upon the bridge was such as to endanger its giving way. But Mr. Maddison, as is affirmed, having escaped among the first, was no sooner safe on the opposite bank of the river, than he gave orders that the bridge should be broken down; which being obeyed, the rest were obliged to return, and to trust to the clemency of the victors.

In this manner was the night passed by both parties; and at daybreak next morning the light brigade moved into the city, whilst the reserve fell back to a height about half a mile in the rear. Little, however, now remained to be done, because everything marked out for destruction was already consumed. Of the Senate-house, the President's palace, the barracks, the dockyard, &c., nothing could be seen, except heaps of smoking ruins; and even the bridge, a noble structure upwards of a mile in length, was almost entirely demolished. There was, therefore, no further occasion to scatter the troops, and they were accordingly kept together as much as possible on the Capitol Hill.

Of the city of Washington I have purposely declined attempting any minute description, because it possesses no leading features, by catching which I might hope to convey to a person who has not seen it, something like an accurate notion of the whole. It was then, and is, I believe, still in its infancy, few of the streets being finished, and many containing not more than three or four houses, at wide intervals from each other. But its situation gives to it advantages such as few capitals either in the new or old world can boast of, and if it continue to be the head of the American States for another century, it will become, I doubt not, one of the most flourishing cities in existence. America is, and always will be, a commercial nation, nor can a single town throughout the whole of that vast continent boast of a better harbour than Washington. Standing upon the Potomac, one of the most navigable of all the rivers that empty themselves into the Chesapeake, the depth of which is sufficient to float a frigate for some way above the town, it possesses unrivalled facilities for the carrying on of an extensive trade; whilst its distance from the coast is such as to place it, in a great measure, beyond reach of insult from an enemy. Such an assertion, coming from one who has just detailed the particulars of its capture, may, indeed, appear to partake not slightly of the nature of a paradox; but there is no denying that the fall of Washington ought to be attributed much more to the misconduct of the Americans themselves, than to the skill or enterprise of those who effected it. Had the emergency been contemplated, and in a proper manner provided against, or had the most moderate ingenuity and courage been displayed in retarding the progress of our troops, the design, if formed at all, would have been either abandoned immediately, or must have ended in the total destruction of the invaders.

Like other infant towns, Washington is but little ornamented with fine buildings; except the Senate-house, I really know of none worthy to be noticed. This however is, or rather was, an edifice of some beauty. It stood, where its ruins now stand, upon a mound called the Capitol Hill, and near a trifling stream named the Tiber; from which circumstances these modern republicans are led to flatter themselves that the days are coming when it will rival in power and grandeur the Senate-house of ancient Rome herself. It was built entirely of freestone, tastefully worked and highly polished; and, besides its numerous windows, was lighted from the top by a large and handsome cupola. Perhaps it could not be said to belong to any decided style of architecture; but its central appearance was light, airy, and elegant. After traversing a wide and spacious entrance-hall, you arrived at the foot of a handsome spiral hanging staircase; on the right of which were two spacious apartments, one above the other, which were occupied as sitting chambers by the two houses of representatives. From these branched off several smaller rooms, fitted up as offices, and probably used as such by the various officers of state. On the right of the staircase, again, were two other apartments equal in size to those on the left, with a like number of smaller rooms branching off from them. These were furnished as a public library, the two larger being well stocked with valuable books, principally in modern languages, whilst the others, filled with archives, national statutes, acts of legislature, &c., were used as the private rooms of the librarians.

The President's house, on the other hand, though likewise a public building, was remarkable for nothing except the absence of taste exhibited in its structure. It was small, incommodious, and plain; in no respect likely to excite the jealousy of a people peculiarly averse to all pomp or parade, even in their chief magistrate. Besides these, there were also a custom-house, several banking-houses, and a school or college, all claiming to themselves the destruction of public works; but in them there was a plainness amounting almost to coarseness, and a general air of republicanism, by no means imposing. With respect to the number of inhabitants which Washington contained, I confess that I cannot pretend to give an opinion: but if any judgment may be formed from the extent of ground covered by what is considered as the town, I should say that they amounted to somewhere about sixty thousand. George Town, the quarter where the President's house stood, is compact and regular, containing, I should conceive, at least twenty thousand souls within itself; nor can the population of the other quarters be estimated at less than double that number.

Such was then the city of Washington, of which our hasty and unfriendly visit did not allow us to take a very minute survey. I return now to the movements of the British army.

I have stated above that our troops were this day kept as much together as possible upon the Capitol Hill. But it was not alone on account of the completion of their destructive labours that this was done. A powerful army of Americans already began to show themselves upon some heights, at the distance of two or three miles from the city; and as they sent out detachments of horse even to the very suburbs, for the purpose of watching our motions, it would have been unsafe to permit more straggling than was absolutely necessary. The army which we had overthrown the day before, though defeated, was far from annihilated; it had by this time recovered its panic, began to concentrate itself in our front, and presented quite as formidable an appearance as ever. We learnt, also, that it was joined by a considerable force from the back settlements, which had arrived too late to take part in the action, and the report was, that both combined amounted to nearly twelve thousand men.

Whether or not it was their intention to attack, I cannot pretend to say, because it was noon before they showed themselves; and soon after, when something like a movement could be discerned in their ranks, the sky grew suddenly dark, and the most tremendous hurricane ever remembered by the oldest inhabitant in the place came on. Of the prodigious force of the wind it is impossible for one who was not an eye-witness to its effects to form a conception. Roofs of houses were torn off by it, and whirled into the air like sheets of paper; whilst the rain which accompanied it resembled the rushing of a mighty cataract rather than the dropping of a shower. The darkness was as great as if the sun had long set, and the last remains of twilight had come on, occasionally relieved by flashes of vivid lightning streaming through it; which, together with the noise of the wind and the thunder, the crash of falling buildings, and the tearing of roofs as they were stript from the walls, produced the most appalling effect I ever have, and probably ever shall, witness. The storm lasted for nearly two hours without intermission, during which time many of the houses spared by us were blown down, and thirty of our men, besides several of the inhabitants, buried beneath their ruins. Our column was as completely dispersed as if it had received a total defeat; some of the men flying for shelter behind walls and buildings, and others falling flat upon the ground, to prevent themselves from being carried away by the tempest; nay, such was the violence of the wind, that two pieces of light cannon, which stood upon the eminence, were fairly lifted from the ground, and borne several yards to the rear.

Chapter 11
Fighting Outside the Capital

When the hurricane had blown over, the camp of the Americans appeared to be in as great a state of confusion as our own; nor could either party recover themselves sufficiently during the rest of the day to try the fortune of a battle. Of this General Ross did not fail to take advantage. He had already attained all that he could hope, and perhaps more than he originally expected to attain; consequently, to risk another action would only be to spill blood for no purpose. Whatever might be the issue of the contest, he could derive from it no advantage. If he were victorious, it would not do away with the necessity which existed of evacuating Washington; if defeated, his ruin was certain. To avoid fighting was therefore his object, and perhaps he owed its accomplishment to the fortunate occurrence of the storm. Be that, however, as it may, a retreat was resolved upon; and we now only waited for night, to put the resolution into practice.

There was, however, one difficulty to be surmounted in this proceeding. Of the wounded, many were so ill as to preclude all possibility of their removal, and to leave them in the hands of an enemy whom we had beaten was rather a mortifying anticipation. But for this there was no help; and it now only remained to make the best arrangements for their comfort, and to secure for them, as far as could be done, civil treatment from the Americans.

It chanced that, among other prisoners taken at Bladensburg, was Commodore Barney, an American officer of much gallantry and high sense of honour. Being himself wounded, he was the more likely to feel for those who were in a similar condition, and having received the kindest treatment from our medical attendants, as long as he continued under their hands, he became, without solicitation, the friend of his fellow-sufferers. To him, as well as to the other prisoners, was given his parole, and to his care were our wounded, in a peculiar manner, intrusted,—a trust which he received with the utmost willingness, and discharged with the most praiseworthy exactness. Among other stipulations, it was agreed that such of our people as were left behind should be considered as prisoners of war, and should be restored to us as soon as they were able to travel; and that, as soon as they reached the ships, the Commodore and his countrymen would, in exchange, be released from their engagements.

As soon as these arrangements were completed, and darkness had come on, the third brigade, which was posted in the rear of our army, began to withdraw. Then followed the guns, afterwards the second, and last of all the light brigade, exactly reversing the order which had been maintained during the advance. Instead of an advanced guard, this last now furnished a party to cover the retreat, and the whole procession was closed by the mounted drivers.

It being a matter of great importance to deceive the enemy and to prevent pursuit, the rear of the column did not quit its ground upon the Capitol till a late hour. During the day an order had been issued that none of the inhabitants should be seen in the streets after eight o'clock; and as fear renders most men obedient, the order was punctually attended to. All the horses belonging to different officers were removed to drag the guns, no one being allowed to ride, lest a neigh, or even the trampling of hoofs, should excite suspicion. The fires were trimmed, and made to blaze brightly; fuel enough was left to keep them so for some hours; and finally, about half-past nine o'clock the troops formed in marching order, and moved off in the most profound silence. Not a word was spoken, nor a single individual permitted to step one inch out of his place, by which means they passed along the streets perfectly unnoticed, and cleared the town without any alarm being given. Our pace, it will be imagined, was none of the most tardy, consequently it was not long before we reached the ground which had been occupied by the other brigades. Here we found a second line of fires blazing in the same manner as those deserted by ourselves; and the same precautions in every respect adopted, to induce a belief that our army was still quiet.—Beyond these, again, we found two or three solitary fires, placed in such order as to resemble those of a chain of piquets. In a word, the deception was so well managed, that even we ourselves were at first doubtful whether the rest of the troops had fallen back.

When we reached the ground where yesterday's battle had been fought, the moon rose, and exhibited a spectacle by no means enlivening.—The dead were still unburied, and lay about in every direction completely naked. They had been stripped even of their shirts, and having been exposed in this state to the violent rain in the morning, they appeared to be bleached to a most unnatural degree of whiteness. The heat and rain together had likewise affected them in a different manner; and the smell which rose upon the night air was horrible.

There is something in such a scene as this extremely humbling, and repugnant to the feelings of human nature. During the agitation of a battle, it is nothing to see men fall in hundreds by your side. You may look at them, perhaps, for an instant, but you do so almost without being yourself aware of it, so completely are your thoughts carried away by the excitation of the moment and the shouts of your companions.—But when you come to view the dead in an hour of calmness, stripped as they generally are, you cannot help remembering how frail may have been the covering which saved yourself from being the loathsome thing on which you are now gazing.—For myself, I confess that these reflections rose within my mind on the present occasion; and if any one should say that, similarly situated, they would not rise in his, I should give him no credit for a superior degree of courage, though I might be inclined to despise him for his want of the common feelings of a reasonable being.

In Bladensburg the brigade halted for an hour, while those men who had thrown away their knapsacks endeavoured to recover them. During this interval I strolled up to a house which had been converted into an hospital, and paid a hasty visit to the wounded. I found them in great pain, and some of them deeply affected at the thought of being abandoned by their comrades, and left to the mercy of their enemies. Yet, in their apprehension of evil treatment from the Americans, the event proved that they had done injustice to that people; who were found to possess at least one generous trait in their character, namely, that of behaving kindly and attentively to their prisoners.

As soon as the stragglers had returned to their ranks, we again moved on, continuing to march without once stopping to rest during the whole of the night. Of the fatigue of a night march none but those who have experienced it can form the smallest conception. Oppressed with the most intolerable drowsiness, we were absolutely dozing upon our legs; and if any check at the head of the column caused a momentary delay, the road was instantly covered with men fast asleep. It is generally acknowledged that no inclination is so difficult to resist as the inclination to sleep; but when you are compelled not only to bear up against that, but to struggle also with weariness, and to walk at the same time, it is scarcely possible to hold out long. By seven o'clock in the morning, it was found absolutely necessary to pause, because numbers had already fallen behind, and numbers more were ready to follow their example; when throwing ourselves upon the ground, almost in the same order in which we had marched, in less than five minutes there was not a single unclosed eye throughout the whole brigade. Piquets were of course stationed, and sentinels placed, to whom no rest was granted, but, except these, the entire army resembled a heap of dead bodies on a field of battle, rather than living men.

In this situation we remained till noon, when we were again roused to continue the retreat. Though the sun was oppressively powerful, we moved on without resting till dark, when having arrived at our old position near Marlborough, we halted for the night. During this day's march we were joined by numbers of negro slaves, who implored us to take them along with us, offering to serve either as soldiers or sailors, if we would but give them their liberty; but as General Ross persisted in protecting private property of every description, few of them were fortunate enough to obtain their wishes.

We had now proceeded a distance of thirty-five miles, and began to consider ourselves beyond the danger of pursuit. The remainder of the retreat was accordingly conducted with more leisure; our next march carrying us no farther than to Nottingham, where we remained during an entire day, for the purpose of resting the troops. It cannot, however, be said that this resting-time was spent in idleness. A gun-brig, with a number of ships' launches and long-boats, had made their way up the stream, and were at anchor opposite to the town. On board the former were carried such of the wounded as had been able to travel, whilst the latter were loaded with flour and tobacco, the only spoil which we found it practicable to bring off.

Whilst the infantry were thus employed, the cavalry was sent back as far as Marlborough, to discover whether there were any American forces in pursuit; and it was well for the few stragglers who had been left behind that this recognizance was made. Though there appeared to be no disposition on the part of the American General to follow our steps and to harass the retreat, the inhabitants of that village, at the instigation of a medical practitioner called Bain, had risen in arms as soon as we departed; and falling upon such individuals as strayed from the column, put some of them to death, and made others prisoners. A soldier whom they had taken, and who had escaped, gave information of these proceedings to the troopers, just as they were about to return to head-quarters; upon which they immediately wheeled about, and galloping into the village, pulled the doctor out of his bed (for it was early in the morning), compelled him, by a threat of instant death, to liberate his prisoners; and mounting him before one of the party, brought him in triumph to the camp.

The wounded, the artillery, and plunder, being all embarked on the 28th, at daybreak on the 29th we took the direction of St. Benedict's, where we arrived, without any adventure, at a late hour in the evening. Here we again occupied the ground of which we had taken possession on first landing, passing the night in perfect quiet; and next day, the boats of the fleet being ready to receive us, the regiments, one by one, marched down to the beach. We found the shore covered with sailors from the different ships of war, who welcomed our arrival with loud cheers; and having contrived to bring up a larger flotilla than had been employed in the disembarkation, they removed us within a few hours, and without the occurrence of any accident, to our respective vessels.

Such is a plain impartial account of the inroad upon Washington, an affair than which the whole war produced none more brilliant or more daring. In whatever light we may regard it, whether we look to the amount of difficulties which it behoved him to overcome, the inadequacy of the force which he commanded, or the distance which he was called upon to march, in the midst of a hostile population, and through deep and trackless forests, we cannot deny to General Ross the praise which is his due, of having planned and successfully accomplished an expedition which none but a sagacious mind could have devised, and none but a gallant spirit carried into execution. Among the many important transactions which then occupied the public attention, the campaign at Washington was, I believe, but little spoken of; and even now, it is overwhelmed in the recollections of the all-engrossing Waterloo; but the time will probably come, when he who at the head of four thousand men penetrated upwards of sixty miles into an enemy's country; overthrew an army more than double his own in point of numbers; took possession of the capital of a great nation, and having held it as long as it suited his own purposes to hold it, returned again in triumph to his fleet, will be ranked, as he deserves to be ranked, among the number of those who have most successfully contributed to elevate Great Britain to the height of military glory on which she now stands.

It has been said that the entire merit of this brilliant expedition is due, not so much to the brave man who conducted it, as to Sir George Cockburn, at whose suggestion it was undertaken. To the great gallantry and high talents of Sir George Cockburn no one who served within the compass of the Bay of Chesapeake will refuse to bear testimony, nor is it improbable that in attributing to him the original, design of laying Washington itself under contribution, common report speaks truly. But with whomsoever the idea first originated, to General Boss belongs the undivided of having, carried it into effect. From Sir George Cockburn, and indeed from the whole fleet, the army received every assistance which it was in the power of the fleet to bestow; but had no Ross been at the head of the land forces, the capital of the United States would have suffered no insult. I have ventured to make these remarks, not with any design of taking away, in the slightest degree, from the well-earned reputation of the living; but merely as an act of justice towards the memory of the gallant dead, whose services have hardly received all the notice, either from the Government or the country, which they deserved.

Of the degree of military sagacity exhibited on both sides, during the progress of hostilities, it scarcely becomes me to speak. Perhaps our leader delayed something too long in making, up his mind as to the ultimate end to be pursued, after the troop had penetrated so far into the interior as Marlborough. Had he pushed on at once, it is barely possible that Washington might have fallen at a less expense of human life than actually occurred. Perhaps, too, he commenced the attack at Bladensburg with a degree of precipitancy which hindered him from, taking advantage of an open ford, and compelled him to expose his troops to the fire of the enemy's artillery whilst crossing a narrow bridge in a single column. But these errors, if errors they may be termed, were amply compensated by the perfect success of his operations; whilst in every other particular his conduct was beyond the reach of censure. In his choice of ground for halting, in the order both of his advance and retreat, and in the rapidity of his movements as soon as his plans had been arranged, General Ross exhibited himself in the light of an able and diligent commander. No man could possess, more than he a soldier's eye in examining the face of a country; and in what little manoeuvring the circumstances permitted, he displayed the proficiency of one well practised in the arts of campaigning. It will be recollected, that on the 23rd, the day previous to the battle, we fell in with a strong body of the enemy, to deceive whom we wheeled off from the main road, and took the direction of Alexandria. The plan was attended by the most perfect success; the party deceived, being in fact the advanced guard of the main army. Thinking that Alexandria, and not Washington, was threatened, the American General abandoned a strong position, which he had seized on the main road, harassed his troops by a needless march towards that town; and discovered his mistake only time enough to occupy the heights of Bladensburg a very few minutes before we came in sight.

With respect to the Americans, again, criticism necessarily degenerates into unqualified censure. From the beginning to the end of the affair, they acted in no one instance like prudent or sagacious men. In the first place, they ought on no account to have risked a general action in an open country, however strong and steep; and, secondly, they deserved to suffer much more severely than they did suffer, for permitting an enemy's army to penetrate beyond Nottingham. In allowing us to land without opposition, they were perhaps guilty of no great mistake; but having done so, instead of concentrating their forces in one place, they ought to have harassed us with continual skirmishing; felled trees on each side, and thrown them across the road; dug deep ditches at certain intervals; in a word, it was their wisdom to adopt the mode of warfare to which their own habits, as, well as the nature of their country, invited them.

In America, every man is a marksman from his very boyhood, and every man serves in the militia; but to bring an army of raw militia-men, however excellent they might be as marksmen, into a fair field against regular troops, could end in nothing but defeat. When two lines oppose each other, very little depends upon the accuracy with which individuals take aim. It is then that the habit of acting in concert, the confidence which each man feels in his a companions, and the rapidity and good order in which different movements can be executed, are alone of real service. But put these raw militia-men into thick woods, and send your regular troops to drive them out, and you will immediately lose all the advantages of discipline, and reduce your battle to so many single combats.

Here, therefore, lay their principal error: had they left all clear, and permitted us to advance as far as Nottingham, then broken up the roads, and covered them with trees, it would have been impossible for us to go a step beyond. As soon as this was effected, they might have skirmished with us in front, and kept our attention alive with part of their troops, till the rest, acquainted as they doubtless were with every inch of the country, had got into our rear, and, by a similar mode of proceeding, cut off our retreat. Thus we should have been taken in a snare, from which it would have been no easy task to extricate ourselves, and might, perhaps, have been obliged in the end to surrender at discretion.

But so obvious and so natural a plan of defence they chose to reject ad determining to trust all to the fate of a battle, they were guilty of a monstrous error again. Bladensburg ought not to have been left unoccupied. The most open village, if resolutely defended, will cost many men before it falls; whereas Bladensburg, being composed of substantial brick houses, might have been maintained for hours against all our efforts. In the next place, they displayed great want of military knowledge in the disposition of both their infantry and artillery. There was not, in the whole space of their position, a single point where an enemy would be exposed to a cross fire. The troops were drawn up in three straight lines, like so many regiments upon a gala parade; whilst the guns were used as connecting links to a chain, being posted in the same order, by ones and twos, at every interval.

In maintaining themselves, likewise, when attacked, they exhibited neither skill nor resolution. Of the personal courage of the Americans there can be no doubt; they are, individually taken, as brave a nation as any in the world. But they are not soldiers; they have not the experience nor the habits of soldiers. It was the height of folly, therefore, to bring them into a situation where nothing except that experience and those habits will avail; and it is on this account that I repeat what I have already said, that the capture of Washington was more owing to the blindness of the Americans themselves than to any other cause.

Chapter 12
Afloat Again

Whilst the army was thus actively employed, the fleet did not remain idle. A squadron of frigates, with two bomb-ships, under the command of Captain Gordon, of the *Seahorse*, penetrated up the Potomac, and appeared before Alexandria. The whole of the militia of the district was at this time called away for the defence of the capital, consequently no place could be less prepared to resist an invader than that city. A party accordingly landed from the ships without opposition, and having destroyed the barracks, public works, and all the cannon which they found on shore, they seized a number of schooners and other small craft then lying in the harbour, and loading them with flour and tobacco to a considerable amount, prepared to rejoin the fleet in the bay.

But by this time the country was alarmed; a detachment was sent from the main army, and being joined by the reserve of militia, it was determined to intercept the squadron on its return. With this view, several pieces of heavy cannon were mounted upon a steep part of the bank, where the river, in making an angle, narrows considerably in its channel. Thither also hastened large bodies of infantry; and before the frigates had begun to weigh anchor nearly 5000 men were assembled to prevent their passage.

Of these preparations Captain Gordon did not long remain ignorant; nor was he backward in making the best arrangements possible to meet the danger. By shifting the ballast in each of the vessels entirely to one side, he caused them to lean in such a manner as that their artillery could be elevated to a surprising degree, and the shot rise even to the summit of the hill. The guns were then stuffed, rather than loaded, with grape and musket-balls; and the ships, taking their stations according to their draft of water, the lightest keeping nearest to the enemy's shore, set sail, and, favoured by a leading breeze, stood leisurely down the river.

As soon as they arrived within tangible distance, a brisk cannonade was opened upon them from the heights, and the whole of the infantry appeared in line along, the brow of the eminence. Regardless of these formidable salutations, the ships continued to hold their course without changing their order or returning a shot, till they reached the base of the hill upon which the infantry stood, and received a volley of musketry into their decks. Then, indeed, they answered the fire; and with such effect, that at the first broadside the enemy's guns were abandoned, and their infantry took to flight. The Americans had persuaded themselves that no ship could point her guns so as to sweep the top of the hill; and under this idea had drawn up their troops along the ridge, with the intention of overawing the squadron by a display of their numbers. But in the event they found themselves mistaken, for so well had Captain Gordon arranged matters, that not a single shot fell under its mark; and as the ships' artillery had been loaded for the occasion, a shower of balls of every size and description came amongst them, such as it was impossible to withstand. A single broadside was sufficient to secure the safe passage of his squadron; but with this Captain Gordon was not contented. Seeing the enemy driven from their cannon, he immediately landed his marines, spiked the guns, and blew up the expense magazines; when, having received them all safely on board again, he continued his voyage, and regained the Chesapeake without further molestation.

Nor was this the only operation in which the navy were employed. Cruising about in every direction, they threatened the whole line of coast, from the entrance to the very bend of the bay; and thus kept the Americans in a constant state of alarm. Whenever a favourable opportunity presented itself, parties landed, plundered or destroyed the Government stores, laid towns and districts under contribution, and brought off all the shipping which could be reached. In a word, the hostilities carried on in the Chesapeake resembled the expeditions of the ancient Danes against Great Britain, rather than a modern war between civilized nations. But these hasty excursions, though generally successful, were not always performed without loss to the invaders. Many men and some officers were killed and wounded, among whom was Captain Sir Peter Parker, of the *Menelaus* frigate, an officer distinguished for his gallantry and knowledge of naval tactics.

Having learnt that an encampment of 300 men and six pieces of cannon had been formed, at the distance of a few miles from the banks of the Potomac, and about nine leagues below Alexandria, he determined, with part of his ship's crew, to surprise it, and to capture the guns. Running his frigate with this view up the river, he cast anchor opposite to the place where the American forces lay; and leaving on board only a sufficient number of sailors to manage the ship, and to guard against surprise, with the rest, amounting to 200 seamen and marines, he landed, and marched rapidly towards the enemy's camp. But intelligence of his proceedings had already reached them; patrols of horse hovering continually along the coast for the purpose of watching the motions of our fleet. When, therefore, he arrived at the point of destination, he found the bivouac deserted, and the rear-guard in full retreat.

With these a little skirmishing ensued, and he received a rifle-ball in the thigh. Not suspecting that the wound was dangerous, he continued to push forward, till he fell exhausted from loss of blood; when, on examining the hurt, it was found that the femoral artery had been cut; and before any proper assistance could be afforded, he literally bled to death. Seeing their leader killed, and the enemy retiring, apparently with the design of drawing them away from the coast, the sailors now halted; and taking up their dead commander, returned to the river without being able to effect anything which might, in any degree, console them for their loss.

In the meantime the army continued, for some days, quietly on board the ships in the Patuxent. The wounded whose cases appeared most desperate were removed to vessels fitted up for their reception, and sailed, some for Halifax, and others for England. The dispatches were likewise made out and sent off in the *Iphigenia*, whilst a sort of breathing-time was given to those who had been of late so actively employed. Whilst this Sabbath continued, I amused myself by landing; and under the pretext of shooting, strolled sometimes farther up the country than prudence exactly warranted. The houses and villas, upon the immediate banks of the river, I found universally deserted, and thoroughly plundered. The corn, however, was uninjured; and even flocks of sheep were seen grazing within a short distance of the water, protected only by negro slaves. Of these none were taken without an equivalent being as faithfully paid as if they had been sold in the market-place of New York; a circumstance which favoured the belief that the houses had been ransacked, not by the British troops, but by the inhabitants themselves. Whether it was really so or not I cannot say, but this I know, that from the time of our arrival in the Chesapeake, all acts of individual plunder or violence were strictly prohibited, and severely punished.

But this appearance of ruin and desertion extended not more than a mile or two from the coast. Beyond that, I found the cottages occupied by their owners, and everything remaining as if no enemy were within a hundred miles. The young men, indeed, were generally absent, because every man fit to bear arms was now serving with the army; but the old men and the women seemed to live as comfortably as if the most profound peace had reigned throughout the State. Nor did I find them altogether so hostile to our interest as I had expected. They professed to be Federalists; and though they regretted the events of the war, they blamed their own rulers for its commencement.

Tempted by this show of quietness, I one day continued my walk to a greater distance from the fleet than I had yet ventured to do. My servant was with me, but had no arms, and I was armed only with a double-barrelled fowling-piece. Having wearied myself with looking for game, and penetrated beyond my former landmarks, I came suddenly upon a small hamlet, occupying a piece of cleared ground in the very heart of a thick wood. With this, to confess the truth, I was by no means delighted, more especially as I perceived two stout-looking men sitting at the door of one of the cottages. To retire unobserved was, however, impossible, because the rustling which I had made among the trees attracted their attention, and they saw me; probably, before I had seen them. Perceiving that their eyes were fixed upon me, I determined to put a bold face upon the matter; and calling aloud, as if to a party to halt, I advanced, with my servant, towards them. They were dressed in sailors' jackets and trowsers, and rose on my approach, taking off their hats with much civility. On joining them, I demanded to be informed whether they were not Englishmen, and deserters from the fleet, stating that I was in search of two persons very much answering their description. They assured me that they were Americans, and no deserters, begging that I would not take them away; a request to which, after some time, I assented.

They then conducted me into the house, where I found an old man and three women, who entertained me with bread, cheese, and new milk. While I was sitting here, a third youth, in the dress of a labourer, entered, and whispered to one of the sailors, who immediately rose to go out, but I commanded him to sit still, declaring that I was not satisfied, and should certainly arrest him if he attempted to escape. The man sat down sulkily; and the young labourer coming forward, begged permission to examine my gun. This was a request which I did not much relish, and with which I, of course, refused to comply; telling the fellow that it was loaded, and that I was unwilling to trust it out of my own band, on account of a weakness in one of the locks.

I had now kept up appearances as long as they could be kept up, and therefore rose to withdraw; a measure to which I was additionally induced by the appearance of two other countrymen at the opposite end of the hamlet. I therefore told the sailors that, if they would pledge themselves to remain quietly at home, without joining the American army, I would not molest them; warning them, at the same time, not to venture beyond the village, lest they should fall into the hands of other parties, who were also in search of deserters. The promise they gave, but not with much alacrity, when I rose, and keeping my eye fixed upon them, and my gun ready cocked in my hand, walked out, followed by my servant. They conducted us to the door, and stood staring after us till we got to the edge of the wood; when I observed them moving towards their countrymen, who also gazed upon us, without either advancing or flying. The reader will readily believe, that as soon as we found ourselves concealed by the trees, we lost no time in endeavouring to discover the direct way towards the shipping; but plunging into the thickets, ran with all speed, without thinking of aught except an immediate escape from pursuit. Whether the Americans did attempt to follow, or not, I cannot tell. If they did, they took a wrong direction, for in something more than an hour I found myself at the edge of the river, a little way above the shipping, and returned safely on board, fully resolved not again, to expose myself to such risks, without necessity.

In this manner the time was spent till daybreak on the 6th of September, when the whole fleet got under weigh, and stood towards the Chesapeake. The wind was fair, and we speedily cleared the river; but instead of standing up the bay, as we had expected, we ran down a few miles below the mouth of the Patuxent, and there anchored. A signal was then made by telegraph for all ships to send in a return of the number of seamen whom, in addition to marines, they could land with small-arms. Every ship's crew was accordingly mustered, and it was found that, besides the numbers necessary for conveying stores and dragging guns, one thousand sailors could be spared from the fleet. Thus, in spite of our loss at Bladensburg, we were enabled on our next debarkation to bring into the field about five thousand fighting men.

Next morning we again weighed, and directed our course towards the Potomac. We entered this river soon after midday, and continued to stem the stream during the night, and till dusk on the following evening, when we again brought up. Here we were joined by Admiral Cockburn, who had quitted the anchorage some days before the rest of the fleet, with a large flotilla of prizes and small craft; and having on the 9th once more set sail, and steered for a few hours in the direction of Alexandria, we suddenly put about, and, favoured by a fresh breeze, ran down to the bay, turning our heads upwards towards the Patapsco. Baltimore, it was now understood, was the point of attack; and towards the river upon which that town is built we hastened under a heavy press of sail.

The object of this manoeuvring was evidently to deceive the enemy, and by keeping him in suspense as to the place threatened, to prevent his concentrating his forces, or throwing up works for its defence. But in the attainment of our object, the event proved that we were but partially successful. Certain it is, however, that the utmost consternation prevailed in every town or village opposite to which we made our appearance. In passing Anapolis, a considerable town built upon the bay, and possessing a tolerable harbour, we stood in so close as to discern the inhabitants flying from their houses; carts and wagons loaded with furniture hurrying along the roads, and horsemen galloping along the shore, as if watching the fearful moment when the boats should be hoisted out, and the troops quit the vessels. Wherever a lighthouse or signal station was erected, alarm-guns were fired and beacons lighted. In a word, all the horrors of doubt and apprehension seemed to oppress the inhabitants of this devoted district.

The fair wind continuing to blow without interruption, on the 11th we came in sight of the projecting headland, where it was designed to disembark the troops. It was a promontory washed by the Patapsco on one side, and a curvature of the bay itself on the other. It was determined to land here, rather than to ascend the river, because the Patapsco, though broad, is far from deep. It is, in fact, too shallow to admit a line-of-battle ship; and, as no one could guess what impediments might be thrown in the way to obstruct the navigation, prudence forbade that five thousand men should be intrusted to the convoy of the smaller vessels alone. Besides, the distance from the point to Baltimore did not exceed fourteen or fifteen miles, a space which might easily be traversed in a day.

But while the land forces moved in this direction upon Baltimore, it was resolved that the frigates and bomb-ships should endeavour to force their way through every obstacle, and to obtain possession of the navigation of the river, so as, if possible, to co-operate with the army by bombarding the place from the water. A frigate was accordingly dispatched to try the depth, and to take soundings of the channel, whilst the remainder of the fleet came to an anchor off the point. In the meantime all was again bustle and preparation on board the troop-ships and transports. Three days' provisions were cooked, as before, and given to the men; and as we were now to carry everything by a *coup-de-main*, twenty rounds of ammunition were added to the sixty with which soldiers are usually loaded; whilst a smaller quantity of other baggage was directed to be taken on shore. A blanket, with a spare shirt and pair of shoes, was considered enough for each man on an expedition of so rapid a nature; whilst brushes and other articles of that description were divided between comrades, one carrying what would suffice for both. Thus the additional load of twenty cartridges was more than counterbalanced by the clothing and necessaries left behind.

It was dusk when we reached the anchorage, consequently no landing could take place before the morrow. But as the boats were ordered to be in readiness at dawn, every man slept in his clothes, that he might be prepared to start at a moment's warning. There was something in this state of preparation at once solemn and exciting. That we should obtain possession of a place so important as Baltimore without fighting was not to be expected; and, therefore, this arming and this bustle seemed in fact to be the prelude to a battle. But no man of the smallest reflection can look forward to the chance of a sudden and violent death without experiencing sensations very different from those which he experiences under any other circumstances. When the battle has fairly begun, I may say with truth that the feelings of those engaged are delightful; because they are in fact so many gamblers playing for the highest stake that can be offered. But the stir and noise of equipping, and then the calmness and stillness of expectation, these are the things which force a man to think. On the other hand, the warlike appearance of everything about you, the careless faces and rude jokes of the private soldiers, and something within yourself, which I can compare to nothing more seemly than the mirth which criminals are said sometimes to experience and to express previous to their execution; all these combine to give you a degree of false hilarity, I had almost said painful from its very excess. It is an agitation of the nerves, such as we may suppose madmen feel, which you are inclined to wish removed, though you are not unwilling to admit that it is agreeable.

And yet, as if in mockery of these deadly preparations, I do not recollect to have seen a more heavenly night than the present. The heat of the day was past, a full clear moon shone brightly in a sky where not a cloud could be discerned, and a heavy dew falling appeared to refresh the earth, which had been parched and burnt up by the sun. We lay at this time within two miles of the shore, consequently every object there was distinctly visible. Around us were moored numerous ships, which, breaking the tide as it flowed gently onwards, produced a ceaseless murmur like the gushing of a mountain stream. The voices of the sentinels too, as they relieved one another on the decks, and the occasional splash of oars, as a solitary boat rowed backwards and forwards to the Admiral's ship for orders, sounded peculiarly musical in the perfect stillness of a calm night. Though I am far from giving the preference, in all respects, to a sailor's life, it must nevertheless be confessed that it has in it many moments of exquisite enjoyment, and the present seemed to me to be of the number.

CHAPTER 13
Attack on Baltimore

But the stillness of night soon passed away, and at three o'clock in the morning every ship in the fleet began to lower her boats, and the soldiers were roused from their slumbers. The same precautions which had been formerly used to cover the landing were again adopted, several gun-brigs laying themselves within cable's length of the beach, and the leading boats in every division being armed with carronades, loaded and ready for action. But, as had been the case at St. Benedict's, they were unnecessary, for the troops reached the shore without opposition, and leisurely formed in an open field close to the river.

It was seven o'clock before the whole army was disembarked and in order for marching. The same arrangements which had been made on the late expedition were, as far as circumstances would permit, again adopted on this. The light brigade, now commanded by Major Jones of the 4th regiment, led the advance; then followed the artillery, amounting to six field-pieces and two howitzers, all of them drawn by horses; next came the second brigade, then the sailors, and last of all the third brigade. Flank patrols and reconnoitring parties were likewise sent out; in short, the same admirable dispositions regulated the present march which had governed our march to Washington.

The column being put in motion, advanced, without the occurrence of any incident deserving of notice, for about an hour, when it arrived at a piece of ground which appeared as if it had been lately in possession of the enemy. It was a narrow neck of land, confined between the river on one side, and the head of a creek on the other, measuring, perhaps, a mile across. From the river to the creek a breastwork had been begun, and was partly completed. In front of it there were lines drawn, apparently for the purpose of marking out the width of a ditch; in some places the ditch itself was dug, and the commencement of what resembled an enfilading battery in the centre, showed that a considerable degree of science had been displayed in the choice of this spot as a military position. And, in truth, it was altogether such a position as, if completed, might have been maintained by a determined force against very superior numbers. Both flanks were completely protected, not only by water, but by thick wood, while a gentle eminence in the very middle of the line offered the most desirable situation for the projecting battery which had been begun; because a fire from it would have swept the whole, both to the right and left. In its present state, however, it was untenable, unless by a force as able to attack as to defend; consequently the Americans, who acted solely on the defensive, did wisely in choosing another.

But the aspect of the ground was such as led us to conclude that the enemy could not be very distant. The troops were accordingly halted, that the rear might be well up, and the men fresh and ready for action. Whilst this was done part of the flank patrol came in, bringing with them three light-horse men, as prisoners. These were young gentlemen belonging to a corps of volunteers, furnished by the town of Baltimore, who had been sent out to watch our motions, and convey intelligence to the American General. Being but little accustomed to such service, they had suffered themselves to be surprised; and, instead of reporting to their own leader as to the number and dispositions of their adversaries, they were now catechized by General Ross respecting the strength and preparations of their friends. From them we learned that a force of no less than twenty thousand men was embodied for the defence of Baltimore; but as the accounts of prisoners are generally over-rated, we took it for granted that they made their report only to intimidate.

Having rested for the space of an hour, we again moved forward, but had not proceeded above a mile when a sharp fire of musketry was heard in front, and shortly afterwards a mounted officer came galloping to the rear, who desired us to quicken our pace, for that the advanced guard was engaged. At this intelligence the ranks were closed, and the troops advanced at a brisk rate, and in profound silence. The firing still continued, though, from its running and irregular sound, it promised little else than a skirmish; but whether it was kept up by detached parties alone, or by the outposts of a regular army, we could not tell; because, from the quantity of wood with which the country abounded, and the total absence of all hills or eminences, it was impossible to discern what was going on at the distance of half a mile from the spot where we stood.

We were already drawing near to the scene of action, when another officer came at full speed towards us, with horror and dismay in his countenance, and calling loudly for a surgeon. Every man felt within himself that all was not right, though none was willing to believe the whispers of his own terror. But what at first we would not guess at, because we dreaded it so much, was soon realized; for the aide-de-camp had scarcely passed, when the General's horse, without its rider, and with the saddle and housings stained with blood, came plunging onwards. Nor was much time given for fearful surmise as to the extent of our misfortune. In a few moments we reached the ground where the skirmishing had taken place, and beheld General Ross laid by the side of the road, under a canopy of blankets, and apparently in the agonies of death. As soon as the firing began, he had ridden to the front, that he might ascertain from whence it originated, and, mingling with the skirmishers, was shot in the side by a rifleman. The wound was mortal: he fell into the arms of his aide-de-camp, and lived only long enough to name his wife, and to commend his family to the protection of his country. He was removed towards the fleet, but expired before his bearers could reach the boats.

It is impossible to conceive the effect which this melancholy spectacle produced throughout the army. By the courteousness and condescension of his manners, General Ross had secured the absolute love of all who served under him, from the highest to the lowest; and his success on a former occasion, as well as his judicious arrangements on the present, had inspired every one with the most perfect confidence in his abilities. His very error, if error it may be called, in so young a leader—I mean that diffidence in himself which had occasioned some loss of time on the march to Washington, appeared now to have left him. His movements were at once rapid and cautious; nay, his very countenance indicated a fixed determination, and a perfect security of success. All eyes were turned upon him as we passed, and a sort of involuntary groan ran from rank to rank, from the front to the rear of the column.

By the fall of our gallant leader, the command now devolved upon Colonel Brook, of the 44th regiment, an officer of decided personal courage, but, perhaps, better calculated to lead a battalion than to guide an army. Being informed of his unexpected and undesired elevation, he came to the front, and under him we continued to move on; sorrowful, indeed, but not dejected. The skirmishing had now ceased, for the American riflemen were driven in; and in a few minutes we found ourselves opposite to a considerable force, drawn up with some skill, and occupying a strong position. Judging from appearances, I should say that the corps now opposed to us amounted to six or seven thousand men. They covered a neck of land, very much resembling that which we had passed; having both flanks defended by little inland lakes; the whole of their position was well wooded, and in front of their line was a range of high palings, similar to those which intersected the field of Bladensburg. About the centre, though some way advanced, was a farm-house, with its outbuildings and stackyard; and near to the right ran the main road. Their artillery, which could not greatly exceed our own, either in weight of metal or number of guns, was scattered along the line of infantry in nearly the same order as had been preserved at Bladensburg, and their reserve was partly seen, and partly hid by a thick wood.

The whole of this country is flat and unbroken. About half a mile in rear of the enemy's position were some heights, but to occupy these as they should be occupied would have required a much greater number of men than the American army could muster. Their General, therefore, exhibited some judgment in his choice of ground, but, perhaps, he would have exhibited more had he declined a pitched battle altogether. Yet, to do him justice, I repeat that the ground was well chosen; for, besides the covering of wood which he secured for his own people, he took care to leave open fields in his front; by which means we were of necessity exposed to a galling fire, as soon as we came within range. Of one error, however, he was guilty. Either he did not possess himself of the farm-house at all, or he suffered it to be taken from him with very little resistance; for on the arrival of the column at the ground where it was to form, it was in the occupation of our advanced guard. He was likewise to blame in not filling the wood upon our left with skirmishers. In short, he acted unwisely in merely attempting to repel attacks, without ever dreaming that the most effectual mode of so doing is to turn the tables, and attack the assailants.

As our troops came up they filed off to the right and left, and drew up just within cannon shot in the following order. The light brigade, consisting, as I have formerly stated, of the 85th regiment and the light companies of the other corps, in extended order, threatened the whole front of the American army. The 21st remained in column upon the road; the 4th moved off to the right, and advanced through a thicket to turn the enemy's left; and the 44th, the seamen and marines, formed line in rear of the light brigade.

While this formation was going on, the artillery being brought up, opened upon the American army, and a smart cannonade ensued on both sides. That our guns were well served I myself can bear witness; for I saw the Shrapnel shells which were thrown from them strike among the enemy, and make fearful gaps in the line. Our rockets likewise began to play, one of which falling short, lighted upon a haystack in the barn-yard belonging to the farm-house, and immediately set it on fire. The house itself, the stables, barns, and outhouses, as well as all the other stacks, one after another caught the flames, and were quickly in a state of conflagration; and the smoke and blaze which they emitted, together with the roar of cannon and flashes of the guns, produced altogether a very fine effect.

In the meantime the American artillery was not idle. Pushing forward two light field-pieces upon the road, they opened a destructive fire of grape upon the 21st regiment, and such of the sailors as occupied that point. Three other guns were directed against our artillery, between which and several of our pieces a sort of duel was maintained; and the rest played without ceasing upon the 85th and the light companies, who had lain down while the other regiments took up their ground. Neither was their infantry altogether quiet. They marched several strong bodies from the right to the left, and withdrew others from the left to the right of their line, though for what end this marching and countermarching was undertaken I am at a loss to conceive. While thus fluctuating it was curious to observe their dread of every spot where a cannon-ball had struck. Having seen the shots fall, I kept my eye upon one or two places, and perceived that each company as it drew near to those points hung back; and then assuming as it were a momentary courage, rushed past, leaving a vacancy between it and the company which next succeeded.

All this while the whole of our infantry, except the 4th

regiment, lay or stood in anxious expectation of an order to advance. This, however, was not given till that corps had reached the thicket through which it was to make its way; when Colonel Brook, with his staff, having galloped along the line to see that all was ready, commanded the signal to be made. The charge was accordingly sounded, and echoed back from every bugle in the army, when, starting from the ground where they had lain, the troops moved on in a cool and orderly manner. A dreadful discharge of grape and canister shot, of old locks, pieces of broken muskets, and everything which they could cram into their guns, was now sent forth from the whole of the enemy's artillery, and some loss was on our side experienced. Regardless of this, our men went on without either quickening or retarding their pace, till they came within a hundred yards of the American line. As yet not a musket had been fired, nor a word spoken on either side, but the enemy, now raising a shout, fired a volley from right to left, and then kept up a rapid and ceaseless discharge of musketry. Nor were our people backward in replying to these salutes; for giving them back both their shout and their volley, we pushed on at double-quick, with the intention of bringing them to the charge.

The bayonet is a weapon peculiarly British; at least it is a weapon which in the hands of a British soldier is irresistible. Though they maintained themselves with great determination, and stood to receive our fire till scarcely twenty yards divided us, the Americans would not hazard a charge. On the left, indeed, where the 21st advanced in column, it was not without much difficulty and a severe loss that any attempt to charge could be made; for in that quarter seemed to be the flower of the enemy's infantry, as well as the main body of their artillery; towards the right, however, the day was quickly won. The only thing to be regretted, indeed, was that the attack had not been for some time longer deferred; because the Americans were broken and fled, just as the 4th regiment began to show itself upon the brink of the water which covered their flank; and before a shallow part could be discovered, and the troops were enabled to pass, they had time to escape.

As soon as their left gave way, the whole American army fell into confusion; nor do I recollect on any occasion to have witnessed a more complete rout. Infantry, cavalry, and artillery were huddled together, without the smallest regard to order or regularity. The sole object of anxiety seemed to be, which should escape first from the field of battle; insomuch, that numbers were actually trodden down by their countrymen in the hurry of the flight. Yet, in spite of the short duration of the action, which lasted little more than two hours from its first commencement, the enemy's loss was severe. They stood in some respects better than at Bladensburg, consequently we were more mingled with them when they gave way, and were thus enabled to secure some prisoners, an event which their more immediate flight had on the other occasion prevented. In the capture of guns, however, we were not so fortunate. Their pieces being light, and well supplied with horses, they contrived to carry off all except two; both of which would have also escaped but for the shooting of the leaders.

I have said that the number of killed and wounded in the American army was very great; in ours, on the other hand, the casualties were fewer by far than might have been expected. The 21st and seamen suffered a good deal, the 85th and light companies a little; but had our gallant General been spared, we should have pronounced this a glorious, because a comparatively bloodless day. In the loss of that one man, however, we felt ourselves more deeply wounded than if the best battalion in the army had been sacrificed.

In following up the flying enemy the same obstacles which presented themselves at Bladensburg again came in the way. The thick woods quickly screened the fugitives, and as even our mounted drivers were wanting, their horses having been taken for the use of the artillery, no effectual pursuit could be attempted. We accordingly halted upon the field of battle, of necessity content with the success which we had obtained;

and having collected the stragglers and called in the pursuers, it was resolved to pass the night in this situation. Fires were speedily lighted, and the troops distributed in such a manner as to secure a tolerable position in case of attack; and the wounded being removed into two or three houses scattered along the ground, the victors lay down to sleep under the canopy of heaven.

Having thus given a distinct and connected detail of this affair, I shall beg leave to finish the present chapter with one or two anecdotes, which may not be unamusing. It is said that when Admiral Cockburn, who accompanied the army, and attended General Ross with the fidelity of an aide-de-camp, was in the wood where the latter fell, he observed an American rifleman taking deliberate aim at him from behind a tree. Instead of turning aside, or discharging a pistol at the fellow, as any other man would have done, the brave Admiral, doubling his fist, shook it at his enemy, and cried aloud, "O you d—d Yankee, I'll give it you!" upon which the man dropped his musket in the greatest alarm, and took to his heels.

It is likewise told of an officer of engineers, that having overtaken an American soldier, and demanded his arms, the fellow gave him his rifle very readily, but being ordered to resign a handsome silver-hilted dagger and silver-mounted cartouch-box, which graced his side, he refused to comply, alleging that they were private property, and that, by our own proclamations, private property should be respected. This was an instance of low cunning which reminded me of my own adventure with the squirrel-hunters, and which was attended with equal success.

One other anecdote, of a different nature, and for the truth of which I can myself answer, may likewise be related. In strolling over the field of battle, I came unexpectedly upon a wounded American, who lay among some bushes with his leg broken. I drew near to offer him assistance, but on seeing me the wretch screamed out, and appeared in the greatest alarm; nor was it without some difficulty that I could persuade him he had nothing to fear. At last, being convinced that I intended him no harm, the fellow informed me that it was impressed upon the minds of the American levies that from the British they might expect no quarter; and that it was consequently their determination to give no quarter to the British troops. The fellow might belie his countrymen, and I hope and believe he did, but such was his report to me. To convince him of the erroneousness of his notions, I removed him to one of our hospitals, where his leg was amputated; and he saw himself, as well as many others of his wounded comrades, treated with the same attention which was bestowed upon our own soldiers.

CHAPTER 14
Back to the Ships

At an early hour on the 13th the troops were roused from their lairs, and forming upon the ground, waited till daylight should appear. A heavy rain had come on about midnight, and now fell with so much violence, that some precautions were necessary, in order to prevent the firelocks from being rendered useless by wet. Such of the men as were fortunate enough to possess leathern cases, wrapped them round the locks of their muskets, whilst the rest held them in the best manner they could, under their elbows; no man thinking of himself, but only how he could best keep his arms in a serviceable condition.

As soon as the first glimmering of dawn could be discerned, we moved to the road, and took up our wonted order of march; but before we pushed forward, the troops were desired to lighten themselves still further, by throwing off their blankets, which were to be left under a slender guard till their return. This was accordingly done; and being now unencumbered, except by a knapsack almost empty, every man felt his spirits heightened in proportion to the diminution of his load. The grief of soldiers is seldom of long duration, and though I will not exactly say that poor Ross was already forgotten, the success of yesterday had reconciled at least the privates to the guidance of their new leader; nor was any other issue anticipated than what would have attended the excursion had he still been its mainspring and director.

The country through which we passed resembled, in every particular, that already described. Wood and cultivation succeeded each other at intervals, though the former surpassed the latter in tenfold extent; but instead of deserted villages and empty houses, which had met us on the way to Washington, we found most of the inhabitants remaining peaceably in their homes, and relying upon the assurance of protection given to them in our proclamations. Nor had they cause to repent of that confidence. In no instance were they insulted, plundered, or ill-treated; whereas every house which was abandoned fell a prey to the scouts and reconnoitring parties.

But our march to-day was not so rapid as our motions generally were. The Americans had at last adopted an expedient which, if carried to its proper length, might have entirely stopped our progress. In most of the woods they had felled trees, and thrown them across the road; but as these abattis were without defenders, we experienced no other inconvenience than what arose from loss of time; being obliged to halt on all such occasions till the pioneers had removed the obstacle. So great, however, was even this hindrance, that we did not come in sight of the main army of the Americans till evening, although the distance travelled could not exceed ten miles.

It now appeared that the corps which we had beaten yesterday was only a detachment, and not a large one, from the force collected for the defence of Baltimore; and that the account given by the volunteer troopers was in every respect correct. Upon a ridge of hills, which concealed the town itself from observation, stood the grand army, consisting of twenty thousand men. Not trusting to his superiority in numbers, their General had there entrenched them in the most formidable manner, having covered the whole face of the heights with breastworks, thrown back his left so as to rest it upon a strong fort erected for the protection of the river, and constructed a chain of field redoubts which covered his right and commanded the entire ascent. Along the side of the hill were likewise fleches and other projecting works, from which a cross fire might be kept up; and there were mounted throughout this commanding position no less than one hundred pieces of cannon.

It would be absurd to suppose that the sight of preparations so warlike did not in some degree damp the ardour of our leader; at least it would have been madness to storm such works without pausing to consider how it might best be attempted. The whole of the country within cannon-shot was cleared from wood, and laid out in grass and corn-fields; consequently there was no cover to shelter an attacking army from any part of the deadly fire which would be immediately poured upon it. The most prudent plan, therefore, was to wait till dark; and then, assisted by the frigates and bombs, which he hoped were by this time ready to co-operate, to try the fortune of a battle.

Having resolved thus to act, Colonel Brook halted his army; and, secured against surprise by a well-connected line of piquets, the troops were permitted to light fires and to cook their provisions. But though the rain still fell in torrents, no shelter could be obtained; and as even their blankets were no longer at hand, with which to form gipsy-tents, this was the reverse of an agreeable bivouac to the whole army.

Darkness had now come on, and as yet no intelligence had arrived from the shipping. To assail such a position, however, without the aid of the fleet, was deemed impracticable; at least our chance of success would be greatly diminished without their co-operation. As the left of the American army extended to a fort built upon the very brink of the river, it was clear that could the ships be brought to bear upon that point, and the fort be silenced by their fire, that flank of the position would be turned. This once effected, there would be no difficulty in pushing a column within their works; and as soldiers entrenched always place more reliance upon the strength of their entrenchments than upon their own personal exertions, the very sight of our people on a level with them would in all probability decide the contest. At all events, as the column was to advance under cover of night, it might easily push forward and crown the hill above the enemy, before any effectual opposition could be offered; by which means they would be enclosed between two fires, and lose the advantage which their present elevated situation bestowed. All, however, depended upon the ability of the fleet to lend their assistance; for without silencing the fort, this flank could scarcely be assailed with any chance of success, and, therefore, the whole plan of operations must be changed.

Having waited till it was considered imprudent to wait longer, without knowing whether he was to be supported, Colonel Brook determined, if possible, to open a communication with the fleet. That the river could not be far off we knew, but how to get to it without falling in with wandering parties of the enemy was the difficulty. The thing, however, must be done; and as secrecy, and not force, was the main object, it was resolved to dispatch for the purpose a single officer without an escort.

On this service a particular friend of mine chanced to be employed. Mounting his horse, he proceeded to the right of the army, where, having delayed a few minutes till the moon rising gave light enough through the clouds to distinguish objects, he pushed forward at a venture, in as straight a line as he could guess at. It was not long before his progress was stopped by a high hedge. Like knights-errant of old, he then gave himself up to the guidance of his horse, which taking him towards the rear, soon brought him into a narrow lane, that appeared to wind in the direction of the enemy's fort: this lane he determined to follow, and holding a cocked pistol in his hand, pushed on, not perhaps entirely comfortable, but desirous at all hazards of executing his commission.

He had not ridden far, when the sound of voices through the splashing of the rain arrested his attention. Pulling up, he listened in silence, and soon discovered that they came from two American soldiers, whether stragglers or sentinels it was impossible to divine; but whoever they were, they seemed to be approaching. It now struck him that his safest course would be to commence the attack, and having therefore waited till he saw them stop short, as if they had perceived him, he rode forward, and called out to them to surrender. The fellows turned and fled, but galloping after them, he overtook one, at whose head he presented a pistol, and who instantly threw down his rifle, and yielded himself prisoner; whilst the other, dashing into a thicket, escaped, probably to tell that he had been attacked by a whole regiment of British cavalry.

Having thus taken a prisoner, my friend resolved to make him of some use; with this view he commanded him to lay hold of his thigh, and to guide him directly to the river, threatening, if he attempted to mislead or betray him into the hands of the Americans, that he would instantly blow out his brains.

Finding himself completely in my friend's power, the fellow could not refuse to obey; and accordingly, the man resting his hand upon the left thigh of the officer, they proceeded along the lane for some time, till they came to a part where it branched off in two directions. My friend here stopped for a moment; and again repeated his threat, swearing that the instant his conduct became suspicious should be the last of his life. The soldier assured him that he would keep his word, and moreover informed him that some of our ships were almost within gun-shot of the fort; a piece of information which was quickly confirmed by the sound of firing, and the appearance of shells in the air. They now struck to the right, and in half an hour gained the brink of the river: where my friend found a party just landed from the squadron, and preparing to seek their way towards the camp. By them he was conducted to the Admiral, from whom he learnt that no effectual support could be given to the land force; for such was the shallowness of the river, that none except the very lightest craft could make their way within six miles of the town; and even these were stopped by vessels sunk in the channel, and other artificial bars, barely within a shell's longest range of the fort. With this unwelcome news he was accordingly forced to return; and taking his unwilling guide along with him, he made his way, without any adventure, to our advanced posts; where, having thanked the fellow for his fidelity, he rewarded it more effectually by setting him at liberty.

Having brought his report to head-quarters, a council of war was instantly summoned to deliberate upon what was best to be done. Without the help of the fleet, it was evident that, adopt what plan of attack we could, our loss must be such as to counterbalance even success itself; whilst success, under existing circumstances, was, to say the least of it, doubtful. And even if we should succeed, what would be gained by it? We could not remove anything from Baltimore, for want of proper conveyances. Had the ships been able to reach the town, then, indeed, the quantity of booty might have repaid the survivors for their toil, and consoled them for the loss of comrades; but as the case now stood, we should only fight to give us an opportunity of reacting repeating the scenes of Washington. To distress an enemy is, no doubt, desirable, but, in the present instance, that distress, even if brought upon the Americans, would cost us dear; whereas, if we failed, it was hardly possible to avoid destruction.

Such was the reasoning which influenced the council of war to decide that all idea of storming the enemy's lines should be given up. To draw them from their works would require manoeuvring, and manoeuvring requires time; but delays were all in their favour, and could not possibly advantage us. Every hour brought in reinforcements to their army, whereas ours had no source from which even to recruit its losses; and it was, therefore, deemed prudent, since we could not fight at once, to lose no time in returning to the shipping.

About three hours after midnight the troops were accordingly formed upon the road, and began their retreat, leaving the piquets to deceive the enemy, and to follow, as a rear-guard. The rain, which had continued with little interruption since the night before, now ceased, and the moon shone out bright and clear. We marched along, therefore, not in the same spirits as if we had been advancing, but feeling no debasement at having thus relinquished an enterprise so much beyond our strength.

When the day broke, our piquets, which had withdrawn about an hour before, rejoined us, and we went on in a body. Marching over the field where the battle of the 12th had been fought, we beheld the dead scattered about, and still unburied; but so far different from those which we had seen at Bladensburg, that they were not stripped, every man lying as he had fallen. One object, however, struck me as curious. I saw several men hanging lifeless among the branches of trees, and learnt that they had been riflemen, who chose, during the battle, to fix themselves in these elevated situations, for the combined purposes of securing a good aim and avoiding danger. Whatever might be their success in the first of these designs, in the last they failed; for our men soon discovered them, and, considering the thing as unfair, refused to give them quarter, and shot them on their perches.

Here we paused for about an hour, that the soldiers might collect their blankets and refresh themselves; when we again moved forward, passing the wood where the gallant Ross was killed. It was noon, and as yet all had gone on smoothly with out any check or alarm. So little indeed was pursuit dreamt of, that the column began to straggle, and to march without much regard to order; when suddenly the bugle sounded from the rear, and immediately after some musket shots were heard. In an instant the men were in their places, and the regiments wheeled into line, facing towards the enemy. The artillery turned round and advanced to the front; indeed I have never seen a manoeuvre more coolly or more steadily performed on a parade in England than this rally. The alarm, however, turned out to be groundless, being occasioned only by the sudden appearance of a squadron of horse, which had been sent out by the American General to track our steps. These endeavoured to charge the rearguard, and succeeded in making two prisoners; but a single Shrapnel checked their farther advance, and sent them back at full speed to boast of the brave exploit which they had performed.

Seeing that no attack was seriously intended, the army broke once more into the line of march, and proceeded to a favourable piece of ground, near the uncompleted position which I have already described, where we passed the night under little tents made with blankets and ramrods. No alarm occurring, nor any cause of delay appearing, at daybreak we again got under arms, and pushed on towards the shipping, which in two hours were distinguishable.

The infantry now halted upon a narrow neck of land, while the artillery was lifted into boats, and conveyed on board the fleet. As soon as this was done, brigade after brigade fell back to the water's edge and embarked, till finally all, except the light troops, were got off. These being left to cover the embarkation, were extended across the entire space which but a little before contained the whole army; but as no attempt was made to molest them, they had only the honour of being the last to quit the shore.

Were I to enter into a review of the military proceedings in this expedition, I should be condemned to repeat, almost word for word, the remarks which I ventured to make upon the operations previous to the capture of Washington. On the present occasion, however, neither hesitation nor precipitancy was displayed by the British General. He threw his valuable life away, indeed, by exposing his person unnecessarily in a trifling skirmish; but who will blame a soldier for excess of courage, or a leader for excess of alertness? Like other able men, he was unwilling to trust to the report of his subalterns, when it was in his power to ascertain what he sought to know by personal observation; and, like other brave men, he would not be deterred from prosecuting his design by the apprehension of danger. In the plan of the expedition here, he displayed both skill and resolution. Instead of wasting time by an attempt to ascend the river, he chose to land where he was least likely to meet with immediate opposition; and such was the celerity of his motions, that, had he lived, the chances are that we should have fought two battles in one day. But of what a man might have done, I have nothing to say; let me rather do justice to his successor and his advisers. Of these latter, there is one whom it would be improper not to mention by name—I mean Lieutenant Evans, Deputy-Assistant Quartermaster-General. The whole arrangement of our troops in order of battle was committed to him; and the judicious method in which they were drawn up, proved that he was not unworthy of the trust. With respect to the determination of the council of war, I choose to be silent. Certain it is, that the number of our forces would hardly authorise any desperate attempt; yet had the attempt been made, I have very little doubt that it would have been made successfully.

On the part of the Americans, again, the same blunders were committed which marked their proceedings during the incursion to Washington, with this exception, that more science was displayed now than formerly in the distribution of their forces along their principal position. At Bladensburg, indeed, there existed no works, and the troops were badly arranged in an open country: here there were not only fortifications, but fortifications constructed in a scientific manner, and troops drawn up in such order, as that, even without their works, many cross fires would have protected their front. But they neglected numerous favourable opportunities of harassing both our advance and retreat. They felled trees, but left no guards to keep them from being removed, and took no advantage of the delays which their removal created. They risked a battle with a part of their army, when there was no necessity for it; in a word, they committed all those errors which men generally commit who are not soldiers, and yet love war.

Chapter 15
To Sea Again

Having once more received the troops on board, the fleet remained quietly at anchor till the 17th, when, at an early hour, we set sail and stood towards the Patuxent. In this voyage we passed close to Sent Island, and again threw the inhabitants of Anapolis into alarm by approaching almost within gun-shot of their town; but at neither place were hostilities attempted, and on the 19th we arrived, without any adventure, at our former anchorage in the river. Here we brought up, and parties were sent on shore to dig wells in the sand, to which the boats resorted in great numbers for water. Cattle and sheep were likewise purchased from the natives; some of the flour which had been captured was converted into biscuit; and every preparation seemed to be making for a long voyage.

To facilitate these operations, the fleet now separated, part remaining here, and part proceeding under Admiral Malcolm to the Potomac; whilst Sir Alexander Cochrane, in the Tonnant, with several frigates and gun-brigs, quitted us altogether, and set sail, as it was given out, for Halifax. But our situation was by no means agreeable. The climate of this part of America is, at certain seasons, far from healthy; and the prevalence of dysentery through the armament proved that the unhealthy season had already commenced. Neither did there appear to be any prospect of further employment. No one talked of a future enterprise, nor was the slightest rumour circulated as to the next point of attack. The death of General Ross seemed to have disorganized the whole plan of proceedings, and the fleet and army rested idle, like a watch without its main spring.

Whilst things were in this state, whilst the banks of the rivers continued in our possession, and the interior was left unmolested to the Americans, a rash confidence sprang up in the minds of all, insomuch that parties of pleasure would frequently land without arms, and spend many hours onshore. On one of these occasions, several officers from the 85th regiment agreed to pass a day together at a farm-house, about a quarter of a mile from the stream; and taking with them ten soldiers, unarmed, to row the boat, a few sailors, and a young midshipman, not more than twelve years of age, they proceeded to put their determination into practice. Leaving the men, under the command of their youthful pilot, to take care of the boat, the officers went on to the house; but they had not remained there above an hour, when they were alarmed by a shout, which sounded as if it came from the river. Looking, out, they beheld their party surrounded by seventy or eighty mounted riflemen; the boat dragged upon the beach, and set on fire. Giving themselves up for lost, they continued for an instant in a sort of stupor; but the master of the house, to whom some kindness had been shown by our people, proved himself grateful, and, letting them out by a back door, directed them to bide themselves in the wood, whilst he should endeavour to turn their pursuers on a wrong scent. As they had nothing to trust to except the honour of this American, it cannot be supposed that they felt much at ease; but, seeing no better course before them, they resigned themselves to his guidance, and plunging into the thicket, concealed themselves as well as they could among the underwood. In the mean time the American soldiers, having secured all that were left behind, except the young midshipman, who fled into the wood in spite of their fire, divided into two bodies, one of which approached the house, whilst the other endeavoured to overtake the brave boy. It so chanced that the party in pursuit passed close to the officers in concealment, but by the greatest good fortune failed to observe them. They succeeded, however, in catching a glimpse of the midshipman, just as he had gained the water's edge, and was pushing off a light canoe which he had loosened from the stump of a tree. The barbarians immediately gave chase, firing at the brave lad, and calling out to surrender; but the gallant youth paid no attention either to their voices or their bullets. Launching his little bark, he put to sea with a single paddle, and, regardless of the showers of balls which fell about him, returned alone and unhurt to the ship. Whilst one party was thus employed, the other hastened to the house in full expectation of capturing the British officers. But their host kept his word with great fidelity, and, having directed his countrymen towards another farm-house at some distance from his own, and in an opposite quarter from the spot where his guests lay, he waited till they were out of sight, and then joined his new friends in their lurking-place. Bringing with him such provisions as he could muster, he advised them to keep quiet till dark, when, their pursuers having departed, he conducted them to the river, supplied them with a large canoe, and sent them off in perfect safety to the fleet.

On reaching their ship, they found the 85th regiment under arms, and preparing to land, for the purpose of either releasing their comrades from captivity, or inflicting exemplary punishment upon the farmer by whose treachery it was supposed that they had suffered. But when the particulars of his behaviour were related, the latter alternative was at once abandoned; and it was determined to force a dismissal of the captives, by advancing up the country, and laying waste every thing with fire and sword. The whole of the light brigade was accordingly carried on shore, and halted on the beach, whilst a messenger was sent forward to demand back the prisoners. Such, however, was the effect of his threatening, that the demand was at once complied with, and they returned on board without having committed any ravages, or marched above two miles from the boats.

Besides this trifling debarkation, another little excursion was made by the second and third brigades, the light troops being left most unaccountably on board of ship, Colonel Brook, having heard that an encampment was formed a few miles from the left bank of the Potomac, determined, if possible, to come up with and engage the force there stationed. With this view, two brigades were landed on the night of the 4th of October, and pushed forward at a brisk pace; but the enemy, being on the alert, had timely notice of the movement, and retired; by which means our people returned on the 5th, without effecting anything.

By this time the whole fleet was once more collected together; and crowded the Potomac with their keels. The *Diadem* being an old ship and a bad sailor, it was determined to remove from her the troops which she had formerly carried, to fill her with American prisoners, and to send her to England. The *Menelaus* was likewise dispatched with such officers and soldiers as required the benefit of their native air to complete the cure of their wounds; and the rest, getting under weigh on the 6th, stood directly towards the mouth of the Chesapeake. When we reached the James River, we anchored, and were joined by an American schooner bearing a flag of truce. She brought with her Colonel Thornton, Lieut. Colonel Wood, with the rest of the officers and men who had been left behind at Bladensburg, and, being under the guidance of Commodore Barney, that gentleman was enabled to discharge his trust even to the very letter.

It may readily be supposed that the meeting between friends thus restored to each other was very agreeable. But there was another source of comfort which this arrival communicated, of greater importance than the pleasure bestowed upon individuals. In Colonel Thornton we felt that we had recovered a dashing and enterprising officer; one as well calculated to lead a corps of light troops, and to guide the advance of an army, as any in the service. On the whole, therefore, the American schooner was as welcome as if she had been a first-rate man-of-war filled with reinforcements from England.

The wounded being now sent off, and Colonel Wood among the number, the remainder of the fleet again set sail, and reached the mouth of the bay without interruption. Here they were met by a frigate and two brigs, which spoke to the Admiral, and apparently communicated some important intelligence; for we immediately put about and stood once more up the Chesapeake. The wind, however, blew with great violence, and directly against us. After beating about, therefore, for some time, without making any progress, we turned our heads towards the ocean, and flying between the Capes with amazing velocity, stood out to sea, directing our course towards the S.S.E., and proceeding at the rate of seven miles an hour under bare poles. The sea ran tremendously high, and the sky was dark and dreary; insomuch that by a landsman the gale might safely be accounted a storm. Under these circumstances, the ship rolling as if she would dip her topmasts in the water, and the waves breaking in at the back windows of the cabin, nothing remained to be done but to go to bed. Thither most of us accordingly repaired, and holding ourselves in our berths by clinging to the posts, we amused ourselves by watching the motions of stools, books, trunks, and other articles, as they floated majestically from one side of the cabin to the other. But the effects of the gale were not in every respect ludicrous. Two small schooners, which had been captured at Alexandria and converted into tenders, foundered and went down, without an opportunity being afforded of saving an individual of their crews.

At length the wind began to moderate, and on the 18th there was a dead calm. In point of comfort, however, I cannot say that much change was experienced; for though the gale had ceased, the swell still continued; and the motion produced by a heavy sea after a storm is even more disagreeable than that occasioned by the storm itself. But on this day the minds of all were set at ease as to the place whither we were going, a telegraph signal being made to steer for Jamaica. It was likewise understood that we should be there joined by strong reinforcements, and proceed upon a secret expedition against some place on the southern borders of the United States.

The calm which had succeeded the storm did not last long, for on the 19th a fair breeze sprang up, and sent us at a moderate and agreeable rate upon our course. The heat, however, was most oppressive; even awnings being unable to afford sufficient shelter. We were fast approaching the tropic of Cancer, and every day experienced a greater degree of sultriness; till at length, on the 25th, we crossed that imaginary boundary. Here we were visited, according to custom, by Neptune and his wife; and as the ceremony of shaving may be unknown to some of my readers, I shall beg leave to relate the particulars of that operation.

A clever active seaman, dressed up grotesquely in party-coloured rags, adorned with a long beard made of the stuff which sailors call spun-yarn, and armed with a tri-pronged harpoon, personates the God of the Ocean. Another seaman, arrayed in like manner, except that, instead of a beard, he wears a hideous mask, performs the part of the lady. These are attended by a troop of sea-gods and nymphs, similarly equipped; and advancing from the bow of the vessel, as if just stepped on board, they come forward to the mainmast, and summon before them all such persons as have never sworn the oaths or previously visited their capital. At the foot of the mast is placed a large tub full of sea-water, and covered by a piece of canvas, which is held tight by four of their attendants. Upon this unsteady throne is the luckless wight, whom they design to initiate, compelled to sit; and being asked several questions, which he cannot answer, and taking several oaths, very much resembling those said to be administered at Highgate, Neptune proceeds to confer upon him the honour of filiation, by rather an extraordinary process. Two of the sea-nymphs, generally tall stout fellows, pinion his arms to his sides; and another, bringing a bucket filled with grease and slops from the kitchen, sets it down at his godship's feet, putting a small painting-brush into his hand. Neptune now dips his brush into the filth, and proceeds to spread a lather over the face of the novice, taking care to ask questions during the whole process; and if the adopted be simple enough to reply, the brush is instantly thrust into his mouth. As soon as a sufficient quantity of grease is laid upon the face, Neptune seizes a piece of rusty iron, generally the broken hoop of some water-cask, with which he scrapes off all that has been applied. If the novice take all this patiently, his face is washed, and he is permitted to descend from his throne in peace; but if he lose his temper, which most men are apt to do, a bucket of sea-water is poured upon his head. If this be sufficient to cool his wrath, he suffers no more; but if it only increase his indignation, bucket after bucket is emptied over him, and at last, the holders of the sail-cloth suddenly retiring, he is plunged overhead into the tub. To crown all, the unfortunate wretch who has endured these miseries is fined by his tormentor in a gallon of ruin; a fine which the force of custom compels him to pay. It must be confessed that this is a barbarous amusement, much resembling that of the boys in the fable of the boys and the frogs. Though very agreeable to those who act and to the lookers on, it is not so to him that suffers.

In this manner many persons were treated, till at length Neptune, growing weary from the number of novices, was content to admit the rest to the privileges of initiation, on condition that the fines should be punctually paid; an agreement into which most of us very thankfully entered.

Next morning, the first object which met our eyes was the land of Caycos island. We were so close to the shore, when daylight discovered it, that had the wind been at all adverse we must unquestionably have struck; but being assisted by a fair and gentle breeze, the ships put about immediately, and escaped the danger. Standing out to sea, the fleet now doubled the promontory, and steering round by the other side, sailed on without losing sight of the land till late in the evening.

On the following day, a signal was made from the Admiral's ship, that the Golden Fleece transport, under convoy of the Volcano bomb, should proceed to Port Royal, whilst the rest of the fleet held their course towards Negril Bay. These two vessels accordingly set all sail, and pushed forward by themselves; the others keeping on at a more moderate rate, that none might stray from the convoy: for the West India seas at this time swarmed with American privateers, and it was of great consequence to keep the store-ships and heavy transports in the middle of the squadron.

It so chanced that I took my passage in one of the two ships which proceeded forward by themselves. The wind was fair, and we made great progress, insomuch that before dark the high land of St. Domingo on one side, and the mountains of Cuba on the other, were discernible. In spite of the heat, therefore, our voyage soon became truly delightful. Secure of getting on under the influence of the trade winds, we had nothing to distract our thoughts, or keep us from feasting our eyes upon the glorious shores of these two islands; whilst in addition to the sight of land, which of itself was cheering, we were amused with waterspouts, apparently playing about us in every direction. One of these, however, began to form within a little distance of the ship, and as they are dangerous as well as interesting, a cannon was got ready to break it before it should reach us. But it did not complete its formation, though I cannot tell why; for, after one spout had risen into the air some height, and another bent down from the clouds to meet it, they were suddenly carried away in different directions, and fell into the sea with the noise of a cataract.

Among other sources of amusement, our attention was drawn, on the 29th, to a shark, which made its appearance at the stern of the vessel. A strong hook was immediately prepared, and baited with a piece of salt pork, which being thrown over, was instantly gulped by the voracious monster. But as soon as he felt the pain occasioned by the book in his jaws, he plunged towards the bottom of the sea with such violence, as to render the very tafferel hot, by the rapidity of the cord gliding over it. Having permitted him to go a certain length, he was again hauled up to the surface, where he remained without offering further resistance, till a boat was lowered, and a strong noose thrown over his head. Being thus made fast to the gunwale of the boat, he was brought round to the gangway, when the end of the noose being cast over the main-yard, he was lifted out of the sea and swung upon the ship's deck. Hitherto he had suffered quietly enough, in apparent stupefaction from the pain of his jaw; but he began now to convince us that neither life nor strength had deserted him; lashing his tail with such violence as speedily to clear the quarter-deck, and biting in the most furious manner at everything within his reach.

One of the sailors, however, who seemed to understand these matters more than his comrades, took an axe, and watching his opportunity, at one, blow chopped off his tail. He was now perfectly harmless, unless, indeed, one had chosen to thrust one's hand into his mouth; and the same sailor accordingly proceeded to lay him open, and to take out his entrails. And now it was that the tenacity of life, peculiar to these animals, displayed itself. After his heart and bowels were taken out; the shark still continued to exhibit proofs of animation, by biting with as much force as ever at a bag of carpenter's tools that happened to lie within his reach.

Being cut up, he was distributed in portions among the soldiers and the ship's crew. The tail part only was reserved as the chief delicacy for our cabin, which, though dry and hard, with little flavour or taste, was on the present occasion considered as agreeable food, because it was fresh.

Chapter 16
We Battle an American Privateer

But what I principally relished, in this part of our voyage, was the exquisite beauty of its night-scenery. To an inhabitant of Great Britain, the splendour of a night-scene in these climates is altogether unknown. Shining broad and full in a sky perfectly cloudless, the moon sends forth a clear and mellow lustre, little inferior, in point of brilliancy, to the full twilight in England. By this means you never lose sight of land, either by night or day, as long as your course lies between Cuba and St. Domingo; whilst the delicious coolness, which follows the setting of the sun, tempts you, in spite of all the whispers of prudence, to expose yourself to dews and damps, rather than forego the pleasures of which they are the bane. Besides, you have constantly the satisfaction of observing yourself move steadily on at the most agreeable of all rates, about five or six miles an hour; a satisfaction far from trifling in a sea-life. Then the ocean is so smooth, that scarcely a ripple is seen to break the moon-beams as they fall; whilst the quiet dash of little waves against the ship's side, and the rushing noise occasioned by the moving of her bow through the water, produce altogether an effect which may, without affectation, be termed absolutely refreshing. It was my common practice to sit for hours after night-fall upon the tafferel, and strain my eyes in the attempt to distinguish objects on shore or strange sails in the distance.

It happened that, on the 30th, I was tempted to indulge in this idle but bewitching employment, even beyond my usual hour for retiring, and did not quit the deck till towards two o'clock in the morning of the 31st. I had just entered my cabin, and was beginning to undress, when a cry from above, of an enemy in chase, drew me instantly to the quarter-deck. On looking astern, I perceived a vessel making directly after us, and was soon convinced of the justice of the alarm, by a shot which whistled over our heads. All hands were now called to quarters, the small sails were taken in, and having spoken to our companion, and made an agreement as to position, both ships cleared for action. But the stranger, seeing his signal obeyed with so much alacrity, likewise slackened sail, and, continuing to keep us in view, followed our wake without approaching nearer. In this state things continued till daybreak, we still holding our course, and he hanging back; but as soon as it was light, he set more sail and ran to windward, moving just out of gun-shot, in a parallel direction with us. It was now necessary to fall upon some plan of deceiving him, otherwise there was little probability that he would attack. In the bomb, indeed, the height of the bulwark served to conceal some of the men; but in the transport no such screen existed. The troops were, therefore, ordered below, and only the sailors, a few blacks, and the officers, kept the deck. The same expedient was likewise adopted, in part, by Captain Price, of the *Volcano*; and in order to give to his ship a still greater resemblance than it already had to a merchantman, he displayed an old faded scarlet ensign, and drew up his fore and mainsail in what sailors term a *lubberly* manner.

As yet the stranger had shown no colours, but, from her build and rigging, there was little doubt as to her country. She was a beautiful schooner, presenting seven ports on a side, and apparently crowded with men, circumstances which immediately led us to believe that she was an American privateer. The *Volcano*, on the other hand, was a clumsy strong-built ship, carrying twelve guns; and the *Golden Fleece* mounted eight; so that, in point of artillery, the advantage was rather on our side; but the American's sailing was so much superior to that of either of us, that this advantage was more than counterbalanced.

Having dodged us till eight o'clock, and reconnoitred with great exactness, the stranger began to steer gradually nearer and nearer, till at length it was judged that she had arrived within range. A gun was accordingly fired from the *Volcano*, and another from the transport, the balls from both of which passed over her and fell into the sea. Finding herself thus assaulted, she instantly threw off her disguise, and hung out an American ensign; when, putting her helm up, she poured a broadside, with a volley of musketry, into the transport; and ran alongside of the bomb, which sailed to windward.

As soon as her flag was displayed, and her intention of attacking discerned, all hands were ordered up, and she received two well-directed broadsides from the *Volcano*, as well as a warm salute from the *Golden Fleece*. But such was the celerity of her motion, that she was alongside of the bomb in less time than can be imagined; and actually dashing her bow against the other, attempted to carry her by boarding. Captain Price, however, was ready to receive them. The boarders were at their posts in an instant, and the enemy discovering, when it was too late, the mistake into which he had fallen, left about twenty of his men upon the *Volcano's* bowsprit, all of whom were thrown into the sea; and filling his sails, sheered off with the same speed with which he had borne down. In attempting to escape, he unavoidably fell somewhat to leeward, and exposed the whole of his deck to the fire of the transport. A tremendous discharge of musketry saluted him as he passed; and it was almost laughable to witness the haste with which his crew hurried below, leaving none upon deck except such as were absolutely wanted to work his vessel.

The *Volcano* had by this time filled, and gave chase, firing with great precision at the privateer's yards and rigging, in the hope of disabling him. But as fortune would have it, none of his important ropes or yards were cut; and we had the mortification to see him, in a few minutes, beyond our reach.

In this affair, a marine officer and two men were killed on board the bomb; and some of the tackling was shot away. The transport suffered nothing in killed or wounded, having been in a great degree protected from the enemy's fire by her commodore; and only one rope, not, I believe, an important one, was destroyed.

The battle having ended, and the chase being given up as fruitless, we continued our course without any other adventure; and before dark were able to distinguish the blue mountains of Jamaica. St. Domingo and Cuba had both disappeared, and this was now the only land visible; but it was not till the 1st of November that we could obtain a distinct view of it. Then, indeed, we found ourselves within a few miles of the shore, and seldom has landscape appeared more attractive to the eyes of a voyager, than the romantic shores of Jamaica now appeared to ours.

Jamaica is in general a bold and mountainous island, but on this side it is peculiarly so. It appeared to me that even the Pyrenees, magnificent as they are, were not to be compared, in point of altitude, to the hills now before me; and early in the morning, while yet the mists hung upon their summits and concealed them, no prospect can be imagined more sublime than that which they presented. It was, in truth, a glorious scene; and as the wind blew light and uncertain, we were permitted, from the slowness of the ship's progress, to enjoy it to the full. Towards evening, indeed, the breeze died entirely away, which compelled us to anchor about eight miles from the harbour of Port Royal.

In spite of the little rest which I had procured during the two preceding nights, having sat up till an early hour this morning, to watch several strange sails that hovered about us, I could not bring myself to quit the deck till after midnight, so beautiful, in all respects, were the objects around me. The moon shone with her accustomed brilliancy, and exhibited every crag and tree upon the land, changed and confounded in shape, but still plainly; whilst the perfume, borne off upon the breeze, was odoriferous in the highest degree. The sound of the waves, likewise, breaking upon the rocks, and the occasional cry of seamen, as they adjusted ropes and sails, together with the sight of several vessels which took advantage of the night-wind and stood to sea, with canvas glittering in the moonbeams, produced so delightful a combination, as completely riveted me to my seat; nor was it without much reluctance that I at length yielded to the drowsy god, and descended to my cabin.

Next morning, the ship got under weigh at an early hour, but, owing to the unsteadiness of the breeze, it was ten o'clock before we made any satisfactory progress. As we approached the bay which forms the harbour of Port Royal, a novel and pleasing sight presented itself. The hills dying gradually away, gave place to gentle slopes and green knolls, till, towards the entrance, the coast became perfectly level. Pushing forward, we soon found ourselves in a narrow channel between two projecting headlands, beautifully ornamented with cocoa-nut trees, and so near to each other, that I could with ease have thrown a biscuit from the ship's deck upon either. At the extremity of these necks, just where the bay begins its sweep, stand two well-built forts, bristling with cannon; and at the opposite side may be seen a third, ready to sink whatever hostile fleet should be fortunate enough to force an entrance. But these were not the most striking parts of the scene. The water in this strait is remarkably clear, and exhibits with great distinctness the tops and chimneys of houses at the bottom. It will be recollected, that many years ago, an earthquake not only demolished great part of the town of Port Royal, but likewise covered it with the sea; by which means, the site of the harbour was completely changed, and that which was formerly dry land, and a town, became part of the entrance of the bay.

Having doubled the promontories, a rich and extensive prospect meets the eye. You find yourself, as it were, in a large inland lake, the banks of which are covered with plantations of sugar cane, groves of cocoa-nut and plantain trees, and other woods peculiar to these regions, beautifully interspersed with seats and villages. On your right is the town of Port Royal, lying almost on a level with the water, and strongly protected by fortifications, whilst in various other directions are castles and batteries, adding an appearance of security to that of plenty. The banks, though not lofty, slope gently upwards, with occasional falls or glens, and the background is composed in general of the rugged tops of distant mountains.

Having waited till the ship dropped anchor, I put myself into a sort of barge rowed by four negroes, and proceeded to Kingston. Though not the capital of the island, Kingston is the largest town in Jamaica. It stands upon the brink of a frith, about nine miles above Port Royal, and thence enjoys all the advantages of the chief mart in this trading country. Like most other mercantile seaports, it is built without much regard to regularity. The streets, though wide, are in general the reverse of elegant, being composed almost entirely of wooden houses, and by no means remarkable for cleanliness. Of public buildings it possesses none worthy of notice. Its inns are, however, excellent; and though certainly not moderate in their charges, they are at least more so than those of Bermuda. In a word, it is exactly such a town as one would expect to find holding the principal commercial rank in a colony where men's minds seldom aspire beyond the occupations of trade.

Of the intense heat in this place, none but those who have experienced it can form a notion. It is impossible to walk out with any comfort, except before the sun has risen, or after he has set; and even within doors, with the aid of thorough draughts and all the other expedients usually adopted on such occasions, it is with the utmost difficulty that you can contrive to keep your blood in a moderate degree of temperature. In the town itself, therefore, few of the higher classes reside, the closeness produced by a proximity of houses being in this climate peculiarly insupportable. These inhabit for the most part little villas, called Pens, about three or four miles in the country, the master of each family generally, retaining a suite of apartments, or, perhaps an entire mansion, in some open street for his own use, when business obliges, him, to exchange the comfort of fresh air for the suffocating atmosphere of Kingston. Towards the outskirts, indeed, in one direction, a few gentile families inhabit one or two handsome houses, surrounded by extensive gardens and shrubberies; but these are not numerous, and they are so far removed from the heart of the town, as to be in great measure beyond the influence of its smoke and other nuisances.

During our sojourn in this place we received the most hospitable attention from several persons of the first distinction. Balls and other entertainments were given, at which all the beauty and fashion in this part of the island attended; and for some days I had little leisure or inclination for any other pursuit than the enjoyment of civilized pleasure, a pursuit which, from long disuse, possessed more than ordinary zest. But at length having seen as much of Kingston and its vicinity as, I desired to see, I determined to take advantage of the opportunity which fortune had placed within my reach, and to make an excursion into the heart of the Blue Mountains. To this I was additionally induced by an invitation from an old friend to visit him at Annotto bay; and as, along with his letter, he sent a horse for my own conveyance, and a mule for the conveyance of my baggage, no difficulty respecting a mode of being transported stood in the way to obstruct my design.

Having made up my mind to this journey, I waited, till sunset on the 9th, when, starting in the cool of the evening, I reached a little tavern called the Plum Tree, about half an hour after dark. My ride carried me through an open and fertile country covered with sugar-canes, coffee, and such other plants as are cultivated in the low grounds of Jamaica. It was a short one, not more than twelve miles in extent, but I was forced to halt where I did, because I had gained the foot of the mountains; and if I had passed the Plum Tree, well known as a sort of half-way house on such tours, I might have travelled all night without finding any place of accommodation.

As darkness set in, one of the, beautiful peculiarities of a tropical climate, which I had not previously witnessed, came under my observation. The air was filled with fire-flies, which, emitting a phosphoric light something similar to the light of the glow-worm, only more red and brilliant, danced around me like sparks from a smith's anvil when he is beating a bar of red-hot iron. These creatures flutter about with a humming noise, and frequently settle in large swarms upon branches of trees, giving them the semblance of so many pieces of timber taken newly out of a fire. When viewed by daylight they are in no way remarkable for their elegance, resembling in the shape of the body a long beetle which may be seen in the fields after sunset, without wings or scales. In colour they are a dingy brown, and, like the glow-worm, carry their light in the tail.

As I had not before chanced to see anything of the kind, and forgot at the moment that such an insect as the fire-fly existed, I was for a few minutes at a loss to what cause to attribute the phenomenon, and was at last indebted to my negro guide for refreshing my memory on the subject. The effect, however, cannot be conceived without being witnessed. A cluster of two or three glow-worms shine so brilliantly, that they will furnish subject for the commendatory eloquence of any one fortunate enough to perceive them together; but their brilliancy is to a farthing candle to the sun, when compared with that of the fire-fly. Not two, or three, but thousands of these creatures dance around, filling the air with a wavering and uncertain glimmer, of the extreme beauty of which no words can convey an adequate conception.

Having passed the night at this tavern, a small cottage kept by a free negro and his wife, I rose two hours before dawn, and prosecuted my journey. From the moment I quitted the Plate Tree I began gradually to ascend, till at daybreak I found myself in the midst of the most glorious scenery that the imagination of man can conceive. Everything around was new and romantic. The hills, towering into the very sky, were covered from top to bottom with the richest herbage and the most luxuriant wood. Rarely could a barren crag be discerned, and when it did appear it was only a sharp point, or a bald projection pushing itself forward from the midst of the thickest foliage. But what to me formed the most bewitching part of the prospect was the elegance of the trees and their perfect dissimilitude to any which had previously beheld. The cocoa-nut and plantain were mingled with the wild pine and lime-tree; while the cashew and wild coffee, with numberless other shrubs, loaded at once with fruit and blossom, formed the underwood to these graceful forests.

As yet I had been favoured with a wide and good road, but now it began gradually to narrow, till at last it ended in a path little more distinct than the sheep-tracks over the hills in Scotland. Winding along the sides of the mountains, it brought me frequently to spots where the wood parting, as if artificially, displayed deep ravines, to look down which, without becoming dizzy, required no little strength of head; whilst above, the same hill continued to stretch itself to a height far beyond any I had before gazed upon. Presently after it conducted me gently down into valleys completely shut out from the rest of the world; and as I descended I could hear the roar of water, though neither, the stream nor the bottom of the glen could be perceived. On one of these occasions, after passing through a thick grove, I beheld a river of some width dashing along the glen, and chafing so as to produce the noise of a mighty waterfall. Towards the brink of this river my guide conducted me; when, plunging in, we made our way with some difficulty to the opposite bank, and again began to ascend.

For several hours, the same scenery surrounded me, only varied by the occasional appearance of clusters of negro huts. Than these, it is impossible to imagine any species of huts or dwellings more beautifully picturesque. They are constructed of strong limbs of trees, thatched over with straw, and usually ending in a cone; having no windows, but only two, or sometimes four doors, for the purpose of admitting a free current of air. The spots chosen for their erection, are generally small platforms or terraces in the sides of the hills. A little path, similar to that along which I travelled, winds down from their doors to the bottom of the valley, and conducts to the edge of the river, from whence the inhabitants are supplied with water. Other tracks likewise branch off in different directions, some towards the summit, and others along the sides of the mountains; leading, probably, to the fields or spots where the inhabitants labour. These huts have no chimney, but only a large hole in the roof, to give free passage to the smoke; and I could perceive, by its rise at present, that fires were now burning.

It would be labour lost, were I to attempt any more minute description of this delightful journey. Every step I took presented something new, and something more grand and sublime than I had just quitted; whilst the continual fording of the swollen river (for I crossed the same stream no fewer than eight-and-twenty times) gave an additional interest to the scene, arising from the sense of danger. The rainy season having just ended, this stream, the Wag-water, a most appropriate name, had not as yet returned to its natural size; but at the fords, which in general would not cover a horse's knees, the depth was such as to moisten the saddle-girths. So great a quantity of water, in a furious mountain-torrent, pouring on with all the violence produced by a steep descent, occasioned no slight pressure upon my steed; nor was it without considerable floundering on his part, and some anxiety on mine, that once or twice we succeeded in making good our passage.

Chapter 17
Jamaica

Noon was approaching when my sooty fellow-traveller directed my attention to a neat cottage, romantically situated on the top of a low mound, which stood alone in the middle of stupendous mountains. It commanded one of the most exquisite prospects that fancy can represent. A sort of glen surrounded it on every side, richly and beautifully wooded; behind, rose some of the most lofty of the Blue Mountains; on the right there was an opening, which admitted a fine view of Annotto Bay; whilst in the other direction, the hills sloping gradually upwards, presented an inclined plane, covered with fields of sugar-cane, and ending, at a considerable distance, in one abrupt and broken ridge.

The cottage in question was the residence of my friend, and the resting-place whither my steps were turned; nor did I experience any regret at finding myself so near my journey's end. The heat had for some time been almost intolerable, and having eaten nothing since the night before, nature began to cry out for repose and repletion; and, in truth, the welcome which I experienced, was of a nature to take away all desire of wandering farther. We had not met for several years—not, indeed, since I was a child—and in the interval, some melancholy changes had occurred in the family of my host; but he received me with the cordial hospitality which a warm heart produces, and forgot his private sorrows for a time, that he might not throw a damp upon my enjoyments.

The remainder of this day I spent, as a powerful sensation

of fatigue warned me to spend it, within doors; but on the following morning I set out at an early hour, for the purpose of gratifying my curiosity on a number of points which had frequently exercised it. In this excursion, and indeed in all the excursions which I undertook during my residence at his Pen, my friend accompanied me; and an excellent and most intelligent guide he proved to be. We made the tour of several estates, saw the process of making sugar, visited the sugar and coffee plantations, and inspected several hospitals, with one of which each estate is supplied, for the accommodation and cure of sick negroes. In the course of these rambles, I made it my business to inquire into the condition and treatment of the slave population; inspecting their huts, and even examining their provisions; and I frankly confess that, though I began my researches under the influence of as many prejudices as, on such a subject, are wont to be entertained by Englishmen in general, the result of the whole was to convince me that I had done glaring injustice to the character of the Jamaica planters, as well as fostered notions of the wretchedness of the negroes, utterly and iniquitously erroneous. It is no business of mine, and, if it were, this is no proper place to take part in what has of late been termed the West-Indian controversy; but, as an eye-witness, I may venture to speak out on one point, by affirming, that a countless proportion of the stories with which the British public is amused, touching the barbarous treatment of slaves by owners and overseers, are, if not absolute fables, at all events gross exaggerations. I am aware that my residence in the island was too brief, and my acquaintance with it too limited, to entitle my opinions to the weight which a more protracted sojourn might have obtained for them; but it is but justice to state, that whilst I was there, I enjoyed opportunities of seeing the negro at all times, and under all circumstances, such as few casual visitors can boast of. My host was not a planter, but a medical practitioner; and one prejudiced rather against the slave system than in favour of it: there was therefore no disposition on his part to cast dust into my eyes, or to present to them only the bright side of the picture. Under his guidance, I beheld the negro at work in the fields, in the bosom of his family, in the sick ward, and at market; and I never saw him other than a contented and light-hearted being. No doubt there are instances of cruelty on the part of overseers in Jamaica, exactly as there are instances of tyranny on the part of parish officers and county magistrates in England; but had these been as numerous, or as flagrant, as they are represented to be, I cannot doubt but that something of the kind must have passed under my eyes, even within the space of one week. No such event, however, took place; and, as far as I could learn, no such event was to be expected.

Far be it from me to stand forward as the advocate of personal bondage in the abstract—it is a grievous evil; and wherever men are so far civilized as to render its abolition desirable, it is an evil which ought to be abolished. But it is an evil of long standing, authorized in the Bible, and therefore, we may presume, not without its counterbalancing benefits. He, therefore, who would seek, at all hazards and under all circumstances, to dissolve the tie which binds a master to his slave, and a slave to his master—whilst he would be doing that which the Apostles never did, and which Christians are nowhere commanded to do—would run no slight hazard of causing a quantity of mischief to both parties, for which the benefits bestowed upon either would not compensate. With respect to our own colonies, in particular, it is manifest that the whole matter resolves itself into one consideration. If the negroes be in such a state, as that the boon of universal freedom would be productive to them of universal benefit, by all means let it be bestowed at once, even though it be attended by so much national expense, as the fair demands of the proprietors for compensation shall impose upon us. If they be not thus situated, let every practicable method be adopted to advance them on the scale of civilization; but till they be advanced far beyond their present station, let no false hopes be excited that the moment of their liberation is at hand. Many measures for their improvement have been adopted since the year 1814, and many more are in daily process of adoption; but it is greatly to be apprehended that much of the benefit which these measures promised to bring about, has been obstructed by the indiscreet zeal of those who profess, and probably feel, the liveliest interest in their welfare.

Besides adding to my stock of knowledge as to the cultivation of the sugar-cane, the making of sugar, rum, &c. &c.; I had an opportunity of seeing something of the Maroons, or free Negroes, who inhabit the mountains. These people dwell apart from the European settlers, holding very little intercourse with them, though a single European generally resides in each of their villages, as a sort of chief or magistrate. They struck me to be a lazy, indolent, and harmless race of human beings; and they formed, in all their habits, a striking contrast with their enslaved brethren. Whilst the latter devote their spare hours to the culture of their own little spots, to cudgel-playing, dancing, or other gambols, the former appear to spend their whole time in a state between sleeping and waking, at the doors of their huts, or under the shelter of trees. Some of the Maroon females, I observed, were really handsome, their features being high, and their persons elegantly formed; but in general they differed nothing from the other negroes, from whom, indeed, they are principally descended.

I heard that the men carry on a petty trade in feathers, but that their principal occupation, at least that from which they derive the largest emolument, consists in apprehending, and leading back to their masters, run-away slaves. For their services in this department, they were wont to receive a pension from the Government; and they are still, I believe, supplied with muskets and ammunition at the expense of the colonial authorities. But enough of these details.

My sojourn in St. Mary's having extended considerably

beyond the limits which prudence would have imposed upon it, I set out on the morning of the 13th, on my return towards Kingston. The country through which I travelled differed in many respects from that which I had crossed in my way hither: it was in general less wild, and less mountainous; but it possessed features of striking beauty, rich corn-fields being interspersed amidst graceful forests, and here and there a wild hill-side rising as a contrast to both. The most remarkable variety, and not perhaps the least agreeable, was, however, to be found in the absence of the Wag-water; my guide having led me in a direction by which its tortuous course was avoided.

As it was late before I started, my ride soon became toilsome on account of the heat, and I was fain to stop short for the night at a place called Stoney Hill, about twelve miles from Kingston. Here I was hospitably entertained by the officers of the 102nd regiment; and, rising at an early hour on the following morning, I contrived to complete my journey before breakfast. And it was well that no further time had been expended in my progress. The ships, I found, were preparing to put to sea; the stock was all embarked, and the crews on board; nothing therefore remained for me but to follow the general example, and to establish myself with as little delay as possible in my cabin.

In spite of these preparations, the 15th and 16th of November both passed away without any movement being made. It was, however, my custom not to neglect any opportunities which chanced to come in my way of viewing strange places, and obtaining an acquaintance with strange people; neither on the present occasion did I fail to make the most of the interval, by landing and wandering over the town of Port Royal. But to describe minutely a place so little deserving of description, would hardly repay me for the labour of writing, or the reader for the toil of perusing what I write. It is sufficient to observe, that except to him who takes delight in beholding a well-constructed military work, there is nothing in the busy, bustling town of Port Royal which will at all compensate for the heat and fatigue which he must undergo who, like myself, traverses its streets and lanes at noon-day.

The long looked-for signal to weigh was hung out at last; and at an early hour on the 17th we put to sea. Our point of destination was Negril Bay, the appointed place of rendezvous for the whole armament; and we reached it without the occurrence of mishap or adventure on the evening of the 19th. We found here a large fleet already assembled; but the horses were all landed, many officers were dwelling in tents on the shore, and everything gave indication that some further delay might be expected. To say the truth, I experienced no degree of satisfaction at this prospect; for the point of the island opposite to which we now lay was neither remarkable for its natural beauty nor very thickly inhabited; and had the contrary been the case, I had seen as much of Jamaica and its people as I was at all desirous to see. Besides, it was impossible not to feel that whatever the object of our expedition might be, it was not likely to be furthered by this tardy mode of entering upon it; and rumours already began to spread abroad, of discoveries incautiously and untimely made. It was, therefore, with no slight degree of pleasure that, on the morning of the 24th, the topmasts of a numerous squadron were seen over the eastern promontory, in full sail towards us; and it was with still greater delight that in a short time we were able to discern the flags of Sir Alexander Cochrane and Admiral Malcolm floating in the breeze. By and bye the Tonnant and Royal Oak showed their hulls in the offing; and a short while afterwards, these ships, followed by a large fleet of troopers and transports, majestically entered the bay. As may be imagined, our curiosity was strongly excited to learn what reinforcements they contained, and what intelligence they brought; insomuch, that they had scarcely dropped anchor when they were boarded from almost every one of the ships which they came to join.

It appeared that this powerful reinforcement consisted of the following corps:—the 93rd regiment, a fine battalion of

Highlanders, mustering nine hundred bayonets; six companies of the 95th rifle corps; two West India regiments, each eight hundred strong; two squadrons of the 14th Dragoons dismounted; detachments of artillery, rockets, sappers, and engineers; recruits for the different corps already in this part of the world; and though last, not least, Major-General Keane to take upon himself the command of the whole. The intelligence brought was likewise interesting, for it informed us of the point whither we were to proceed; and it was soon known throughout the fleet, that the conquest of New Orleans was the object in view.

But before I pursue my narrative further, having arrived, as it were, at a second commencement, it may be well if I state in full the number of men of which the army now consisted. In the first place, then, there were the 4th, 44th, and 85th regiments, originally dispatched from Bordeaux, and the 21st, which joined the expedition at Bermuda. These battalions, being considerably reduced by past service, could not at present muster conjunctly above two thousand two hundred men; and being likewise deprived of the Marine battalion, which had fought beside them in the Chesapeake, they retained no followers except the artillery, sappers, &c. which had accompanied them from the first. The whole amount of this corps may, therefore, be estimated at two thousand five hundred men.

Without computing the individual strength of each detachment now arrived, I will venture to fix the aggregate at two thousand five hundred; and thus the whole, taken collectively, will amount to five thousand combatants. That it might somewhat exceed or fall under this computation, I do not deny; but neither the excess nor deficiency could be considerable; and therefore my statement may be received as correct, with very little allowance.

This, it must be confessed, was a formidable force, and such as, had all its parts been trustworthy, might have done much. But on the black corps little reliance could be placed, especially if the climate should prove colder than was anticipated;

consequently, there were not more than three thousand four hundred men upon whom a General could fully depend.

Together with these forces were brought out abundant stores of ammunition, some clothing for the troops, and tents to be used when an opportunity should offer. There were also numerous additions to the commissariat and medical departments; in short, the materiel of the army was increased in proportion to its increase in number.

To find himself in the chief command of the army, exceeded the expectation, and perhaps the desire, of General Keane. Being a young and dashing officer, he had been selected as most fit to serve under General Ross; and having sailed from England before the death of that gallant chief was known, he reached Madeira before his elevation was communicated to him. Young as he was, however, his arrival produced much satisfaction throughout the armament; for though no one entertained a doubt as to the personal courage of Colonel Brook, it was felt that a leader of more experience was wanted on the present expedition.

As soon as the newly-arrived squadron had anchored, the Bay was covered with boats, which conveyed parties of officers from ship to ship, hastening to salute their comrades, and to inquire into the state of things at home. Greetings and hearty embraces were interchanged between friends thus again brought together; and a few passing ejaculations of sorrow bestowed upon those who could not now take part in the meeting. Many questions were put, relative to persons and places in England; in a word, the day was spent in that species of employment, which can be completely known only to those who have been similarly situated.

Chapter 18
To New Orleans

But the period granted for such indulgence was not of long duration, for on the following morning the *Tonnant*, *Ramilies*, and two brigs stood to sea; and on the 26th the rest of the fleet got under weigh and followed the Admiral. It is impossible to conceive a finer sea-view than this general stir presented. Our fleet amounted now to upwards of fifty sail, many of them vessels of war, which shaking loose their topsails, and lifting their anchors at the same moment, gave to Negril Bay an appearance of bustle such as it has seldom been able to present. In half an hour all the canvas was set, and the ships moved slowly and proudly from their anchorage, till, having cleared the headlands, and caught the fair breeze which blew without, they bounded over the water with the speed of eagles, and long before dark the coast of Jamaica had disappeared.

There is something in rapidity of motion, whether it be along a high road or across the deep, extremely elevating; nor was its effect unperceived on the present occasion. It is true that there were other causes for the high spirits which now pervaded the armament, but I question if any proved more efficient in their production than the astonishing rate of our sailing. Whether the business we were about to undertake would prove bloody or the reverse entered not into the calculations of a single individual in the fleet. The sole subject of remark was the speed with which we got over the ground, and the probability that existed of our soon reaching the point of debarkation. The change of climate, likewise, was not without its effect in producing pleasurable sensations. The farther we got from Jamaica, the more cool and agreeable became the atmosphere; from which circumstance we were led to hope that, in spite of its southern latitude, New Orleans would not be found so oppressively hot as we had been taught to expect.

The breeze continuing without interruption, on the 29th we came in sight of the island of Grand Cayman. It is a small speck in the middle of the sea, lying so near the level of the water as to be unobservable at any considerable distance. Though we passed along with prodigious velocity, a canoe nevertheless ventured off from the shore, and making its way through waves which looked as if they would swallow it up, succeeded in reaching our vessel. It contained a white man and two negroes, who brought off a quantity of fine turtle, which they gave us in exchange for salt pork; and so great was the value put upon salt provisions, that the bartered a pound and a half of the one for a pound of the other. To us the exchange was very acceptable, and thus both parties remained satisfied with their bargain.

Having lain-to till our turtle-merchants left us, we again filled and stood our course. The land of Cayman was soon invisible; nor was any other perceived till the 2nd of December, when the western shores of Cuba presented themselves. Towards them we now directed the ship's head, and reaching in within a few miles of the beach, coasted along till we had doubled the promontory, which forms one of the jaws of the Mexican Gulf. Whilst keeping thus close to the shore, our sail was more interesting than usual, for though this side of Cuba be low, it is nevertheless picturesque, from the abundance of wood with which it is ornamented. There are likewise several points where huge rocks rise perpendicularly out of the water, presenting the appearance of old baronial castles, with their battlements and lofty turrets; and it will easily be believed that none of these escaped our observation. The few books which we had brought to sea were all read, many of them twice and three times through; and there now remained nothing to amuse except what the variety of the voyage could produce.

But the shores of Cuba were quickly passed, and the old prospect of sea and sky again met the gaze. There was, however, one circumstance from which we experienced a considerable diminution of comfort. As soon as we entered the gulf, a short disagreeable swell was perceptible; differing in some respects from that in the Bay of Biscay, but to my mind infinitely more unpleasant. So great was the motion, indeed, that all walking was prevented; but as we felt ourselves drawing every hour nearer and nearer to the conclusion of our miseries, this additional one was borne without much repining. Besides, we found some amusement in watching, from the cabin windows, the quantity and variety of weed with which the surface of the gulf is covered. The current being here extremely rapid, the weed sails continually in the same direction; that is to say, it goes round by the opposite side of Cuba towards the banks of Newfoundland, and is carried sometimes as far as Bermuda, and even to the Western Isles.

It is not, however, my intention to continue the detail of this voyage longer than may be interesting; I shall therefore merely state that, the wind and weather having undergone some variations, it was the 10th of December before the shores of America could be discerned. On that day we found ourselves opposite to the Chandeleur Islands, and near the entrance of Lake Borgne. There the fleet anchored, that the troops might be removed from the heavy ships into such as drew least water; and from this and other preparations it appeared that to ascend this lake was the plan determined upon.

But before I pursue my narrative further, it will be well if I endeavour to give some account of the situation of New Orleans, and of the nature of the country against which our operations were directed.

New Orleans is a town of some note, containing from twenty to thirty thousand inhabitants. It stands upon the eastern bank of the Mississippi, in 30 degrees north latitude, and about 110 miles from the Gulf of Mexico. Though in itself unfortified, it is difficult to conceive a place capable of presenting greater obstacles to an invader; and at the same time more conveniently situated with respect to trade. Built upon a narrow neck of land, which is confined on one side by the river, and on the other by impassable morasses, its means of defence require little explanation; and as these morasses extend to the distance of only a few miles, and are succeeded by Lake Pontchartrain, which again communicates through Lake Borgne with the sea, its peculiar commercial advantages must be equally apparent. It is by means of the former of these lakes, indeed, that intercourse is maintained between the city and the northern parts of West Florida, of which it is the capital; a narrow creek, called in the language of the country a bayo or bayouke, navigable for vessels drawing less than six feet water, running up through the marsh, and ending within two miles of the town. The name of this creek is the Bayouke of St. John, and its entrance is defended by works of considerable strength.

But to exhibit its advantages in a more distinct point of view, it will be necessary to say a few words respecting that mighty river upon which it stands. The Mississippi (a corruption of the word Mechasippi, signifying, in the language of the natives, "the father of rivers ") is allowed to be inferior, in point of size and general navigability, to few streams in the world. According to the Sioux Indians it takes its rise from a large swamp, and is increased by many rivers emptying themselves into its course as far as the Fall of St. Anthony, which, by their account, is upwards of 700 leagues from its source. But this fall, which is formed by a rock thrown across the channel, of about twelve feet perpendicular height, is known to be 800 leagues from the sea; and therefore the whole course of the Mississippi, from its spring to its mouth, may be computed at little short of 5000 miles.

Below the fall of St. Anthony, again, the Mississippi is joined by a number of rivers, considerable in point of size, and leading out of almost every part of the continent of America. These are the St. Pierre, which comes from the west; St. Croix, from the eat; the Moingona, which is said to run 150 leagues from the west, and forms a junction about 250 below the fall; and the Illinois, which rises near the lake Michigan, 200 leagues east of the Mississippi.

But by far the most important of these auxiliary streams is the Missouri, the source of which is as little known as that of the Father of Rivers himself. It has been followed by traders upwards of 400 leagues, who traffic with the tribes which dwell upon its banks, and obtain an immense return for European goods. The mouth of this river is five leagues below that of the Illinois, and is supposed to be 800 from its source, which, judging from the flow of its waters, lies in a northwest direction from the Mississippi. It is remarkable enough that the waters of this river are black and muddy, and prevail over those of the Mississippi, which running with a clear and gentle stream till it meets with this addition, becomes from that time both dark and rapid.

The next river of note is the Ohio, which taking its rise near Lake Erie, runs from the north-east to the south-west, and joins the Mississippi about 70 leagues below the Missouri. Besides this there are the St. Francis, an inconsiderable stream, and the Arkansas, which is said to originate in the same latitude with Santa Fe in New Mexico, and which, holding its course nearly 300 leagues, falls in about 200 above New Orleans. Sixty leagues below the Arkansas, comes the Yazous from the northeast; and about 58 nearer to the city is the Rouge, so called from the colour of its waters, which are of a reddish dye, and tinge those of the Mississippi at the time of the floods. Its source is in New Mexico, and after running about 200 leagues it is joined by the Noir 30 miles above the place where it empties itself into the Mississippi.

Of all these rivers there is none which will not answer the

purposes of commerce, at least to a very considerable extent; and as they join the Mississippi above New Orleans, it is evident that this city may be considered as the general mart of the whole. Whatever nation, therefore, chances to possess this place, possesses in reality the command of a greater extent of country than is included within the boundary-line of the whole United States since from every direction are goods, the produce of East, West, North, and South America, sent down by the Mississippi to the Gulf. But were New Orleans properly supplied with fortifications, it is evident that no vessels could pass without the leave of its governor; and therefore is it that I consider that city as of greater importance to the American government than any other within the compass of their territories.

Having said so much on its commercial advantages, let me now point out more distinctly than I have yet done the causes which contribute to its safety from all hostile attempts. The first of these is the shallowness of the river at its mouth, and the extreme rapidity of the current. After flowing on in one prodigious sheet of water, varying in depth from one hundred to thirty fathoms, the Mississippi, previous to its joining the Mexican Gulf, divides into four or five mouths, the most considerable of which is encumbered by a sandbank continually liable to shift. Over this bank no vessel drawing above seventeen feet water can pass; when once across, however, there is no longer a difficulty in being floated; but to anchor is hazardous, on account of the huge logs which are constantly carried down the stream. Should one of these strike the bow of the ship, it would probably dash her to pieces; whilst, independent of this, there is always danger of drifting or losing anchors, owing to the number of sunken logs which the under-current bears along within a few feet of the bottom. All vessels ascending the river are accordingly obliged, if the wind be foul, to make fast to the trees upon the banks; because without a breeze at once fair and powerful, it is impossible to stem the torrent.

But besides this natural obstacle to invasion, the mouth of the river is defended by a fort, which from its situation may be pronounced impregnable. It is built upon an artificial causeway, and is surrounded on all sides by swamps totally impervious, which extend on both sides of the river to a place called the Detour des Anglais, within twenty miles of the city. Here two other forts are erected, one on each bank. Like that at the river's mouth, these are surrounded by a marsh, a single narrow path conducting from the commencement of firm ground to the gates of each. If, therefore, an enemy should contrive to pass both the bar and the first fort, he must here be stopped, because all landing is prevented by the nature of the soil; and however fair his breeze may have hitherto been, it will not now assist his further progress. At this point the Mississippi winds almost in a circle, insomuch that vessels which arrive are necessitated to make fast till a change of wind occur.

From the *Detour des Anglais* towards New Orleans the face of the country undergoes an alteration. The swamp does not indeed end, but it narrows off to the right, leaving a space of firm ground, varying, from three to one mile in, width, between it and the river. At the back of this swamp, again, which may be about six or eight miles across, come up the waters of Lake Pontchartrain, and thus a neck of arable land is formed, stretching for some way above the city. The whole of these morasses are covered as far as the Detour with tall reeds; a little wood now succeeds, skirting the open country, but the wood measures no more than one mile in depth, when it again gives place to reeds. Such is the aspect of that side of the river upon which the city is built; with respect to the other I can speak with less confidence, having seen it but cursorily. It appears, however, to resemble this in almost every particular, except that it is more wooded and less confined with marsh. Both sides are flat, containing no broken ground, nor any other cover, for military movements; for on the open shore there are no trees, except a few in the gardens of those houses which skirt the rivers; the whole being laid out in large fields of sugar-cane; separated from one another by rails and ditches.

From the preceding brief account of the country, the advantages possessed by a defending army must; be apparent. To approach by the river is out of the question, and therefore an enemy can land only from the lake. But this can be done nowhere, except where creeks or bayos offer convenience for that purpose, because the banks of the lake are universally swampy; and can hardly supply footing for infantry, far less for the transportation of artillery. Of these, however, there are not above one or two which could be so used. The Bayo of St. John is one; but it is too well defended, and too carefully guarded for any attempts; and the Bayo of Catiline is another, about ten miles below the city. That this last might be found useful in an attack, was proved by the landing affected by our army at that point; but what is the consequence? The invaders arrive upon a piece of ground, where the most consummate generalship will be of little If the defenders can but retard their progress—which, by crowding the Mississippi with armed vessels, may very easily be done, the labour of a few days will cover the narrow neck with entrenchments; whilst the opposite bank remaining in their hands, can at all times gall their enemy with a close and deadly cannonade. Of wood, as I have already said, or broken ground which might conceal an advance, there exists not a particle. Every movement of the assailants must, therefore, be made under their eyes; and as one flank of their army will be defended by a morass, and the other by the river, they may bid defiance to all attempts at turning.

Such are the advantages of New Orleans; and now it is only fair that I should state its disadvantages: these are owing solely the climate. From the swamps with which it is surrounded, there arise, during the summer months, exhalations extremely fatal to the health of its inhabitants. For some months of the year, indeed, so deadly are the effects of the atmosphere, that the garrison is withdrawn, and most of the families retire from their houses to more genial spots, leaving the town as much deserted as if it had been visited by a pestilence. Yet, in spite of these cautions, agues and intermittent fevers abound here at all times. Nor is it wonderful that the case should be so; for independent of the vile air which the vicinity of so many putrid swamps occasions, this country is more liable than perhaps any other to sudden and severe changes of temperature. A night of keen frost sufficiently powerful to produce ice a quarter of an inch in thickness, frequently follows a day of intense heat; whilst heavy rains and bright sunshine often succeed each other several times in the course of a few hours. But these changes, as may supposed, occur only during the winter; the summer being one continued series of intolerable heat and deadly fog.

Of all these circumstances the conductors of the present expedition were not ignorant. To reduce the forts which command the navigation of the river was regarded as a task too difficult to be attempted; and for any ships to pass without their reduction seemed impossible. Trusting, therefore, that the object of the enterprise was unknown to the Americans, Sir Alexander Cochrane and General Keane determined to effect a landing somewhere on the banks of the lake; and pushing directly on, to take possession of the town, before any effectual preparation could be made for its defence. With this view the troops were removed from the larger into the lighter vessels, and these, under convoy of such gun-brigs as the shallowness of the water would float, began on the 13th to enter Lake Borgne. But we had not proceeded far, when it was apparent that the Americans were well acquainted with our intentions, and ready to receive us. Five large cutters, armed with six heavy guns each, were seen at anchor in the distances: and as all endeavours to land, till these were captured, would have been useless, the transports and largest of the gun-brigs cast anchor, whilst the smaller craft gave chase to the enemy.

But these cutters were built purposely to act upon the lake. They accordingly set sail as soon as the English cruisers arrived within a certain distance, and running on, were quickly out of sight, leaving the pursuers fast aground. To permit them to remain in the hands of the enemy, however, would be fatal, because, as long as they commanded the navigation of the lake, no boats could venture to cross. It was therefore determined at all hazards, and at any expense, to take them; and since our lightest craft could not float where they sailed, a flotilla of launches and ships' barges was got ready for the purpose.

This flotilla consisted of fifty open boats; most of them armed with a carronade in the bow, and well manned with volunteers from the different ships of war. The command was given to Captain Lockier, a brave and skilful officer, who immediately pushed off; and about noon came in sight of the enemy, moored fore and aft, with broadsides pointing towards him. Having pulled a considerable distance, he resolved to refresh his men before he hurried them into action; and, accordingly, letting fall grapplings just beyond the reach of the enemy's guns, the crews of the different boats coolly ate their dinner.

As soon as that meal was finished, and an hour spent in resting, the boats again got ready to advance. But, unfortunately, a light breeze which had hitherto favoured them, now ceased to blow, and they were in consequence compelled to make way only with the oar. The tide also ran strong against them, at once increasing their labour and retarding their progress; but all these difficulties appeared trifling to British sailors; and, giving a hearty cheer, they moved steadily onward in one extended line.

It was not long before the enemy's guns opened upon them, and a tremendous shower of balls saluted their approach. Some boats were sunk, others disabled, and many men were killed and wounded; but the rest pulling with all their might, and occasionally returning the discharges from their carronades, succeeded, after an hour's labour, in closing with the Americans. The marines now began a deadly fire of musketry; whilst the seamen, sword in hand, sprang up the vessels' sides in spite of all opposition; and sabring every man that stood in their way, hauled down the American ensign, and hoisted the British flag in its place.

One cutter alone, which bore the commodore's broad pendant, was not so easily subdued. Having noted its pre-eminence, Captain Lockier directed his own boat against it; and happening to have placed himself in one of the lightest and fastest sailing barges in the flotilla, he found himself alongside of his enemy before any of the others were near enough to render him the smallest support. But nothing dismayed by odds so fearful, the gallant crew of this small bark, following their leader, instantly leaped on board the American. A desperate conflict ensued, in which Captain Lockier received several severe wounds; but after fighting from the bow to the stern, the enemy were at length overpowered; and other barges coming up to the assistance of their commander, the commodore's flag shared the same fate with the others.

Having destroyed all opposition in this quarter, the fleet again weighed anchor, and stood up the lake. But we had not been many hours under sail, when ship after ship ran aground: such as still floated were, therefore, crowded with the troops from those which could go no farther, till finally the lightest vessel stuck fast; and the boats were of necessity hoisted out, to carry us a distance of upwards of thirty miles. To be confined for so long a time as the prosecution of this voyage would require, in one posture, was of itself no very agreeable prospect; but the confinement was but a trifling misery when compared with that which arose from the change in the weather. Instead of a constant bracing frost, heavy rains, such as an inhabitant of England cannot dream of, and against which no cloak could furnish protection, began. In the midst of these were the troops embarked in their new and straitened transports, and each division, after an exposure of ten hours, landed upon a small desert spot of earth, called Pine Island, where it was determined to collect the whole army, previous to its crossing over to the main.

Than this spot it is scarcely possible to imagine any place more completely wretched. It was a swamp, containing a small space of firm ground at one end, and almost wholly unadorned with trees of any sort or description. There were, indeed, a few stunted firs upon the very edge of the water, but these were so diminutive in size as hardly to deserve a higher classification than among the meanest of shrubs. The interior was the resort of wild ducks and other water-fowl; and the pools and creeks with which it was intercepted abounded in dormant alligators.

Upon this miserable desert the army was assembled, without tents or huts, or any covering to shelter them from the inclemency of the weather; and in truth we may fairly affirm that our hardships had here their commencement. After having been exposed all day to a cold and pelting rain, we landed upon a barren island, incapable of furnishing even fuel enough to supply our fires. To add to our miseries, as night closed, the rain generally ceased, and severe frosts set in, which, congealing our wet clothes upon our bodies, left little animal warmth to keep the limbs in a state of activity; and the consequence was, that many of the wretched negroes, to whom frost and cold were altogether new, fell fast asleep, and perished before morning.

For provisions, again, we were entirely dependent upon the fleet. There were here no living creatures which would suffer themselves to be caught; even the water-fowl being so timorous that it was impossible to approach them within musket-shot. Salt meat and ship biscuit were, therefore, our food, moistened by a small allowance of rum; fare which, though no doubt very wholesome, was not such as to reconcile us to the cold and wet under which we suffered.

On the part of the navy, again, all these hardships were experienced in a four-fold degree. Night and day were boats pulling from the fleet to the island, and from the island to the fleet; for it was the 21st before all the troops were got on shore; and as there was little time to inquire into men's turns of labour, many seamen were four or five days continually at the oar. Thus they had not only to bear up against variety of temperature, but against hunger, fatigue, and want of sleep in addition; three as fearful burdens as can be laid upon the human frame. Yet in spite of all this, not a murmur nor a whisper of complaint could be heard throughout the whole expedition. No man appeared to regard the present, whilst every one looked forward to the future. From the General, down to the youngest drum-boy, a confident anticipation of success seemed to pervade all ranks; and in the hope of an ample reward in store for them, the toils and grievances of the moment were forgotten. Nor was this anticipation the mere offspring of an overweening confidence in themselves. Several Americans had already deserted, who entertained us with accounts of the alarm experienced at New Orleans. They assured us that there were not at present 5000 soldiers in the State; that the principal inhabitants had long ago left the place; that such as remained were ready to join us as soon as we should appear among them; and that, therefore, we might lay our account with a speedy and bloodless conquest. The same persons likewise dilated upon the wealth and importance of the town, upon the large quantities of Government stores there collected, and the rich booty which would reward its capture; subjects well calculated to tickle the fancy of invaders, and to make them unmindful of immediate afflictions, in the expectation of so great a recompense to come.

Chapter 19
Marching Towards the Attack

It is well known that, at the period to which my narrative refers, an alliance, offensive and defensive, subsisted between the Government of Great Britain and the heads of as many Indian nations or tribes as felt the aggressions of the settlers upon their ancient territories, and were disposed to resent them. On this side of the continent our principal allies were the Chaktaws and Cherokees, two nations whom war and famine had reduced from a state of comparative majesty to the lowest ebb of feebleness and distress. Driven from hunting-ground to hunting-ground, and pursued like wild beasts wherever seen, they were now confined to a narrow tract of country, lying chiefly along the coasts of the gulf and the borders of the lakes which adjoin to it. For some time previous to the arrival of the expedition, the warriors of these tribes put themselves under the command of Colonel Nickolls, of the Royal Marines, and continued to harass the Americans by frequent incursions into the cultivated districts. It so happened, however, that, being persuaded to attempt the reduction of a fort situated upon Mobile Point, and being, as might be expected, repulsed with some loss, their confidence in their leader, and their dependence upon British aid, had begun of late to suffer a serious diminution. Though not very profitable as friends, their local position and desultory mode of warfare would have rendered them at this period exceedingly annoying to us as enemies; it was accordingly determined to dispatch an embassy to their settlements, for the purpose of restoring them to good humour, or at least discovering their intentions.

Whilst the troops were assembling upon Pine Island, a cutter, having proper officers on board, and carrying presents of clothing, arms, and rum, was dispatched upon this business. It reached its place of destination in safety, and the ambassadors found very little difficulty in bringing back the fickle Indians to their wonted reliance upon British support. Several of the chiefs and warriors, indeed, requested and obtained permission to visit our Admiral and General, and to follow the fortunes of our troops; and a very grotesque and singular appearance they presented as they stood upon the quarter-deck of the Tonnant. But the costume, habits, and customs of these savages have been too frequently and too accurately described elsewhere, to render any account of them on the present occasion desirable. It is sufficient to observe, that whilst they gazed upon everything around them with a look expressive of no astonishment whatever, they were themselves objects of eager curiosity to us; and that they bore our close inspection and somewhat uncourteous deportment with the most perfect philosophy. But to my tale.

The enemy's cutters having fallen into our hands, at an early hour on the morning of the 16th the disembarkation of the troops began. So deficient, however, was the fleet in boats and other small craft fit to navigate the lakes, that it was late on the evening of the 21st before the last division took up its ground upon Pine Island, and even then the inconveniences of our descent were but beginning. The troops had yet to be arranged in corps and brigades; to each of these its proportion of Commissaries, Purveyors, and Medical attendants, &c., &c., required to be allotted; and some attempt at establishing depots of provisions and military stores behoved to be made. In adjusting these matters the whole of the 22nd was occupied, on which day the General likewise reviewed the whole of the army. This being ended, the force was next distributed into divisions, or corps; and the following is the order it assumed.

Instead of a light brigade, the General resolved to set apart three battalions as an advanced guard. The regiments nominated to that service were the 4th, the 85th Light Infantry, and the 95th. Rifles; and he selected Colonel Thornton of the 85th, as an officer of talent and enterprise, to command them. Attached to this corps were a party of rocket-men, with two light three-pounders— a species of gun convenient enough, where celerity of movement is alone regarded, but of very little real utility in the field. The rest of the troops were arranged, as before, into two brigades. The first, composed of the 21st, 44th, and one black regiment, was intrusted to Colonel Brook; and the second, containing the 93rd and the other black corps, to Colonel Hamilton, of the 7th West India regiment. To each of these, a certain proportion of artillery and rockets was allotted: whilst the dragoons, who had brought their harness and other appointments on shore, remained as a sort of bodyguard to the General, till they should provide themselves with horses.

The adjustment of these matters having occupied a considerable part of the 22nd, it was determined that all things should remain as they were till next morning. Boats, in the mean time, began to assemble from all quarters, supplies of ammunition were packed, so as to prevent the possibility of damage from moisture, and stores of various descriptions were got ready. But it appeared that, even now, many serious inconveniences must be endured, and obstacles surmounted, before the troops could reach the scene of action. In the first place, from Pine Island to that part of the main towards which prudence directed us to steer, was a distance of no less than 80 miles. This, of itself, was an obstacle, or at least an inconvenience, of no slight nature; for should the weather prove boisterous, open boats, heavily laden with soldiers, would stand little chance of escaping destruction in the course of so long a voyage. In the next place, and what was of infinitely greater importance, it was found that there were not, throughout the whole fleet, a sufficient number of boats to transport above one third of the army at a time. But to land in divisions would expose our forces to be attacked in detail, by which means one party might be cut to pieces before the others could arrive to its support. The undertaking was, therefore, on the whole, extremely dangerous, and such as would have been probably abandoned by more timid leaders. Ours, however, were not so to be alarmed. They had entered upon a hazardous business, in whatever way it should be prosecuted; and since they could not work miracles, they resolved to lose no time in bringing their army into the field in the best manner which circumstances would permit.

With this view, the advance, consisting of 1600 men and two pieces of cannon, was next morning embarked. I have already stated that there is a small creek, called the Bayo de Catiline, which runs up from Lake Pontchartrain through the middle of an extensive morass, about ten miles below New Orleans. Towards this creek were the boats directed, and here it was resolved to effect a landing. When we set sail, the sky was dark and lowering, and before long a heavy rain began to fall. Continuing without intermission during the whole of the day, towards night, it, as usual, ceased, and was succeeded by a sharp frost; which, taking effect upon men thoroughly exposed, and already cramped by remaining so long in one posture, rendered our limbs completely powerless. Nor was there any means of dispelling the benumbing sensation, or effectually resisting the cold. Fires of charcoal, indeed, being lighted in the sterns of the boats, were permitted to burn as long as daylight lasted; but as soon as it grew dark, they were of necessity extinguished, lest the flame should be seen by row-boats from the shore, and an alarm be thus communicated. Our situation was, therefore, the reverse of agreeable; since even sleep was denied us, from the apprehension of fatal consequences.

Having remained in this uncomfortable state till midnight, the boats cast anchor and hoisted awnings. There was a small piquet of the enemy stationed at the entrance of the creek by which it was intended to effect our landing. This it was absolutely necessary to surprise; and whilst the rest lay at anchor, two or three fast-sailing barges were pushed on to execute the service. Nor did they experience much difficulty in accomplishing their object. Nothing, as it appeared, was less dreamt of by the Americans than an attack from this quarter, consequently no persons could be less on their guard than the party here stationed. The officer who conducted the force sent against them, found not so much as a single sentinel posted! but having landed his men at two places, above and below the but which they inhabited, extended his ranks so as to surround it, and closing gradually in, took them all fast asleep, without noise or resistance.

When such time had been allowed as was deemed sufficient for the accomplishment of this undertaking, the flotilla again weighed anchor, and without waiting for intelligence of success, pursued their voyage. Hitherto we had been hurried along at a rapid rate by a fair breeze, which enabled us to carry canvas; but this now left us, and we made way only by rowing. Our progress was therefore considerably retarded, and the risk of discovery heightened by the noise which that labour necessarily occasions; but in spite of these obstacles, we reached the entrance of the creek by dawn; and about nine o'clock, were safely on shore.

The place where we landed was as wild as it is possible to imagine. Gaze where we might, nothing could be seen except one huge marsh covered with tall reeds; not a house nor a vestige of human industry could be discovered; and even of trees there were but a few growing upon the banks of the creek. Yet it was such a spot as, above all others, favoured our operations. No eye could watch us, or report our arrival to the American General. By remaining quietly among the reeds, we might effectually conceal ourselves from notice; because, from appearance of all around, it was easy to perceive that the place which we occupied had been seldom, if ever before, marked with a human footstep. Concealment, however, was the thing of all others which we required; for be it remembered that there were now only sixteen hundred men on the mainland. The rest were still at Pine Island, where they must remain till the boats which had transported us should return for their conveyance, consequently many hours must elapse before this small corps could be either reinforced or supported. If, therefore, we had sought for a point where a descent might be made in secrecy and safety, we could not have found one better calculated for that purpose than the present; because it afforded every means of concealment to one part of our force, until the others should be able to come up.

For these reasons, it was confidently expected that no movement would be made previous to the arrival of the other brigades; but, in our expectations of quiet, we were deceived. The deserters who had come in, and accompanied us as guides, assured the General that he had only to show himself, when the whole district would submit. They repeated, that there were not five thousand men in arms throughout the State: that of these, not more than twelve hundred were regular soldiers, and that the whole force was at present several miles on the opposite side of the town, expecting an attack on that quarter, and apprehending no danger on this. These arguments, together with the nature of the ground on which we stood, so ill calculated for a proper distribution of troops in case of attack, and so well calculated to hide the movements of an army acquainted with all the passes and tracks which, for aught we knew, intersected the morass, induced our leader to push forward at once into the open country. As soon, therefore, as the advance was formed, and the boats had departed, we began our march, following an indistinct path along the edge of the ditch or canal. But it was not without many checks that we were able to proceed. Other ditches, similar to that whose course we pursued, frequently stopped us by running in a cross direction, and falling into it at right angles. These were too wide to be leaped, and too deep to be forded; consequently, on all such occasions, the troops were obliged to halt, till bridges were hastily constructed of such materials as could be procured, and thrown across.

Having advanced in this manner for several hours, we at length found ourselves approaching a more cultivated region. The marsh became gradually less and less continued, being intersected by wider spots of firm ground; the reeds gave place, by degrees, to wood, and the wood to inclosed fields. Upon these, however, nothing grew, harvest having long ago ended. They accordingly presented but a melancholy appearance, being covered with the stubble of sugar-cane, which resembled the reeds which we had just quitted, in everything except altitude. Nor as yet was any house or cottage to be seen. Though we knew, therefore, that human habitations could not be far off, it was impossible to guess where they lay, or how numerous they might prove; and as we could not tell whether our guides might not be deceiving us, and whether ambuscades might not be laid for our destruction as soon as we should arrive where troops could conveniently act, our march was insensibly conducted with increased caution and regularity.

But in a little while some groves of orange-trees presented selves; on passing which two or three farm-houses appeared. Towards these, our advanced companies immediately hastened, with the hope of surprising the inhabitants, and preventing any from being raised. Hurrying on at double-quick time, they surrounded the buildings, succeeded in securing the inmates, capturing several horses; but becoming rather careless in watching their prisoners, one man contrived to effect his escape. Now, then, all hope of eluding observation might be laid aside. The rumour of our landing would, we knew, spread faster than we could march; and it only remained to make that rumour as terrible as possible.

With this view, the column was commanded to widen its files, and to present as formidable an appearance as could be assumed. Changing our order, in obedience to these directions, we marched, not in sections of eight or ten abreast, but in pairs, and thus contrived to cover with our small division as large a tract or ground as if we had mustered thrice our present numbers. Our steps were likewise quickened, that we might gain, if possible, some advantageous position, where we might be able to cope with any force that might attack us; and thus hastening on, we soon arrived at the main road which leads directly to New Orleans. Turning to the right, we then advanced in the direction of that town for about a mile; when, having reached a spot where it was considered that we might encamp in comparative safety, our little column halted; the men piled their arms, and a regular bivouac was formed.

The country where we had now established ourselves, answered, in every respect, the description which I have already given of the neck of land on which New Orleans is built. It was a narrow plain of about a mile in width, bounded on one side by the Mississippi, and on the other by the marsh from which we had just emerged. Towards the open ground this marsh was covered with dwarf wood, having the semblance of a forest rather than of a swamp; but on trying the bottom, it was found that both characters were united, and that it was impossible for a man to make his way among the trees, so boggy was the soil upon which they grew. In no other quarter, however, was there a single hedge-row, or plantation of any kind; excepting a few apple and other fruit trees in the gardens of such houses as were scattered over the plain, the whole being laid out in large fields for the growth of sugar-cane, a plant which seems as abundant in this part of the world as in Jamaica.

Looking up towards the town, which we at this time faced, the marsh is upon your right, and the river upon your left. Close to the latter runs the main road, following the course of the stream all the way to New Orleans. Between the road and the water is thrown up a lofty and strong embankment, resembling the dykes in Holland, and meant to serve a similar purpose; by means of which the Mississippi is prevented from overflowing its banks, and the entire flat is preserved from inundation. But the attention of a stranger is irresistibly drawn away from every other object, to contemplate the magnificence of this noble river. Pouring along at the prodigious rate of four miles an hour, an immense body of water is spread out before you; measuring a full mile across, and nearly a hundred fathoms in depth. What this mighty stream must be near its mouth, I can hardly imagine, for we were here upwards of a hundred miles from the ocean.

Such was the general aspect of the country which we had entered;—our own position, again, was this. The three regiments turning off from the road into one extensive green field, formed three close columns within pistol-shot of the river. Upon our right, but so much in advance as to be of no service to us, was a large house, surrounded by about twenty wooden huts, probably intended for the accommodation of slaves. Towards this house there was a slight rise in the ground, and between it and the camp was a small pond of no great depth. As far to the rear as the first was to the front, stood another house, inferior in point of appearance, and skirted by no outbuildings: this was also upon the right; and here General Keane, who accompanied us, fixed his head-quarters; but neither the one nor the other could be employed as a covering redoubt, the flank of the division extending, as it were, between them. A little way in advance, again, where the outposts were stationed, ran a dry ditch and a row of lofty palings; affording some cover to the front of our line, should it be formed diagonally with the main road. The left likewise was well secured by the river; but the right and the rear were wholly unprotected. Though in occupying this field, therefore, we might have looked very well had the country kind us been friendly, it must be confessed that our situation hardly deserved the title of a military position.

Chapter 20
Hand to Hand Fighting

Noon had just passed, when the word was given to halt, by which means every facility was afforded of posting the piquet's leisure and attention. Nor was this deemed enough to secure tranquillity: parties were sent out in all directions to reconnoitre, who returned with an account that no enemy nor any trace of an enemy could be discerned. The troops were accordingly suffered to light fires, and to make themselves comfortable, only their accoutrements were not taken off, and the were piled in such form as to be within reach at a moment's notice.

As soon as these agreeable orders were issued, the soldiers to obey them both in letter and in spirit. Tearing up a number of strong palings, large fires were lighted in a moment; water was brought from the river, and provisions were cooked. But their bare rations did not content them. Spreading themselves over the country as far as a regard to safety would permit, they entered every house, and brought away quantities of hams, fowls, and wines of various descriptions; which being divided among them, all fared well, and none received too large a quantity. In this division of good things, they were not unmindful of their officers; for upon active warfare the officers are considered by the privates as comrades, to whom respect and obedience are due, rather than as masters.

It was now about three o'clock in the afternoon, and all had as yet remained quiet. The troops having finished their meal, lay stretched beside their fires, or refreshed themselves by bathing, for to-day the heat was such as to render this latter employment extremely agreeable, when suddenly a bugle from the advanced posts sounded the alarm, which was echoed back from all in the army. Starting up, we stood to our arms, and prepared for battle, the alarm being now succeeded by some firing; but we were scarcely in order, when intelligence arrived from the front that there was no danger, only a few horse having made their appearance, who were checked and put to flight at the first discharge. Upon this information, our wonted confidence returned, and we again betook ourselves to our former occupations, remarking that, as the Americans had never yet dared to attack, there was no great probability of their doing so on the present occasion.

In this manner the day passed without any further alarm; and darkness having set in, the fires were made to blaze with increased splendour, our evening meal was eaten, and we prepared to sleep. But about half-past seven o'clock, the attention of several individuals was drawn to a large vessel, which seemed to be stealing up the river till she came opposite to our camp; when her anchor was dropped, and her sails leisurely furled. At first we were doubtful whether she might not be one of our own cruisers which had passed the fort unobserved, and had arrived to render her assistance in our future operations. To satisfy this doubt, she was repeatedly hailed; but returning no answer, an alarm immediately spread through the bivouac, and all thought of sleep was laid aside. Several musket-shots were now fired at her with the design of exacting a reply, of which no notice was taken; till at length, having fastened all her sails, and swung her broadside towards us, we could distinctly hear some one cry out in a commanding voice, "Give them this for the honour of America." The words were instantly followed by the flashes of her guns, and a deadly shower of grape swept down numbers in the camp.

Against this destructive fire we had nothing whatever to oppose. The artillery which we had landed was too light to bring into competition with an adversary so powerful; and as she had anchored within a short distance of the opposite bank, no musketry could reach her with any precision or effect. A few rockets were discharged, which made a beautiful appearance in the air; but the rocket is at the best an uncertain weapon, and these deviated too far from their object to produce even terror amongst those against whom they were directed. Under these circumstances, as nothing could be done offensively, our sole object was to shelter the men as much as possible from the iron hail. With this view, they were commanded to leave the fires, and to hasten under the dyke. Thither all accordingly repaired, without much regard to order and regularity, and laying ourselves along wherever we could find room, we listened in painful silence to the pattering of grape-shot among our huts, and to the shrieks and groans of those who lay wounded beside them.

The night was now as dark as pitch, the moon being but young, and totally obscured with clouds. Our fires deserted by us, and beat about by the enemy's shot, began to burn red and dull, and, except when the flashes of those guns which played upon us cast a momentary glare, not an object could be distinguished at the distance of a yard. In this state we lay for nearly an hour, unable to move from our ground, or offer any opposition to those who kept us there; when a straggling fire of musketry called our attention towards the piquets, and warned us to prepare for a closer and more desperate struggle. As yet, however, it was uncertain from what cause this dropping fire arose. It might proceed from the sentinels, who, alarmed by the cannonade from the river, mistook every tree for an American; and till the real state of the case should be ascertained, it would be improper to expose the troops by moving any of them from the shelter which the bank afforded. But these doubts were not permitted to continue long in existence. The dropping fire having paused for a few moments, was succeeded by a fearful yell; and the heavens were illuminated on all sides by a semi-circular blaze of musketry. It was now manifest that we were surrounded, and that by a very superior force; and that no alternative remained, except to surrender at discretion, or to beat back the assailants.

The first of these plans was never for an instant thought of; the second was immediately put into force. Rushing from under the bank, the 85th and 95th flew to support the piquets, whilst the 4th, stealing to the rear of the encampment, formed close column, and remained as a reserve. And now began a battle of which no language were competent to convey any distinct idea; because it was one to which the annals of modern warfare furnish no parallel. All order, all discipline were lost. Each officer, as he succeeded in collecting twenty or thirty men about him, plunged into the midst of the enemy's ranks, where it was fought hand to hand, bayonet to bayonet, and sabre to sabre.

I am well aware that he who speaks of his own deeds in the field of battle lies fairly open to the charge of seeking to make a hero of himself in the eyes of the public; and feeling this, it is not without reluctance that I proceed to recount the part which I myself took in the affair of this night. But, in truth, I must either play the egotist awhile, or leave the reader without any details at all; inasmuch as the darkness and general confusion effectually prevented me from observing how others, except my own immediate party, were employed.

Offering this as my apology for a line of conduct which I should otherwise blush to pursue, and premising that I did nothing, in my own person, which was not done by my comrades at least as effectually, I go on to relate as many of the particulars of this sanguinary conflict as came under the notice of my own senses.

My friend Grey and myself had been supplied by our soldiers with a couple of fowls taken from a neighbouring henroost, and a few bottles of excellent claret, borrowed from the cellar of one of the houses near. We had built ourselves a sort of hut, by piling together, in a conical form, a number of large stakes and broad rails torn up from one of the fences;

and a bright wooden fire was blazing at the door of it. In the wantonness of triumph, too, we had lighted some six or eight wax-candles; a vast quantity of which had been found in the store-rooms of the chateaux hard by; and having done ample justice to our luxurious supper, we were sitting in great splendour and in high spirits at the entrance of our hut, when the alarm of the approaching schooner was communicated to us. With the sagacity of a veteran, Grey instantly guessed how matters stood: he was the first to hail the suspicious stranger; and on receiving no answer to his challenge, he was the first to fire a musket in the direction of her anchorage. But he had scarcely done so when she opened her broadside, causing the instantaneous abandonment of fires, viands, and mirth throughout the bivouac.

As we contrived to get our men tolerably well around us, Grey and myself were among the first who rushed forth to support the piquets and check the advance of the enemy upon the right. Passing as rapidly as might be through the ground of encampment amidst a shower of grape-shot from the vessel, we soon arrived at the pond; which being forded, we found ourselves in front of the farm-house of which I have already spoken as composing the head-quarters of General Keane. Here we were met by a few stragglers from the outposts, who reported that the advanced companies were all driven in, and that a numerous division of Americans was approaching. Having attached these fugitives to our little corps, we pushed on, and in a few seconds reached the lower extremity of a sloping stubble-field, at the other end of which we could discern a long line of men, but whether they were friends or foes the darkness would not permit ups to determine. We called aloud for the purpose of satisfying our doubts; but the signal being disregarded, we advanced.

A heavy fire of musketry instantly opened upon us; but so fearful was Grey of doing injury to our own troops, that he would not permit it to be returned. We accordingly pressed on, our men dropping by ones and twos on every side of us, till having arrived within twenty or thirty yards of the object of our curiosity, it became to me evident enough that we were in front of the enemy. Grey's humane caution still prevailed; he was not convinced, till he, should be convinced it was but natural that he should alter his plans. There chanced to be near the spot where we were standing a huge dungheap, or rather a long solid stack of stubble, behind which we directed the men to take shelter whilst one of us should creep forward alone, for the purpose of more completely ascertaining a fact of which all except my brave and noble-minded comrade were satisfied.

The event proved that my sight had not deceived me: I approached within sabre's length of the line; and having ascertained beyond the possibility of doubt that the line was composed of American soldiers, I returned to my friend and again urged him to charge. But there was an infatuation upon him that night for which I have ever been unable to account: he insisted that I must be mistaken; he spoke of the improbability which existed that any part of the enemy's army should have succeeded in taking up a position in rear of the station of one of our outposts, and he could not be persuaded that the troops now before him were not the 95th Rifle corps. At last it was agreed between us that we should separate; that Grey with one half of the party should remain where he was, whilst I with the other half should make a short detour to the right, and come down upon the flank of the line from whose fire we had suffered so severely. The plan was carried into immediate execution. Taking with me about a dozen or fourteen men, I quitted Grey, and we never met again.

How or when he fell I know not; but, judging from the spot and attitude in which I afterwards found his body, I conceive that my back could have been barely turned upon him when the fatal ball pierced his brain. He was as brave a soldier and as good a man as the British army can boast of; beloved by his brother officers and adored by his men. To me he was as a brother; nor have I ceased even now to feel, as often as the

23rd of December returns, that on that night a tie was broken than which the progress of human life will hardly furnish one more tender or more strong. But to my tale.

Leaving Grey—careless as he ever was in battle of his own person, and anxious as far as might be to secure the safety of his followers—I led my little party in the direction agreed upon, and fortunately falling in with about an equal number of English riflemen, I caused them to take post beside my own men, and turned up to the front. Springing over the paling, we found ourselves almost at once upon the left flank of the enemy; and we lost not a moment in attacking it. But one volley was poured in, and then bayonets, musket-butts, sabres, and even fists, came instantly into play. In the whole course of my military career remember no scene at all resembling this. We fought with the savage ferocity of bull-dogs; and many a blade which till to-night had not drunk blood became in a few minutes crimsoned enough.

Such a contest could not in the nature of things be of very long continuance. The enemy, astonished at the vigour of our assault, soon began to waver, and their wavering was speedily converted into flight. Nor did we give them a moment's time to recover from their panic. With loud shouts we continued to press upon them; and amidst the most horrible din and desperate carnage drove them over the field and through the little village of huts, of which notice has already been taken as surrounding the mansion on our advanced right. Here we found a number of our own people prisoners, and under a guard of Americans. But the guard fled as we approached, and our countrymen catching up such weapons as came first to hand, joined in the pursuit.

In this spot I halted my party, increased by the late additions to the number of forty; among whom were two gallant young officers of the 95th. We had not yet been joined, as I expected be joined, by Grey; and feeling that we were at least far enough in advance of our own line, we determined to attempt nothing further except to keep possession of the village should it be attacked. But whilst placing the men in convenient situations, another dark line was pointed out to us considerably to the left our position. That we might ascertain at once of what troops was composed, I left my brother officers to complete the arrangements which we had begun, and walking down the field, demanded in a loud voice to be informed who they were that kept post in so retired a situation. A voice from the throng made answer that they were Americans, and begged of me not fire upon my friends. Willing to deceive them still further, I asked to what corps they belonged; the speaker replied that they were the second battalion of the first regiment, and inquired what had become of the first battalion. I told him that it was upon my right, and assuming a tone of authority, commanded him not to move from his present situation till I should join him with a party of which I was at the head.

The conversation ended here, and I returned to the village; when, communicating the result of my inquiries to my comrades, we formed our brave little band into line and determined to attack. The men were cautioned to preserve a strict silence, and not to fire a shot till orders were given; they observed these injunctions, and with fixed bayonets and cautious tread advanced along the field. As we drew near, I called aloud for the commanding officer of the second regiment to step forward, upon which an elderly man, armed with a heavy dragoon sabre, stepped out of the ranks. When he discovered by our dress that we were English, this redoubtable warrior lost all self-command; he resigned his sword to me without a murmur, and consented at once to believe that his battalion was surrounded, and that to offer any resistance would but occasion a needless loss of blood. Nor was he singular in these respects: his followers, placing implicit reliance in our assurances that they were hemmed in on every side by a very superior force, had actually begun to lay down their arms, and would have surrendered, in all probability, at discretion, but for the superior gallantry of one man. An American officer, whose sword I demanded, instead of giving it up as his commander had done, made a cut at my head, which with some difficulty I managed to ward off; and a few soldiers near him, catching ardour from his example, discharged their pieces among our troops. The sound of firing was no sooner heard than it became general, and as all hope of success by stratagem might now be laid aside, we were of necessity compelled to try the effect of violence. Again we rushed into the middle of the throng, and again was the contest that of man to man, in close and desperate strife; till a panic arising among the Americans, they dispersed in all directions and left us masters of the field.

In giving a detail so minute of my own adventures this night, I beg to repeat what has been stated already, that I have no wish whatever to persuade my readers that I was one whit more cool or more daring than my companions. Like them I was driven to depend, from first to last, upon my own energies; and I believe the energies of few men fail them when they are satisfied that on them alone they must depend. Nor was the case different with my comrades. Attacked unexpectedly, and in the dark, surrounded, too, by a numerous enemy, and one who spoke the same language with ourselves, it is not to be wondered at if the order and routine of civilised warfare were everywhere set at nought. Each man who felt disposed to command was obeyed by those who stood near him, without any question being asked as to his authority; and more feats of individual gallantry were performed in this single night than many regular campaigns might furnish an opportunity to perform.

The night was far spent, and the sound of firing had begun to wax faint, when, checking the ardour of our brave followers, we collected them once more together and fell back into the village. Here likewise considerable numbers from other detachments assembled, and here we learned that the Americans were repulsed on every side. The combat had been long and obstinately contested: it began at eight o'clock in the evening and continued till three in the morning—but the victory was ours. True, it was the reverse of a bloodless one, not fewer than two hundred fifty of our best men having fallen in the struggle: but even at the expense of such a loss, we could not but account ourselves fortunate in escaping from the snare in which we had confessedly taken.

To me, however, the announcement of the victory brought no rejoicing, for it was accompanied with the intelligence that my friend was among the killed. I well recollect the circumstances under which these sad news reached me. I was standing with a sword in each hand—my own and that of the officer who had surrendered to me, and, as the reader may imagine, in no bad humour with myself or with the brave fellows about me, when a brother officer stepping forward abruptly told the tale. It came me upon me like a thunderbolt; and casting aside my trophy, thought only of the loss which I had sustained.

Regardless of every other matter I ran to the rear, and found Grey lying behind the dung-heap, motionless and cold. A little pool of blood which had coagulated under his head, pointed out the spot where the ball had entered, and the position of his limbs gave proof that he must have died without a struggle. I cannot pretend to describe what were then my sensations, but of whatever nature they might be, little time was given for their indulgence; the bugle sounding the alarm, I was compelled to leave him as he lay, and to join my corps. Though the alarm proved to be a false one, it had the good effect of bringing all the troops together, by which means a regular line was now, for the first time since the commencement of the action, formed. In this order, having defiled considerably to the left, so as to command the highway, we stood in front of our bivouac till dawn began to appear; when, to avoid the fire of the schooner, we once more moved to the river's bank and lay down. Here, during the whole of the succeeding day, the troops were kept shivering in the cold frosty air, without fires, without provisions, and exhausted with fatigue; nor was it till the return of night that any attempt to extricate them from their comfortless situation could be made.

Whilst others were thus reposing, I stole away with two or three men for the purpose of performing the last sad act of affection which it was possible for me to perform to my friend Grey. As we had completely changed our ground, it was not possible for me at once to discover the spot where he lay; indeed I traversed a large portion of the field before I hit upon it. Whilst thus wandering over the arena of last night's contest, the most shocking and most disgusting spectacles everywhere met my eyes. I have frequently beheld a greater number of dead bodies within as narrow a compass, though these, to speak the truth, were numerous enough, but wounds more disfiguring or more horrible I certainly never witnessed. A man shot through the head or heart lies as if he were in a deep slumber; insomuch that when you gaze upon him you experience little else than pity. But of these, many had met their deaths from bayonet wounds, sabre cuts, or heavy blows from the butt ends of muskets; and the consequence was, that not only were the wounds themselves exceedingly frightful, but the very countenances of the dead exhibited the most savage and ghastly expressions. Friends and foes lay together in small groups of four or six, nor was it difficult to tell almost the very hand by which some of them had fallen. Nay, such had been the deadly closeness of the strife, that in one or two places an English and American soldier might be seen with the bayonet of each fastened in the other's body.

Having searched for some time in vain, I at length discovered friend lying where during the action we had separated, and where, when the action came to a close, I had at first found him, shot through the temples by a rifle bullet so remarkably small as scarcely to leave any trace of its progress. I am well aware that this is no fit place to introduce the working of my own personal feelings, but he was my friend, and such a friend as few men are happy enough to possess. We had known and loved each other for years; our regard had been cemented by a long participation in the same hardships and dangers, and it cannot; therefore surprise, if even now I pay that tribute to his worth and our friendship which, however unavailing it may be, they both deserve.

When in the act of looking for him I had flattered myself that I should be able to bear his loss with something like philosophy, but when I beheld him pale and bloody, I found all my resolution evaporate. I threw myself on the ground beside him and wept, like a child. But this was no time for the indulgence of useless sorrow. Like the royal bard, I knew that I should to him, but he could not return to me, and I knew not whether an hour would pass before my summons might arrive. Lifting him therefore upon a cart, I had him carried down to head-quarter house, now converted into an hospital, and having dug for him a grave at the bottom of the garden, I laid him there as a soldier should be laid, arrayed, not in a shroud, but in his uniform. Even the privates whom I brought with me to assist at his funeral mingled their tears with mine, nor are many so fortunate as to return to the parent dust more deeply or more sincerely lamented.

Retiring from the performance of this melancholy duty, I strolled into the hospital and visited the wounded. It is here that war loses its grandeur and show, and presents only a real picture of its effects. Every room in the house was crowded with wretches mangled, and apparently in the most excruciating agonies. Prayers, groans, and, I grieve to add, the most horrid exclamations, smote upon the ear wherever I turned. Some lay at length upon straw, with eyes half closed and limbs motionless; some endeavoured to start up, shrieking with pain, while the wandering eye and incoherent speech of others indicated the loss of reason, and usually foretold the approach of death. But there was one among the rest whose appearance was too horrible ever to be forgotten. He had been shot through the windpipe, and the breath making its way between the skin and the flesh had dilated him to a size absolutely terrific. His head and face were particularly shocking. Every feature was enlarged beyond what can well be imagined; whilst his eyes were so completely hidden by the cheeks and forehead as to destroy all resemblance to a human countenance.

Passing through the apartments where the private soldiers lay, I next came to those occupied by officers. Of these there were five or six in one small room, to whom little better accommodation could be provided than to their inferiors. It was a sight peculiarly distressing, because all of them chanced to be personal acquaintances of my own. One had been shot in the head, and lay gasping and insensible; another had received a musket- ball in the belly, which had pierced through and lodged in the backbone. The former appeared to suffer but little, giving no signs of life, except what a heavy breathing produced; the latter was in the most dreadful agony, screaming out, and gnawing the covering under which he lay. There were many besides these, some severely and others slightly hurt; but as I have already dwelt at sufficient length upon a painful subject, I shall only observe, that to all was afforded every assistance which circumstances would allow, and that the exertions of their medical attendants were such as deserved and obtained the grateful thanks of even the most afflicted among the sufferers themselves.

Chapter 21
Piquets & Raiders

In the mean time the rest of the troops were landing as fast as possible, and hastening to join their comrades. Though the advance had set out from Pine Island by themselves, they did not occupy all the boats in the fleet. Part of the second brigade, therefore, had embarked about twelve hours after their departure; and rowing leisurely on, were considerably more than half way across the lakes when the action began. In the stillness of night, however, it is astonishing at what distance a noise is heard. Though they must have been at least twenty miles from the Bayo when the schooner first opened her fire, the sound reaching them roused the rowers from their indolence, who, pulling with all their might, hurried on, whilst the most profound silence reigned among the troops, and, gaining the creek in little more an three hours, sent fresh reinforcements to share in the danger and glory of the night.

Nor was a moment lost by the sailors in returning to the island. Intelligence of the combat spread like wildfire; the boats were loaded even beyond what was strictly safe, and thus, by exerting themselves in a degree almost unparalleled, our gallant seamen succeeded in bringing the whole army into position before dark on the 24th. The second and third brigades, therefore, now took up their ground upon the spot where the late battle had been fought, and, resting their right upon the woody morass, extended so far towards the river, as that the advance by wheeling up might continue the line across the entire plain.

But instead of taking part in this formation, the advance was still fettered to the bank, from which it was additionally prevented from moving by the arrival of another large ship, which, cast anchor about a mile above the schooner. Thus were three battalions kept stationary by the guns of these two formidable floating batteries, and it was clear that no attempt to extricate them could be made without great loss, unless under cover of night. During the whole of the 24th, therefore, they remained in this uncomfortable situation; but as soon as darkness had well set in, a change of position was effected. Withdrawing the troops, company by company, from behind the bank, General Keane stationed them in the village of huts, by which means the high road was abandoned to the protection of a piquet, and the left of the army covered by a large chateau.

Being now placed beyond risk of serious annoyance from the shipping whole army remained quiet for the night. How long we were to continue in this state nobody appeared to know; not whisper was circulated as to the time of advancing, nor a surmise ventured respecting the next step likely to be taken. In our to whose rumours we had before listened with avidity, no confidence was reposed. It was quite evident, either that they had purposely deceived us, or that their information was gathered from a most imperfect source; and hence, though they were not exactly placed in confinement, they were strictly watched, and treated more like spies than deserters. Instead of an easy conquest, we had already met with a vigorous opposition; instead of finding the inhabitants ready and eager to join us, we found the houses deserted, the cattle and horses driven away, and every appearance of hostility. To march by the only road was rendered impracticable; so completely was it commanded by the shipping. In a word, all things had turned out diametrically opposite to what had been anticipated; and it appeared that, instead of a trifling affair more likely to fill our pockets than to add to our renown, we had embarked in an undertaking which presented difficulties not to be surmounted without patience and determination.

Having effected this change of position, and covered the

front of his army with a strong chain of outposts, General Keane, as I have said, remained quiet during the remainder of the night, and on the morrow was relieved from further care and responsibility by the unexpected arrival of Sir Edward Pakenham and General Gibbs. As soon as the death of Ross was known in London, the former of these officers was dispatched to take upon himself the command of the army.

Sailing immediately with the latter as his second in command, he had been favoured during the whole voyage by a fresh and fair wind, and now arrived in time to see his troops brought into a predicament from which all his abilities could scarcely expect to extricate them. Nor were the troops themselves ignorant of the unfavourable circumstances in which they stood. Hoping everything, therefore, from a change, they greeted their new leader with a hearty cheer; whilst the confidence which past events had tended in some degree to dispel, returned once more to the bosoms of all.

It was Christmas-day, and a number of officers, clubbing their little stock of provisions, resolved to dine together in memory of former times. But at so melancholy a Christmas dinner I do not recollect at any time to have been present. We dined in a barn; of plates, knives, and forks, there was a dismal scarcity; nor could our fare boast of much either in intrinsic good quality or in the way of cooking. These, however, were mere matters of merriment; it was the want of many well-known and beloved faces that gave us pain; nor were any other subjects discussed besides the amiable qualities of those who no longer formed part of our mess, and never would again form part of it.

A few guesses as to the probable success of future attempts alone relieved this topic, and now and then a shot from the schooner drew our attention to ourselves; for though too far removed from the river to be in much danger, we were still within cannon-shot of our enemy. Nor was she inactive in her attempts to molest. Elevating her guns to a great degree, she contrived occasionally to strike the wall of the building within which we sat; but the force of the ball was too far spent to penetrate, and could therefore produce no serious alarm.

Whilst we were thus sitting at table a loud shriek was heard after one of these explosions, and on running out we found that a shot had taken effect in the body of an unfortunate soldier. I mention this incident because I never beheld in any human being so great a tenacity of life. Though fairly cut in two at the lower part of the belly, the poor wretch lived for nearly an hour, gasping for breath and giving signs even of pain.

But to return to my narrative. As soon as he reached the camp Sir Edward proceeded to examine with a soldier's eye every point and place within view. Of the American army nothing, whatever could be perceived except a corps of observation, composed of five or six hundred mounted riflemen, which hovered along our front and watched our motions. The town itself was completely hid; nor was it possible to see beyond the distance of a very few miles either in front or rear, so flat and unbroken was the face of the country. Under these circumstances little insight into the state of affairs could be obtained by reconnoitring. The only, thing, indeed, which he could learn from it was, that while the vessels kept their present station upon river no advance could be made; and as he felt that every moment's delay was injurious to us and favourable to the enemy, he resolved to remove these incumbrances and to push forward as soon as possible.

With this view nine field-pieces, two howitzers, and one mortar were brought down to the brink of the stream as soon as it dark. Working parties were likewise ordered out, by whom was thrown up opposite to the schooner; and having got all things in readiness, at dawn on the 26th a heavy cannonade was opened upon her with red-hot shot. It was not long before we could perceive her crew hastening into their boats, whilst the smoke which began to rise from her decks proved that the balls had taken effect. She was, in fact, on fire, and being abandoned without resistance, in little more than an hour she blew up. In itself the sight was a fine one, but to us it was peculiarly gratifying, for we could not but experience something like satiated revenge at the destruction of a vessel from which we had suffered so much damage. A loud shout accordingly followed the explosion, and the guns were immediately turned against the ship. But the fate of her companion had warned her not to remain till she herself should be attacked. Setting every inch of canvas, and hoisting out her boats, she began, to stem the stream at the very instant the schooner took fire, and being impelled forward both by towing and sailing, she succeeded in getting beyond the range of shot before the guns could be brought to bear. One shell, however, was thrown with admirable precision, which falling upon her deck caused considerable execution; but excepting this, she escaped without injury, and did not anchor again till she had got too far for pursuit.

Having thus removed all apparent obstacles to his future progress, the General made dispositions for a speedy advance. Dividing the army into two columns, he appointed General Gibbs to the command of one, and General Keane to the command of the other. The left column, led on by the latter officer, consisted of the 95th, the 85th, the 93rd, and one black corps; the right, of the 4th, 21st, 44th, and the other black corps. The artillery, of which we had now ten pieces in the field, though at present attached to the left column, was designed to act as circumstances and the nature of the ground would permit; whilst the dragoons, few of whom had as yet provided themselves with horses, were appointed to guard the hospitals, and to secure the wounded from any sudden surprise or molestation from the rear.

But the day was too far spent in making these arrangements, and in clearing the way for future operations, to permit any movement before the morrow. The whole of the 26th was therefore spent in bringing up stores, ammunition, and a few heavy guns from the ships, which being placed in battery upon the banks of the river, secured us against the return of our floating adversary. All this was done quietly enough, nor was there any cause of alarm till after sunset; but from that time till towards dawn, we were kept in a constant state of anxiety and agitation. Sending down small bodies of riflemen, the American General harassed our piquets, killed and wounded a few of the sentinels, and prevented the main body from obtaining any sound refreshing sleep. Scarcely had the troops lain down when they were roused by a sharp firing at the outposts, which lasted only till they were in order, and then ceased; but as soon as they had dispersed and had once more addressed themselves to repose, the same cause of alarm returned, and they were again called to their ranks. Thus was the entire night spent in watching, or at best in broken and disturbed slumbers, than which nothing is more trying, both to the health and spirits of an army.

With the piquets, again, it fared even worse. For the outposts of an army to sleep is at all times considered as a thing impossible; but in modern and civilized warfare they are nevertheless looked upon as in some degree sacred. Thus, whilst two European armies remain inactively facing each other, the outposts of neither are molested, unless a direct attack upon the main body be intended; nay, so far is this tacit good understanding carried, that I have myself seen French and English sentinels not more than twenty yards apart. But the Americans entertained no such chivalric notions. An enemy was to them an enemy, whether alone or in the midst of five thousand companions; and they therefore counted the death of every individual as so much taken from the strength of the whole. In point of fact they no doubt reasoned correctly, but to us at least it appeared an ungenerous return to barbarity. Whenever they could approach unperceived within proper distance of our watch-fires, six or eight riflemen would fire amongst the party that sat around them, while one or two, stealing as close to each sentinel as a regard to their own safety would permit, acted the part of assassins rather than that of soldiers, and attempted to murder him in cold blood. For the officers, likewise, when going their rounds, they constantly lay in wait, and thus, by a continued dropping fire, they not only wounded some of those against whom their aim was directed, but occasioned considerable anxiety and uneasiness throughout the whole line.

It was on this night, and under these circumstances, that I was indebted to the vigilance of my faithful dog for my life. Amid all the bustle of landing, and throughout the tumult of the nocturnal battle, she never strayed from me; at least if she did lose me for a time, she failed not to trace me out again as soon as order was restored, for I found her by my side when the dawn of the 24th came in, and I never lost sight of her afterwards. It was my fortune on the night of the 26th to be put in charge of an outpost on the left front of the army; on such occasions I seldom experienced the slightest inclination to sleep; and on the present, I made it a point to visit my sentinels at least once in every, half-hour. Going my rounds for this purpose, it was necessary that I should pass a little copse of low underwood, just outside the line of our videttes; and I did pass it again and again, without meeting with any adventure. But about an hour after midnight, my dog, which, as usual, trotted a few paces before me, suddenly stopped short at the edge of the thicket, and began to bark violently, and in great apparent anger. I knew the animal well enough to be aware that some cause must exist for such conduct; and I too stopped short, till I should ascertain whether danger were near. It was well for me that I had been thus warned; for at the instant of my halting, about half a dozen muskets were discharged from the copse, the muzzles of which, had I taken five steps forward, must have touched my body. The balls whizzed harmlessly past my head; and, on my returning the fire with the pistol which I carried in my hand, the ambuscade broke up, and the party composing it took to their heels. I was Quixote enough to dash sword in hand into the thicket after them: but no one waited for me; so I continued my perambulations in peace.

Chapter 22
Before the Breastworks

Having continued this detestable system of warfare till towards morning, the enemy retired and left us at rest. But as soon as day began to break, our piquets were called in, and the troops formed in order of attack. The right column, under General Gibbs, took post near the skirts of the morass, throwing out skirmishers half way across the plain, whilst the left column drew up upon the road covered by the rifle corps, which in extended order met the skirmishers from the other. With this last division went the artillery, already well supplied with horses; and, at the signal given the whole moved forward.

It was a clear frosty morning, the mists had dispersed, and the sun shone brightly upon our arms when we began our march. The enemy's corps of observation fell back as we advanced, without offering in any way to impede our progress, and it was impossible to guess, ignorant as we were of the position of his main body, at what moment opposition might be expected. Nor, in truth, was it matter of much anxiety. Our spirits, in spite of the troubles of the night, were good, and our expectations of success were high, consequently many rude jests were bandied about, and many careless words spoken: for soldiers are, of all classes of men, the freest from care, and on that account, perhaps, the most happy. By being continually exposed to it, danger, with them, ceases to be frightful; of death they have no more terror than the beasts that perish; and even hardships, such as cold, wet, hunger, and broken rest, lose at least part of their disagreeableness, by the frequency of their recurrence.

Moving on in this merry mood, we advanced about four or five miles without the smallest check or hindrance; when, at length, we found ourselves in view of the enemy's army, posted in a very advantageous manner. About forty yards in their front was a canal, which extended from the morass to within a short distance of the high road. Along their line were thrown up breastworks, not indeed completed, but even now formidable. Upon the road at several other points were erected powerful batteries; whilst the ship, with a large flotilla of gun-boats, flanked the whole position from the river.

When I say that we came in sight of the enemy, I do not mean that he was gradually exposed to us in such a manner as to leave time for cool examination and reflection. On the right, indeed, he was seen for some time, but on the left a few houses built at a turning in the road entirely concealed him; nor was it till they gained that turning, and beheld the muzzles of his guns pointed towards them, that those who moved in this direction were aware of their proximity to danger. But that danger was indeed near they were quickly taught; for scarcely had the head of the column passed the houses when a deadly fire was opened from both the battery and the shipping. That the Americans are excellent marksmen, as well with artillery as with rifles, we have had frequent cause to acknowledge; but, perhaps, on no occasion did they assert their claim to the title of good artillery-men more effectually than on the present. Scarce a ball passed over or fell short of its mark, but all striking full into the midst of our ranks, occasioned terrible havoc. The shrieks of the wounded, therefore, the crash of firelocks, and the fall of such as were killed; caused at first some little confusion; and what added to the panic was, that from the houses beside which we stood bright flames suddenly burst out. The Americans, expecting this attack, had filled them with combustibles for the purpose; and directing against them one or two guns, loaded with red-hot shot, in an instant set them on fire. The scene was altogether very sublime. A tremendous cannonade mowed down our ranks, and deafened us with its roar; whilst two large chateaux and their outbuildings almost scorched us with the flames, and blinded us with the smoke which they emitted.

The infantry, however, was not long suffered to remain thus exposed; but being ordered to quit the path and to form line in the fields, the artillery was brought up, and opposed to that of the enemy. But the contest was in every respect unequal, since their artillery far exceeded ours, both in numerical strength and weight of metal. The consequence was, that in half an hour two of our field-pieces and one field-mortar were dismounted: many of the gunners were killed; and the rest, after an ineffectual attempt to silence the fire of the shipping, were obliged to retire.

In the mean time the infantry having formed line, advanced under a heavy discharge of round and grape shot, till they were checked by the appearance of the canal. Of its depth they were of course ignorant, and to attempt its passage without having ascertained whether it could be forded might have been productive of fatal consequences. A halt was accordingly ordered, and the men were commanded to shelter themselves as well as they could from the enemy's fire. For this purpose they were hurried into a wet ditch, of sufficient depth to cover the knees, where, leaning forward, they concealed themselves behind some high rushes which grew upon its brink, and thus escaped many bullets which fell around them in all directions.

Thus fared it with the left of the army, whilst the right, though less exposed to the cannonade, was not more successful in its object. The same impediment which checked one column forced the other likewise to pause; and after having driven in an advanced body of the enemy, and endeavoured, without effect, to penetrate through the marsh, it also was commanded to halt. In a word, all thought of attacking was for this day abandoned; and it now only remained to withdraw the troops from their present perilous situation, with as little loss as possible.

The first thing to be done was to remove the dismounted guns. Upon this enterprise a party of seamen were employed, who, running forward to the spot where they lay, lifted them, in spite of the whole of the enemy's fire, and bore them off in triumph. As soon as this was effected, regiment after regiment stole away; not in a body, but one by one, under the same discharge which saluted their approach. But a retreat thus conducted necessarily occupied much time. Noon had therefore long passed before the last corps was brought off; and when we again began to muster twilight was approaching. We did not, however, retire to our former position; but having fallen back only about two miles from the canal, where it was supposed that we should be beyond reach of annoyance from the American artillery, we there established ourselves for the night, having suffered less during the day than, from our exposed situation and the enemy's heavy fire, might have been expected.

The ground which we now occupied resembled, in almost every particular, that which we had quitted. We again extended across the plain, from the marsh to the river; no wood or cover of any description concealing our line, or obstructing the view of either army; while both in front and rear was an open space, laid out in fields and intersected by narrow ditches. Our outposts, however were pushed forward to some houses within a few hundred yards of the enemy's works, sending out advanced sentinels even farther; and the head-quarters of the army were established near the spot where the action of the 23rd had been fought.

In this state we remained during the 28th, the 29th, and 30th, without any efforts being made to fortify our own position, or to annoy that of the enemy. Some attempts were, I believe, set on foot to penetrate into the wood on the right of our line, and to discover a path through the morass, by which the enemy's left might be turned. But all of these proved fruitless, and a few valuable lives having been sacrificed, the idea was finally laid aside. In the meanwhile the American General directed the whole of his attention to the strengthening of his post. Day and night we could observe numerous parties at work upon his lines, whilst from the increased number of tents, which almost every hour might be discerned, it was evident that strong reinforcements were continually pouring into his camp. Nor did he leave us totally unmolested. By giving to his guns a great degree of elevation, he contrived at last to reach our bivouac; and thus were we constantly under a cannonade which, though it did little execution, proved nevertheless extremely annoying. Besides this, he now began to erect batteries on the opposite bank of the river; from which a flanking fire could be thrown across the entire front of his position. In short, he adopted every precaution which prudence could suggest, and for the reception of which the nature of his ground was so admirably adapted.

Under these circumstances it was evident that the longer an attack was delayed the less likely was it to succeed; that something must be done immediately every one perceived, but how to proceed was the difficulty. If we attempted to storm the American lines, we should expose ourselves to almost certain destruction from their artillery; to turn them was impossible; and to draw their troops by any manoeuvring from behind their entrenchments was a thing altogether out of the question. There seemed therefore to be but one practicable mode of assault; which was, to treat these field-works as one would treat a regular fortification; by erecting breaching batteries against them, and silencing, if it were possible, at least some of their guns. To this plan, therefore, our leader had recourse; and, in consequence, the whole of these three days were employed in landing heavy cannon, bringing up ammunition, and making such preparations as might have sufficed for a siege.

At length, having completed his arrangements, and provided such means as were considered sufficient to ensure success, General Pakenham determined to commence operations without delay. One half of the army was accordingly ordered out on the night of the 31st, and marched to the front, passing the piquets, and halting about three hundred yards from the enemy's line. Here it was resolved to throw up a chain of works; and here the greater part of this detachment, laying down their firelocks, applied themselves vigorously to their tasks, whilst the rest stood armed and prepared for their defence.

The night was dark, and our people maintained a profound silence; by which means, not an idea of what was going on existed in the American camp. As we laboured, too, with all diligence, six batteries were completed long before dawn, in which were mounted thirty pieces of heavy cannon; when, falling back a little way, we united ourselves to the remainder of the infantry, and lay down behind some rushes, in readiness to act, as soon as we should be wanted.

In the erection of these batteries, a circumstance occurred worthy of notice, on account of its singularity. I have already stated that the whole of this district was covered with the stubble of sugar-cane; and I might have added, that every storehouse and barn, attached to the different mansions scattered over it, was filled with barrels of sugar. In throwing up these works, the sugar was used instead of earth. Rolling the hogsheads towards the front, they were placed upright in the parapets of batteries; and it was computed that sugar to the value of many thousand pounds sterling was thus disposed of.

Chapter 23

Storm & Slaughter

The infantry having retired, and the gunners taken their station, dawn was anxiously expected. But the morning of the 1st of January chanced to be peculiarly gloomy. A thick haze obscured for a long time the rays of the sun, nor could objects be discerned with any accuracy till a late hour.

But at length the mist gave way, and the American camp was fully exposed to view. Being at this time only three hundred yards distant, we could perceive all that was going forward with great exactness. The different regiments were upon parade; and being dressed in holiday suits, presented really a fine appearance. Mounted officers were riding backwards and forwards through the, ranks, bands were playing, and colours floating in the air; in a word, all seemed jollity and gala; when suddenly our batteries opened, and the face of affairs was instantly changed. The ranks were broken; the different corps dispersing, fled in all directions, whilst the utmost terror and disorder appeared to prevail. Instead of nicely-dressed lines, nothing but confused crowds could now be observed; nor was it without much difficulty that order was finally restored. Oh, that we had charged at that instant!

Whilst this consternation prevailed among the infantry, their artillery remained silent; but as soon as the former rallied, they also recovered confidence, and answered our salute with great rapidity and precision. A heavy cannonade quickly commenced on both sides, and continued during the whole of the day; till, towards evening, our ammunition began to fail, and our fire in consequence to slacken. The fire of the Americans, on the other hand, was redoubled: landing a number of guns from the flotilla, they increased their artillery to a prodigious amount; and directing at the same time the whole force of their cannon on the opposite bank against the flank of our batteries, they soon convinced us that all endeavours to surpass them in this mode of fighting would be useless. Once more, therefore, were we obliged to retire, leaving our heavy guns to their fate; but as no attempt was made by the Americans to secure them, working parties were again sent out after dark, and such as had not been destroyed were removed.

Of the fatigue undergone during these operations by the whole army, from the General down to the meanest sentinel, it would be difficult to form an adequate conception. For two whole nights and days not a man had closed an eye, except such as were cool enough to sleep amidst showers of cannon-ball; and during the day scarcely a moment had been allowed in which we were able so much as to break our fast. We retired, therefore, not only baffled and disappointed, but in some degree disheartened and discontented. All our plans had as yet proved abortive; even this, upon which so much reliance had been placed, was found to be of no avail; and it must be confessed that something like murmuring began to be heard through the camp. And, in truth, if ever an army might be permitted to murmur, it was this. In landing they had borne great hardships, not only without repining, but with cheerfulness; their hopes had been excited by false reports, as to the practicability of the attempt in which they were embarked; and now they found themselves entangled amidst difficulties from which there appeared to be no escape, except by victory. In their attempts upon the enemy's line, however, they had been twice foiled; in artillery they perceived themselves to be so greatly overmatched, that their own could hardly assist them; their provisions, being derived wholly from the fleet, were both scanty and coarse; and their rest was continually broken. For not only did the canon and mortars from the main of the enemy's position play unremittingly upon them both by day and night, but they were likewise exposed to a deadly fire from the opposite bank of the river, where no less than eighteen pieces of artillery were now mounted, and swept the entire line of our encampment. Besides all this, to undertake the duty of a piquet was as dangerous as to go into action. Parties of American sharpshooters harassed and disturbed those appointed to that service from the time they took possession of their post till they were relieved; whilst to light fires at night was impossible, because they served but as certain marks for the enemy's gunners. I repeat, therefore, that a little murmuring could not be wondered at. Be it observed, however, that these were not the murmurs of men anxious to escape from a disagreeable situation by any means. On the contrary, they resembled rather the growling of a chained dog, when he sees his adversary and cannot reach him; for in all their complaints, no man ever hinted at a retreat, whilst all were eager to bring matters to the issue of a battle, at any sacrifice of loves.

Nor was our gallant leader less anxious to fight than his followers. To fight upon something like equal terms was, however, his wish; and for this purpose a new scheme was invented, worthy, for its boldness, of the school in which Sir Edward had studied his profession. It was determined to divide the army, to send part across the river, who should seize the enemy's guns, and turn them on themselves; whilst the remainder should at time make a general assault along the whole entrenchment. But before this plan could be put into execution, it would be necessary to cut a canal across the entire neck of land from the Bayo de Catiline to the river, of sufficient width and depth to admit of boats being brought up from the lake. Upon this arduous undertaking were the troops immediately employed. Being divided into four companies, they laboured by turns, day and night; one party relieving another after a stated number of hours, in such order as that the work should never be entirely deserted. The fatigue undergone during the prosecution of this attempt no words can sufficiently describe; yet it was pursued without repining, and at length, by unremitting exertions, they succeeded in effecting their purpose by the 6th of January.

Whilst these things were going on, and men's minds were anxiously turned towards approaching events, fresh spirit was given to the army by the unexpected arrival of Major-General Lambert, with the 7th and 43rd; two fine battalions, mustering each 800 effective men. By this reinforcement, together with the addition of a body of sailors and marines from the fleet, our numbers amounted now to little short of 6000 men; a force which, in almost any other quarter of America, would have been irresistible. Of the numbers of the enemy, again, various reports were in circulation; some stating them at 20,000, others at 30,000; but I believe that I come nearer the truth when I suppose their whole force to have comprised 12,000 men of all arms. It is, at least, certain that they exceeded us in numbers as much as they did in resources; and that scarcely an hour passed which did not bring in new levies to their camp.

The canal, as I have stated, being finished on the 6th, it was resolved to lose no time in making use of it. Boats were accordingly ordered up for the transportation of 1400 men; and Colonel Thornton, with the 85th regiment, the marines, and a party of sailors, was appointed to cross the river. But a number of untoward accidents occurred, to spoil a plan of operations as accurately laid down as any in the course of the war. The soil through which the canal was dug being soft, part of the bank gave way, and, choking up the channel, prevented the heaviest of the boats from getting forward. These again blocked up the passage, so that none of those which were behind could proceed; and thus, instead of a flotilla for the accommodation of 1400 men, only a number of boats sufficient to contain 350 was enabled to reach their destination. Even these did not arrive at the time appointed. According to the preconcerted plan, Colonel Thornton's detachment was to cross the river immediately after dark. They were to push forward, so as to carry all the batteries, and point the guns before daylight; when, on the throwing up of a rocket, they were to commence firing upon the enemy's line, which at the same moment was to be attacked by the main of our army.

In this manner was one part of the force to act, whilst the rest thus appointed:—Dividing his troops into three columns, Sir Edward directed that General Keane, at the head of the 95th, the light companies of the 21st, 4th, and 44th, together with the two black corps, should make a demonstration, or sham attack, upon the right; that General Gibbs, with the 4th, 21st, 44th, and 93rd, should force the enemy's left, whilst General Lambert, with the 7th and 43rd, remained in reserve, ready to act as circumstances might require. But in storming an entrenched position, something more than bare courage is required. Scaling ladders and fascines had, therefore, been prepared, with which to fill up the ditch and mount the wall; and since to carry these a service of danger, requiring a corps well worthy of dependence, the 44th was for that purpose selected, as a regiment of sufficient numerical strength, and already accustomed to American warfare. Thus were all things arranged on the night the 7th, for the 8th was fixed upon as the day decisive of the fate of New Orleans.

Whilst the rest of the army lay down to sleep till they should be roused up to fight, Colonel Thornton, with the 85th, and a corps of marines and seamen, amounting in all to 1400 men, moved down to the brink of the river. As yet, however, no boats had arrived; hour after hour elapsed before they came; and when they did come, the misfortunes which I have stated above were discovered, for out of all that had been ordered up, only a few made their appearance. Still it was absolutely necessary that this part of the plan should be carried into execution. Dismissing, therefore, the rest of his followers, the Colonel put himself at the head of his own regiment, about fifty seamen, and as many marines, and with this small force, consisting of no more than 340 men, pushed off. But, unfortunately, the loss of time nothing could repair. Instead of reaching the opposite bank at latest by midnight, dawn was beginning to appear before the boats quitted the canal. It was in vain that they rowed on in perfect silence, and with oars muffled, gaining the point of debarkation without being perceived. It was in vain that they made good their landing and formed upon the beach, without opposition or alarm; day had already broke, and the signal-rocket was seen in the air, while they were yet four miles from the batteries, which ought hours ago to have been taken.

In the mean time, the main body armed and moved forward some way in front of the piquets. There they stood waiting for daylight, and listening with the greatest anxiety for the firing which ought now to be heard on the opposite bank. But their attention was exerted in vain, and day dawned upon them long before they desired its appearance. Nor was Sir Edward Pakenham disappointed in this part of his plan alone. Instead of perceiving everything in readiness for the assault, he saw his troops in battle array, but not a ladder or fascine upon the field. The 44th, which was appointed to carry them, had either misunderstood or neglected their orders; and now headed the column of attack, without any means being provided for crossing the enemy's ditch or scaling his rampart.

The indignation of our brave leader on this occasion may be imagined, but cannot be described. Galloping towards Colonel Mullens, who led the 44th, he commanded him instantly to return with his regiment for the ladders, but the opportunity of planting them was lost, and though they were brought up, it was only to be scattered over the field by the frightened bearers. For our troops were by this time visible to the enemy. A dreadful fire was accordingly opened upon them, and they were mowed down by hundreds, while they stood waiting for orders.

Seeing that all his well-laid plans were frustrated, Pakenham gave the word to advance, and the other regiments, leaving the 44th with the ladders and fascines behind them, rushed on to the assault. On the left, a detachment under Colonel Rennie, of the 21st regiment, stormed a three-gun battery, and took it. Here they remained for some time in expectation of support; but none arriving, and a strong column of the enemy forming for its recovery, they determined to anticipate the attack, and pushed on. The battery which they had taken was in advance of the body of the works, being cut off from it by a ditch, across which only a single plank was thrown. Along this plank did these brave men attempt to pass; but being opposed by overpowering numbers, they were repulsed; and the Americans, in turn, forcing their way into the battery, at length succeeded in recapturing it with immense slaughter.

On the right, again, the 21st and 4th, supported by the 93rd, though thrown into some confusion by the enemy's fire, pushed on with desperate gallantry to the ditch; but to scale the parapet without ladders was a work of no slight difficulty. Some few, indeed, by mounting one upon another's shoulders, succeeded in entering the works, but these were speedily overpowered, most of them killed, and the rest taken; whilst as many as stood without were exposed to a sweeping fire, which cut them down by whole companies. It was in vain that the most obstinate courage was displayed. They fell by the hands of men whom they absolutely did not see; for the Americans, without so much as lifting their faces above the rampart, swung their firelocks by one arm over the wall, and discharged them directly upon their heads. The whole of the guns likewise, from the opposite bank, kept up a well-directed wand deadly cannonade upon their flank; and thus were they destroyed without an opportunity being given of displaying their valour, or obtaining so much as revenge.

Sir Edward saw how things were going, and did all that a general could do to rally his broken troops. Riding towards the 44th, which had returned to the ground, but in great disorder, he called out for Colonel Mullens to advance; but that officer disappeared, and was not to be found. He therefore prepared to lead them on himself, and had put himself at their head for that purpose, when he received a slight wound in the knee from a musket-ball, which killed his horse. Mounting another, he again headed the 44th, when a second ball took effect more fatally, and he dropped lifeless into the arms of his aide-de-camp.

Nor were Generals Gibbs and Keane inactive. Riding through the ranks, they strove by all means to encourage the assailants and recall the fugitives; till at length both were wounded, and borne off the field. All was now confusion and dismay. Without leaders, ignorant of what was to be done, the troops first halted and then began to retire; till finally the retreat was changed into a flight, and they quitted the ground in the utmost disorder. But the retreat was covered in gallant style by the reserve. Making a forward motion, the 7th and 43rd presented the appearance of a renewed attack; by which the enemy were so much awed, that they did not venture beyond their lines in pursuit of the fugitives.

Whilst affairs were thus disastrously conducted in this quarter, the party under Colonel Thornton had gained the landing-place. On stepping ashore, the first thing they beheld was a rocket thrown up as a signal that the battle was begun. This unwelcome sight added wings to their speed. Forming in one little column, and pushing forward a single company as an advanced guard, they hastened on, and in half an hour reached a canal, along the opposite bank of which a detachment of Americans was drawn up. To dislodge them was the work of a moment a boat, with a carronade in her bow, got upon their flank, gave them a single discharge of grape, whilst the advanced guard extended its ranks, and approached at double-quick time. But they scarcely waited till the latter were within range, when, firing a volley, they fled in confusion. This, however, was only an outpost: the main body was some way in rear, and amounted to no fewer than 1500 men.

It was not long, however, before they likewise presented themselves. Like their countrymen on the other side, they were strongly entrenched, a thick parapet with a ditch covering their front; whilst a battery upon their left swept the whole position, and two field-pieces commanded the road. Of artillery the assailants possessed not a single piece, nor any means beyond what nature supplied of scaling the rampart. Yet nothing daunted by the obstacles before them, or by the immense odds to which they were opposed, dispositions for an immediate attack were made. The 85th, extending its files, stretched across the entire line of the enemy; the sailors in column prepared to storm the battery, whilst the marines remained some little way in rear of the centre as a reserve.

These arrangements being completed, the bugle sounded, and our troops advanced. The sailors raising a shout, rushed forward, but were met by so heavy a discharge of grape and canister that for an instant they paused. Recovering themselves, however, they again pushed on; and the 85th dashing forward to their aid, they received a heavy fire of musketry, and endeavoured to charge. A smart firing was now for a few minutes kept up on both sides, but our people had no time to waste in distant fighting, and accordingly hurried on to storm the works, upon which a panic seized the Americans, they lost their order, and fled, leaving us in possession of their tents and of eighteen pieces of cannon.

In this affair our loss amounted to only three men killed and about forty wounded, among the latter of whom was Colonel Thornton. Nor could the loss on the part of the enemy greatly exceed our own. Had they stood firm, indeed, it is hardly conceivable that so small a force could have wrested an entrenched position from numbers so superior; at least it could not have been done without much bloodshed. But they were completely surprised. An attack on this side was a circumstance of which they had not dreamed; and when men are assaulted in a point which they deem beyond the reach of danger, it is well known that they defend themselves with less vigour than where such an event was anticipated.

When in the act of storming these lines the word was passed through our ranks that all had gone well on the opposite bank. This naturally added to the vigour of the assault; but we had not followed our flying enemy above two miles when we were commanded to halt. The real state of the case had now reached us, and the same messenger who brought the melancholy news brought likewise an order to return.

The place where we halted was in rear of a canal, across which was thrown a wooden bridge, furnishing apparently the only means of passing. At the opposite end of this bridge stood a collection of wooden cottages and one chateau of some size. Here a company was stationed to serve the double purpose of a piquet and a rear-guard; whilst the main body, having rested for half an hour, began their march towards the point where they had landed.

As soon as the column had got sufficiently on their way the piquet likewise prepared to follow. But in doing so it was evident that some risk must be run. The enemy having rallied, began again to show a front; that is to say, parties of sixty or a hundred men approached to reconnoitre. These, however, must be deceived, otherwise a pursuit might be commenced, and the re-embarkation of the whole corps hindered or prevented. It so happened that the piquet in question was this day under my command; as soon, therefore, as I received information that the main body had commenced its retreat, I formed my men, and made a show of advancing. The Americans perceiving this, fled; when, wheeling about, we set fire to the chateau, and under cover of the smoke destroyed the bridge and retreated. Making all haste towards the rear, we overtook our comrades just as they had begun to embark; when the little corps being once more united, entered their boats, and reached the opposite bank without molestation.

Chapter 24
Defeat & Retreat

As soon as the whole army was re-united, and the broken regiments had recovered their order, a flag of truce was dispatched with proposals for the burial of the dead. To accomplish this end a truce of two days was agreed upon, and parties were immediately sent out to collect and bury their fallen comrades. Prompted by curiosity, I mounted my horse and rode to the front; but of all the sights I ever witnessed, that which met me there was beyond comparison the most shocking and the most humiliating.

Within the narrow compass of a few hundred yards were gathered together nearly a thousand bodies, all of them arrayed in British uniforms. Not a single American was among them; all were English; and they were thrown by dozens into shallow holes, scarcely deep enough to furnish them with a slight covering of earth. Nor was this all. An American officer stood by smoking a cigar, and apparently counting the slain with a look of savage exultation, and repeating over and over to each individual that approached him, that their loss amounted only, to eight men killed and fourteen wounded.

I confess that when I beheld the scene I hung down my head, half in sorrow and half in anger. With my officious informant I had every inclination to pick a quarrel; but he was on duty, and an armistice existed, both of which forbade the measure. I could not, however, stand by and repress my choler, and since to give it vent would have subjected me to more serious inconvenience than a mere duel, I turned my horse's head and galloped back to the camp.

But the change of expression visible there in every countenance no language can portray. Only twenty hours ago, and all was life and animation; wherever you went you were enlivened by the sound of merriment and raillery; whilst the expected attack was mentioned in terms indicative not only of sanguine hope, but, of the most perfect confidence as to its result. Now gloom and discontent everywhere prevailed. Disappointment, grief, indignation, and rage, succeeded each other in all bosoms; nay, so completely were the troops overwhelmed by a sense of disgrace, that for awhile they retained their sorrow without so much as hinting at its cause.

Nor was this dejection occasioned wholly by the consciousness of laurels tarnished. The loss of comrades was to the full as afflicting as the loss of honour; for out of more than 5000 men brought on this side into the field, no fewer than 1500 had fallen. Among these were two generals (for Gibbs survived his wound but a few hours), and many officers of courage and ability; besides which, hardly an individual survived who had not to mourn the loss of some particular and well-known companion.

Yet it is most certain that amidst all this variety of conflicting passions no feeling bordering upon despair or even terror found room. Even among the private soldiers no fear was experienced; for if you attempted to converse with them on the subject of the late defeat, they would end with a bitter curse upon those to whose misconduct they attributed their losses, and refer you to the future, when they hoped for an opportunity of revenge. To the Americans they would allow no credit, laying the entire blame of the failure upon certain individuals among themselves; and so great was the indignation expressed against one corps, that the soldiers of other regiments would hardly exchange words with those who chanced to wear that uniform. Though deeply afflicted, therefore, we were by no means disheartened, and even, yet anticipated, with an eagerness far exceeding what was felt before, a renewal of the combat.

But General Lambert, on whom the chief command had devolved, very prudently determined not to risk the safety of his army by another attempt upon works evidently so much beyond their strength. He considered, and considered justly, that his chances of success were in every respect lessened by the late repulse. In the first place, an extraordinary degree of confidence was given to the enemy; in the next place, the only feasible plan of attack having been already tried, they would be more on their guard to prevent its being again put in execution; and lastly, his own force was greatly diminished in numbers, whilst theirs continued every day to increase. Besides, it would be casting all upon the hazard of a die. If again defeated, nothing could save our army from destruction, because unless it retreated in force no retreat could be effected. A retreat, therefore, whilst yet the measure appeared practicable, was resolved upon, and towards that end were all our future operations directed.

To the accomplishment of this desirable object, however, one great obstacle existed: by what road were the troops to travel, and in what order were they to regain the fleet? On landing we had taken advantage of the creek or bayo, and thus come up by water within two miles of the cultivated country. But to adopt a similar course in returning was impossible. In spite of our losses there were not throughout the armament a sufficient number of boats to transport above one-half of the army at a time. If, however, we should separate, the chances were that both parties would be destroyed; for those embarked might be intercepted, and those left behind would be obliged to cope with the entire American force. Besides, even granting that the Americans might be repulsed, it would be impossible to take to our boats in their presence, and thus at least one division, if not both, must be sacrificed.

To obviate this difficulty prudence required that the road which we had formed on landing should be continued to the very margin of the lake; whilst appearances seemed to indicate the total impracticability of the scheme. From firm ground to the water's edge was here a distance of many miles, through the very centre of a morass where human foot had never before trodden. Yet it was desirable at least to make the attempt; for if it failed we should only be reduced to our former alternative of gaining a battle or surrendering at discretion.

Having determined to adopt this course, General Lambert immediately dispatched strong working parties, under the guidance of engineer officers, to lengthen the road, keeping as near as possible to the margin of the creek. But the task assigned to them was burthened with innumerable difficulties. For the extent of several leagues no firm footing could be discovered on which to rest the foundation of a path; nor any trees to assist in forming hurdles. All that could be done, therefore, was to bind together large quantities of reeds, and lay them across the quagmire; by which means at least the semblance of a road was produced, however wanting in firmness and solidity. But where broad ditches came in the way, many of which intersected the morass, the workmen were necessarily obliged to apply more durable materials. For these, bridges composed in part of large branches brought with immense labour from the woods, were constructed; but they were, on the whole, little superior in point of strength to the rest of the path, for though the edges were supported by timber, the middle was filled up only with reeds.

To complete this road, bad as it was, occupied the space of nine days, during which time our army remained in position without making any attempt to molest the enemy. The Americans, however, were not so inactive. In the course of two days six guns were again mounted upon the bank of the river, from which a continual fire was kept up upon our camp. The same mode of proceeding was adopted in front, and thus, night and day, were we harassed by danger against which there was no fortifying ourselves. Of the extreme unpleasantness of our situation it is hardly possible to convey any adequate conception. We never closed our eyes in peace, for we were sure to be awakened before many minutes elapsed, by the splash of a round shot or shell in the mud beside us. Tents we had none, but lay, some in the open air, and some in huts made of boards, or any materials that could be procured. From the first moment of our landing not a man had undressed excepting to bathe; and many had worn the same shirt for weeks together, Besides all this, heavy rains now set in, accompanied with violent storms of thunder and lightning, which lasting during the entire day, usually ceased towards dark, and gave place to keen frosts. Thus were we alternately wet and frozen: wet all day, and frozen all night. With the outposts again there was constant skirmishing. With what view the Americans wished to drive them in I cannot tell; but every day were they attacked, and compelled to maintain their ground by dint of hard fighting. In one word, none but those who happened to belong to this army can form a notion of the hardships which it endured and the fatigue which it underwent.

Nor were these the only evils which tended to lessen our numbers. To our soldiers every inducement was held out by the enemy to desert. Printed papers, offering lands and money as the price of desertion, were thrown into the piquets, whilst individuals made a practice of approaching our posts, and endeavouring to persuade the very sentinels to quit their stations. Nor could it be expected that bribes so tempting would always be refused. Many desertions began daily to take place, and became before long so frequent, that the evil rose to be of a serious nature.

There occurred, however, one instance of magnanimous fidelity on the part of a British soldier, which I cannot resist the inclination of repeating. A private of the 95th, whose name I should have joyfully mentioned had I not forgotten it, chanced one day to stand sentinel, when he was addressed by an American officer. The American offered him a hundred dollars and a quantity of land if he would come over; representing, at the same time, the superiority of a democratical government, and railing, as these persons generally do, against the title of king. Though the Englishman heard what was said distinctly enough, he nevertheless pretended to be deaf, and begged his tempter to come a little nearer, that, in his own words, "he might tell him all about it." Jonathan, exulting at the prospect of drawing this fine fellow from his duty, approached within twenty paces of where he stood, when just as he had opened his mouth to renew his offer, the sentinel levelled his piece and shot him through the arm. Nor was he contented with inflicting this punishment. Walking forward, he seized his wounded enemy, and reproaching him with dishonourable dealings, brought him in a prisoner to the camp. But, unhappily, conduct such as this was rare; in the course of a week many men quitted their colours, and fled to the enemy.

In the mean time the whole of the wounded, except such as were too severely hurt to be removed, were embarked upon the canal, and sent off to the fleet. Next followed the baggage and stores, with the civil officers, commissaries, purveyors, &c.; and last of all, such of the light artillery as could be withdrawn with out trouble or the risk of discovery. But of the heavy artillery, of which about ten pieces were mounted in front of the bivouac, and upon the bank of the river, no account was taken. They were ship's guns, of little value, and extremely cumbersome; consequently their removal, had it been practicable, would scarcely have rewarded the trouble. It was therefore determined to leave them behind; and they were accordingly permitted to retain their stations to the last.

These preparations being continued for some days, on the 17th no part of our force remained in camp except the infantry. Having therefore delayed only till the abandoned guns were rendered unserviceable, on the evening of the 18th it also began its retreat. Trimming the fires, and arranging all things in the same order as if no change were to take place, regiment after regiment stole away, as soon as darkness concealed their motions; leaving the piquets to follow as a rear-guard, but with strict injunctions not to retire till daylight began to appear. As may be supposed, the most profound silence was maintained; not a man opening his mouth, except to issue necessary orders, and even then speaking in a whisper. Not a cough or any other noise was to be heard from the head to the rear of the column; and even the steps of the soldiers were planted with care, to prevent the slightest stamping or echo. Nor was this extreme caution in any respect unnecessary. In spite of every endeavour to the contrary, a rumour of our intended movement had reached the Americans for we found them of late watchful and prying, whereas they had been formerly content to look only to themselves.

For some time, that is to say, while our route lay along the high road and beside the brink of the river, the march was agreeable enough; but as soon as we began to enter upon the path through the marsh all comfort was at an end. Being constructed of materials so slight, and resting upon a foundation so infirm, the treading of the first corps unavoidably beat it to pieces; those which followed were therefore compelled to flounder on in the best way they could; and by the time the rear of the column gained the morass all trace of a way had entirely disappeared. But not only were the reeds torn asunder and sunk by the pressure of those who had gone before, but the bog itself, which at first might have furnished a few spots of firm footing, was trodden into the consistency of mud. The consequence was, that every step sank us to the knees, and frequently higher. Near the ditches, indeed, many spots occurred which we had the utmost difficulty in crossing at all; and as the night was dark, there being no moon, nor any light except what the stars supplied, it was difficult to select our steps, or even to follow those who called to us that they were safe on the opposite side. At one of these places I myself beheld an unfortunate wretch gradually sink till he totally disappeared. I saw him flounder in, heard his cry for help, and ran forward with the intention of saving him; but before I had taken a second step, I myself sank at once as high as the breast. How I contrived to keep myself from smothering is more than I can tell, for I felt no solid bottom under me, and continued slowly to go deeper and deeper till the mud reached my arms. Instead of endeavouring to help the poor soldier, of whom nothing could now be seen except the head and hands, I was forced to beg assistance for myself: when a leathern canteen strap being thrown to me, I laid hold of it, and was dragged out just as my fellow-sufferer became invisible.

Over roads such as these did we continue our journey during the whole of the night: and in the morning reached a place called Fisherman's huts, upon the margin of the lake. The name is derived from a clump of mud-built cottages, situated in as complete a desert as the eye of man was ever pained by beholding. They stand close to the water, upon a part of the morass rather more firm than the rest. Not a tree or bush of any description grows near them. As far as the eye could reach a perfect ocean of reeds everywhere presented itself, except on that side where a view of the lake changed without fertilizing the prospect. Were any set of human beings condemned to spend their lives here, I should consider their fate as little superior to that of the solitary captive: but during many months of the year these huts are wholly unoccupied, being erected, as their name denotes, merely to shelter a few fishermen while the fishing season lasts.

Here at length we were ordered to halt; and perhaps I never rejoiced more sincerely at any order than at this. Wearied with my exertions, and oppressed with want of sleep, I threw myself on the ground without so much as pulling off my muddy garments, and in an instant all my cares and troubles were forgotten. Nor did I wake from that deep slumber for many hours, when I rose cold and stiff, and creeping beside a miserable fire of reeds, addressed myself to the last morsel of salt pork which my wallet contained.

The whole army had now come up, the piquets having escaped without notice, or at least without annoyance. Forming along the brink of the lake, a line of outposts was planted, and the soldiers were commanded to make themselves as comfortable as they could. But, in truth, the word comfort is one which cannot in any sense be applied to people in such a situation. Without tents or huts of any description (for the few from which the place is named were occupied by the General and other heads of departments), our bed was the morass, and our sole covering the clothes which had not quitted our backs for upwards of a month. Our fires, upon the size and goodness of which much of a soldier's happiness depends, were composed solely of reeds; a species of fuel which, like straw, soon blazes up, and soon expires again, almost without communicating any degree of warmth. But, above all, our provisions were expended, and from what quarter to obtain an immediate supply it defied the most inventive genius to discover. Our sole dependence was upon the boats. Of these a flotilla lay ready to receive us, in which were embarked the black corps, with the 44th; but they had brought with them only food for their own use. It was therefore necessary that they should reach the fleet and return again before they could furnish us with what we so much wanted. But the distance to the nearest of the shipping could not be less than eighty miles; and if the weather should become boisterous or the winds obstinately adverse we might starve before any supply could arrive.

These numerous grievances were, however, without remedy, and we bore them with patience; though for two whole days the only provisions issued to the troops were some crumbs of biscuit and a small allowance of rum. For my own part I did not fare so badly as many others. Having been always fond of shooting, I took a firelock and went in pursuit of wild ducks, which abounded throughout the bog. Wandering along in this quest I reached a lake, by the margin of which I concealed myself and waited for my prey; nor was it long before I had an opportunity of firing. Several large flocks flew over me, and I was fortunate enough to kill three birds. But, alas, those birds, upon which I had already feasted in imagination, dropped into the water: my dog, more tired than her master, would not fetch them out, and they lay about twenty yards off, tantalizing me with the sight of a treasure which I could not reach. Moving off to another point, I again took my station where I hoped for better fortune; but the same evil chance once more occurred, and the ducks fell into the lake. This was too much for a hungry man to endure; the day was piercingly cold, and the edge of the pool was covered with ice; but my appetite was urgent, and I resolved at all hazards to indulge it. Pulling off my clothes, therefore, I broke the ice and plunged in; and though shivering like an aspen-leaf, I returned safely to the camp with a couple of birds. Next day I adopted a similar course with like success, but at the expense of what was to me a serious misery. My stockings of warm wool were the only part of my dress which I did not strip off, and to-day it unfortunately happened that one was lost. Having secured my ducks, I attempted to land where the bottom was muddy; but my leg stuck fast, and in pulling it out off came the stocking; to recover it was beyond my power, for the mud closed over it directly, and the consequence was that till I regained the transport only one of my feet could be warm at a time. To those who can boast of many pairs of fine cotton and woollen hose, this misfortune of mine may appear light, but to me, who had only two stockings on shore, the loss of one was very grievous; and I therefore request that I may not be sneered at when I record it as one of the disastrous consequences of this ill-fated expedition.

Chapter 25
The Seige of Mobile

As soon as the boats returned, regiment after regiment embarked and set sail for the fleet; but the distance being considerable and the wind foul, many days elapsed before the whole could be got off. Excepting in one trifling instance, however, no accident occurred, and by the end of the month we were all once more on board our former ships. But our return was far from triumphant. We, who only seven weeks ago had set out in the surest confidence of glory, and I may add of emolument, were brought back dispirited and dejected. Our ranks were wofully thinned, our chiefs slain, our clothing tattered and filthy, and even our discipline in some degree injured. A gloomy silence reigned throughout the armament, except when it was broken by the voice of lamentation over fallen friends; and the interior of each ship presented a scene well calculated to prove the short-sightedness of human hope and human prudence.

The accident to which I allude was the capture of a single boat by the enemy. About thirty men of the 14th dragoons having crowded into an unarmed barge, were proceeding slowly down the lake, when a boat mounting a carronade in its bow suddenly darted from a creek and made towards them. To escape was impossible, for their barge was too heavily laden to move at a rate of even moderate rapidity; and to fight was equally out of the question, because of the superiority which their cannon gave to the Americans. The whole party was accordingly compelled to surrender to six men and an officer; and having thrown their arms into the lake, their boat was taken in tow and they were carried away prisoners.

This, however, was the only misfortune which occurred. Warned by the fate of their comrades, the rest kept together in little squadrons, each attended by one or more armed launches; and thus rowing steadily on, they gained the shipping without so much as another attempt at surprisal being made.

On reaching the fleet, we found that a considerable reinforcement of troops had arrived from England. It consisted of the 40th foot, a fine regiment, containing nearly a thousand men, which, ignorant of the fatal issue of our attack, had crossed the lakes only to be sent back to the ships without so much as stepping on shore. The circumstance, however, produced little satisfaction. We felt that the coming of thrice the number could not recover what was lost or recall past events; and therefore no rejoicing was heard, nor the slightest regard paid to the occurrence. Nay, so great was the despondency which had taken possession of men's minds, that not even a rumour respecting the next point of attack obtained circulation; whilst a sullen carelessness, a sort of indifference as to what might happen, seemed to have succeeded all our wonted curiosity and confidence of success in every undertaking.

In this state we remained wind-bound till the 4th of February, when, at length getting under weigh, the fleet ran down as far as Cat Island. This is a spot of sandy soil at the mouth of the lake, remarkable for nothing except a solitary Spanish family which possesses it. Completely cut off from the rest of the world, an old man, his wife, two daughters, and a son, dwell here in apparent happiness and contentment. Being at least one hundred and twenty miles from the main, it is seldom that their little kingdom is visited by strangers; and I believe that till our arrival the daughters, though grown up to womanhood, had seen few faces besides those of their parents and brother. Their cottage, composed simply of a few boughs, thatched and in-woven with straw, is beautifully situated within a short distance of the water.

Two cows and a few sheep grazed beside it; whilst a small tract of ground covered with stubble, and a little garden well stocked with fruit-trees and vegetables, at once gave proof of their industry, and showed the source from whence they supplied themselves with bread.

Having remained here till the 7th, we again took advantage of a fair wind and stood to sea. As soon as we had cleared the lake, we directed our course towards the east, steering, as it was rumoured, upon Mobile; nor was it long before we came in sight of the bay which bears that name. It is formed by a projecting headland called Point Bayo, and a large island called Isle Dauphin. Upon the first is erected a small fort, possessing the same title with the promontory which commands the entrance; for though the island is, at least five miles from the main, there is no water for floating a ship of any burthen except within a few hundred yards of the latter. The island is, like Cat Island, uninhabited, except by one family, and unprovided with any works of defence.

As the attack of Mobile was professedly our object, it was clear that nothing could be done previous to the reduction of the fort. The ships accordingly dropped anchor at the mouth of the bay, and immediate preparations were made for the siege. But the fort was too inconsiderable in point of size to require the employment of all our forces in its investment. Whilst one brigade, therefore, was allotted to this service, the rest proceeded to establish themselves on the island, where, carrying tents and other conveniences on shore, the first regular encampment which we had seen since our arrival in this hemisphere was formed.

The spot of ground, of which we had now taken possession, extended twelve miles in length, and from one to three in width. Its soil is in general dry and sandy, well covered with grass, and ornamented by continued groves of pine, cedar, oak, and laurel. On one side only is there a swamp, but not of sufficient size to contaminate the atmosphere of the whole, which is considered so peculiarly healthy, that the place is generally used as a depot for the sick in the American army. At present, as I have said, it was tenanted by no more than a single family, the master of which was a midshipman in the American navy, and banished hither for some misdemeanor; but what was to us of much greater importance, it was likewise stocked with cattle resembling in appearance the black cattle of the Highlands of Scotland, and not behind them in point of wildness.

Whilst the remainder of the army spent their time here, the 4th, 21st, and 44th, being landed above the fort, were busied in the siege. This small work stands, as I have stated, at the extremity of a promontory. Towards the sea its fortifications are respectable enough, but on the land side it is little better than a blockhouse. The ramparts being composed of sand, not more than three feet in thickness, are faced with plank barely cannon-proof; whilst a sand-hill rising within pistol-shot of the ditch, completely commands them. Within, again, the fort is as much wanting in accommodation as it is in strength. There are no bomb-proof barracks, nor any hole or arch under which men might find protection from shells; indeed, so deficient is it in common lodging-rooms, that a great part of the garrison slept in tents. To reduce this place, therefore, occupied but a short time. The troops having assembled on the 8th, drove the enemy within their lines on the 9th, and broke ground the same evening. On the 10th, four eighteen-pounders with two howitzers were placed in battery upon the top of the sand-hill; on the 11th, the fort surrendered; and on the 12th, the garrison, consisting of four hundred men of the second American regiment, marched out with all the honours of war, and laid down their arms upon the glacis.

CHAPTER 26
Peace

With the reduction of this trifling work ended all hostilities in this quarter of America, for the army had scarcely re-assembled when intelligence arrived from England of peace. The news reached us on the 14th, and I shall not deny that it was received with general satisfaction. Though war is the soldier's harvest, yet it must be confessed, that when carried on as it had of late been conducted, it is a harvest of which men in time become weary; and many of us having been absent for several years from our native shores, experienced absolute delight at the prospect of returning once more to the bosom of our families. The communication was therefore welcomed with unfeigned joy, nor could any other topic of conversation gain attention throughout the camp, except the anticipated re-embarkation..

But as the preliminaries only had been signed, and as Mr. Maddison's approval was required before we should be at liberty to depart, our army still continued stationary upon the island. Of the President's conduct, however, no doubts were entertained; all thoughts of future military operations were in consequence laid aside; and the sole aim of every individual thenceforth was to make himself as comfortable as circumstances would permit. To effect this end various expedients were adopted. Among others a theatre was erected, in which such officers as chose to exhibit performed for their own amusement and the amusement of their friends. In shooting and fishing, likewise, much of our time was spent; and thus, by adopting the usual expedients of idle men, we contrived to pass some days in a state of tolerable comfort.

Occupations such as these, however, soon grew insipid, and it was with sincere rejoicing that on the 5th of March we were made acquainted with Mr. Maddison's agreement to the terms proposed. All was now hope and exultation, an immediate departure was anticipated, and those were pitied as unfortunate whose lot it was supposed, might detain them even a day behind their fellows. But as yet no movement took place; our provisions were not sufficient to authorize the undertaking so long a voyage as we must undertake, did we attempt to run for the nearest British settlement; we were therefore compelled to remain where we were, till a frigate should return, which had been sent forward to solicit supplies from the Governor of Cuba.

During this interval, the same occupations were resorted to; and others of a less agreeable nature undertaken. As summer came on, the island sent forth multitudes of snakes from their lurking- places, which infested the camp, making their way in some instances into our very beds. This was bad enough, but it was not the only nuisance to which we were subject. The alligators, which during the winter months lie in a dormant state, now began to awaken, and prowling about the margin of the pool, created no little alarm and agitation. Apparently confounded at our invasion of their territories, these monsters at first confined themselves to the marshy part of the island, but becoming by degrees more familiar, they soon ventured to approach the very precincts of the camp. One of them at length entered a tent; in which only a woman and child chanced to be, and having stared round as if in amazement, walked out again without offering to commit any violence. But the visit was of too serious a nature to be overlooked. Parties were accordingly formed for their destruction, and it was usual on the return of each from an excursion, instead of asking how many birds, to demand how many snakes and alligators they had shot. Of the former, indeed, great numbers were killed, and of the latter not a few, the largest of which measured about nine feet from the snout to the tail.

Another employment, also, deserves to be noted, because it is truly characteristic of the boyish jollity of young soldiers. Wearied with a state of idleness, the officers of the 7th, 43rd, and 14th dragoons made an attack with fir-apples upon those of the 85th, 93rd, and 95th. For the space of some days they pelted each other from morning till night, laying ambuscades and exhibiting, on a small scale, all the stratagems of war; whilst the whole army, not even excepting the Generals themselves, stood by and spurred them on.

But to continue a detail of such proceedings would only swell my narrative, without amusing my reader; I shall therefore content myself with observing, that things remained in this state till the 14th of March, when the long-looked for frigate at length arrived, and on the 15th, the first division of the army embarking, set sail for England. The wind, however, was foul, nor did the ships make any way till the 17th, when a fresh breeze springing up, we stood our course, and by ten o'clock on the 21st could distinguish the high land of Cuba. But the violence of the gale having driven us considerably to leeward, we were forced to bear up, and beat along the coast, on which account it was not till the 23rd that we came opposite to the port of Havannah.

Than the approach to this city, and its first appearance from the water, it is impossible to conceive anything more grand and imposing. A little bay, extremely narrow at the entrance, forms the harbour. On each side of it stand forts of prodigious strength, particularly those on the left, where the ground is considerably elevated, whilst the city itself, with its ramparts and towers, its numerous steeples, spires, and public buildings, gives an assurance of wealth and magnificence peculiarly striking. When we entered, every tower was surmounted by a national banner half-mast high, a circumstance which did not at least diminish the effect of a first view; and the guns from the forts answering our salute, showed us how desperate must be the condition of an enemy that should venture within their range. Why the flags should thus indicate a general mourning, we were at a loss to guess, till the pilot informed us that this was Holy week. Then, indeed, we remembered that we had returned to a Roman Catholic country, and rejoiced at the lucky accident which had brought us thither at such a season.

As it was late before we anchored, I was prevented from landing that night, but on the morrow I went on shore at an early hour, with the intention of seeing as much as my time would allow. But in my proposed visits to the different points worthy of attention I was interrupted. It was Good-Friday, consequently all public places were shut, and neither guides nor carriages could be procured. But if I was disappointed in this, my disappointment was amply compensated by a view of the religious ceremonies peculiar to that day.

Walking into the largest church in the city, I beheld beside the altar a figure of our Saviour as large as life nailed to a cross. Beside this figure stood a number of monks, one of whom presented a rod with a sponge affixed to its mouth, while a second thrust a spear into its side, from which came out a liquor having the colour of blood and water. This being carefully caught in a golden dish, the figure was taken down from the cross, wrapped round with white linen clothes, and laid upon a bier, when an imposing procession began in the following order: First marched a military band playing slow and solemn music; next came a guard of soldiers with heads bent down and arms reversed; then followed about two hundred monks belonging to different orders, arrayed in their dark robes, with hands and feet bare, and crucifixes suspended from their necks. A short interval now succeeded, and another party of monks dressed in white appeared, singing hymns in honour of the Virgin. Next came a splendid couch surmounted by a canopy covered with white silk and sparkling with gold and jewels, upon which sat a waxen image of the Mother of God, clothed in gorgeous apparel. Following this was another party of white-robed monks, chanting a requiem for a departed soul, and then a second interval. At the distance of perhaps twenty yards from these came two monks bearing two large silver nails, then two others bearing a spear and a rod, and then the body of our Saviour stretched at full length upon the bier. After the bier came two monks bearing two other nails, and then another two bearing a small cross and a ladder. Here, again, there was another interval, which was succeeded by a third white-robed party likewise chanting a requiem. Next to these came about twenty canons arrayed in scarlet; then another couch covered with crimson velvet, which supported a figure of Mary Magdalen, likewise in a sitting posture; then a second body of canons, succeeded by about two hundred monks in black; after these another guard of soldiers, and last of all a second military band.

In spite of prejudice I could not avoid being deeply struck by this solemn procession. The airs performed by the bands were slow and mournful, the voices of the singers were deep and musical, the dresses were rich to a degree of splendour, and the whole was gone through with much apparent devotion. No doubt, when regarded with the eye of reflection, the whole may seem something worse than ludicrous, but it is impossible to witness the scene and to reason on its propriety at the same time. As long as the pageant is before your eyes you cannot avoid being powerfully impressed by it; nor is it till after it has disappeared that you are inclined to ask yourself why you gave way to feelings of that nature. Yet among the natives I thought I could observe a considerable degree of levity. It is true that as many as were in the streets or at the windows dropped upon their knees while the procession passed, but their careless looks and suppressed smiles sufficiently proved that they knelt only because they were obliged to kneel.

Commencing at the door of the church where the representation of the crucifixion had been exhibited, the funeral party (for it was neither more nor less) proceeded through the principal streets in the town with a slow and measured pace. As all except the soldiers walked two and two, it covered, I should conceive, little less than a mile in extent, and after winding from lane to lane and from square to square, directed its steps towards a particular convent, where the waxen image was solemnly deposited in a vault. It is said, but with what truth I cannot pretend to determine, that a different image is made use of every year, and that the vault is now so full of waxen corpses, that it will be necessary before long to have some of them destroyed.

Having now got rid of the most sacred part of their burthen, the monks, bearing only the two couches, returned in procession by the same route and in the same order as they had proceeded, only the bands struck up lively airs and the singers chanted hymns of rejoicing and hallelujahs. Instead of walking at a slow pace likewise, they stepped out almost in a sort of dance, and reaching the door of the great church they there separated, each party hastening to its own house to celebrate mass.

Into one or two of the convent chapels I likewise entered, and was present during the performance of their very striking service. I found them ornamented in the most magnificent manner, the rafters of many being gilded over and all the windows crowded with stained glass. Of pictures, and what struck me as something better than mere daubs, there were also great numbers. In a word, it seemed as if I had reached the heart and capital of Roman Catholic splendour. Nothing that I had beheld in the mother-country could at all compare with what was now before me, and I returned in the evening to my ship, not indeed a convert to the principles of that religion, but decidedly astonished and confounded at the solemn magnificence of its ceremonies.

Chapter 27
To England

At an early hour next morning I returned to the city, and found that the face of affairs had undergone a complete revolution. No more melancholy countenances, no closed shops and vacant streets were now to be seen; all was bustle and rejoicing, bells ringing, carriages rattling along, flags flying, and guns firing. The solemnity of Good-Friday ends, it appeared, at ten o'clock on Saturday morning, and from that time the merriments of Easter have their commencement.

The whole of this day I spent in strolling over the different walks and points of view from whence the town and surrounding country may be seen to most advantage; and I certainly must pronounce it to be by far the most magnificent colonial capital which I have visited. The streets are in general wide, clean, and airy; the houses, except in the suburbs, are composed entirely of stone, and being occasionally intermingled with convents, churches, and other public buildings, produce a very striking and handsome effect. Though surrounded by a rampart, Havannah has little of the confined and straitened appearance by which fortified towns are generally disfigured. The works being of great extent, have left within their circumference abundant room for the display of elegance and neatness in its construction, an advantage which has not been neglected; whilst from their situation they command as glorious a prospect as can well be imagined.

When you ascend a bastion which overhangs the harbour, the city, with all its towers and spires, lies immediately and distinctly beneath your gaze. Beyond it, again, you perceive a winding of the bay, which washes three sides of the promontory where the city stands; numerous fields of sugar-cane and Indian corn succeed, intersected by groves of orange and other fruit trees, which extend for some miles in a sort of inclined plane, and are at length bounded by lofty and rugged mountains. On your left, again, is the creek or entrance to the bay, separating you from the Moro, a line of castles remarkable for their strength and extent. Behind sweep the waters of the Gulf of Mexico; and on the right is another view much resembling that which lies before you, only that it is more narrowed; the high ground bearing in this direction closer upon the city. On the whole I do not remember to have been more forcibly struck by any scenery than that which I beheld from this bastion; so well were town and country, castles and convents, land and water, hill and valley combined.

Having spent some hours in wandering through the city, I endeavoured to make my way into the forts, and to examine the state of the works. But in both of these attempts I was interrupted. Without an order from the Governor, I was informed, that none, even of the natives, are permitted to enter the Moro, and all applications on the part of foreigners are uniformly refused. There was a degree of jealousy in this, as needless as it was illiberal; but indeed the whole conduct of the Spanish authorities gave proof of their reluctance to admit their old allies, even to the common rites of hospitality. From the moment we entered the harbour the militia of the island were called out, many of the guns which commanded our shipping were shotted, and artillerymen with lighted fuzes stood constantly beside them. An order was likewise issued, prohibiting more than two persons to land at the same time from each vessel, and many other precautions were taken, little complimentary to the good faith of those to whom Spain must feel that she owes her very existence. In spite of these drawbacks, however, I contrived to spend a week in this city with much satisfaction. The opera and theatre opening on

Easter Sunday, and continuing open during the remainder of our stay, furnished sufficient amusement for the evenings, whilst in walking or riding about, in examining the different churches and chapels, and in chatting with nuns through the grate, or monks within their cells, my mornings passed away more quickly than I desired.

At length our victualling and watering being complete, on the 9th of April we bade adieu to the shores of Cuba, and running along with the Gulf-stream, took our course towards Bermuda. The wind favoured us greatly, and on the 17th we again reached these islands; where we delayed till the 23rd, when, once more setting sail, we steered directly for England. During the remainder of the voyage nothing of importance occurred till the 7th of May, when, reaching in towards the shores of Brest, we were astonished by beholding the tri-coloured flag floating from the citadel. Of the mighty events which dad taken place in Europe, we were as yet in perfect ignorance. Though surprised, therefore, at the first view of that beacon of war, we naturally concluded it to be no more than a signal, and passed on without inquiry. As we ascended the channel, however, we were hailed by a schooner, which professed to communicate some news concerning Buonaparte; but the wind being high, we could not distinctly tell what was said; nor was it till the 9th, when we had anchored off Spithead, that the reappearance of that wonderful man was made known.

The effect of this intelligence it would be difficult to describe. At first it was received with acclamations, but by and bye those who had dreamed of home began to perceive in it the destruction of their visions. Yet we considered that we were soldiers, and certainly no regret was experienced when we were ordered to re-embark, and sail for the Downs.

Chapter 28
An Overview

Having thus brought my narrative to a conclusion, I cannot lay aside my pen without offering a few remarks upon the events of this busy year, and the nature of an American war in general. In doing so, I shall begin with the unfortunate attack upon New Orleans, and endeavour, in as few words as possible, to assign the true causes of its failure.

From the account which I have given of this affair, it will appear that, from its very commencement, it was replete with error, and gave promise of no better result than actually occurred. I do not here allude to the spot fixed upon for landing, because that was as appropriate as could be chosen. Neither do I refer to the groundless rumours brought in by deserters; for to such all assailants are liable; but the error lay in the steps subsequently taken; in the unhappy advance of the first division from a place of concealment into the open country, without pushing forward to the extent required. The fact is, that having reached the main land in safety, one out of two plans might have been selected by General Keane; which, in all probability, would have been equally attended with success. Either he might have remained in the morass till the whole army was assembled, or, if this were deemed too dangerous, he ought to have advanced upon the city with the first division alone. If it be objected that a force of 1600 men was incompetent for an undertaking so important as the latter, I reply that there could be no more hazard in it than in the course actually pursued. New Orleans is not a regular fortification requiring a large army and a powerful battering train for its reduction. In obtaining possession of such a place there would have been no difficulty, because it has since been ascertained that the American troops were, at the time of our landing, some miles above the city; and surely it would not have been more difficult to repulse an attack within a town than in the open country. But neither of these courses was adopted. The advance was drawn from concealment, and halted just where it became most exposed, as if it had been our design to warn the American General of his danger; the consequence of which was a well-directed attack upon our bivouac, and an immediate commencement of those works which afterwards resisted and repelled all our efforts.

The second error evident in this business was the selection of the schooner instead of the ship for destruction. Had the latter, which lay farther up the stream been destroyed, the former never could have passed our battery, nor been of further annoyance to us; whereas, the schooner being burnt, the ship was only removed out of the reach of danger, and posted where she could be infinitely more advantageous to her friends and detrimental to her enemies. This in itself was a grave error, which beyond all doubt contributed, in some degree, to our repulse on the 29th of December.

The third error, and one which continued to exert its influence throughout the whole campaign, was the delay in bringing on a general action. Why our troops fell back on the 29th I confess is to me a mystery. It was not to be supposed that an officer who had shown so much judgment as the American General, Jackson, in his first endeavours to check our advance, would lose the advantage which the nature of his position afforded. That he would fortify the neck of land, indeed, was exactly what might have been expected: and, therefore, every hour during which an attack was deferred, contributed so much to his strength and to our weakness. It is true that we should have suffered, and perhaps suffered severely; but our chances of suffering were certainly not diminished by delay.

We ought, therefore, instead of falling back, to have pursued our operations with vigour on that day; because the American lines, being then incomplete, would have assisted rather than retarded our progress.

It has been said, and perhaps truly, that the movement on the 29th was never intended for more than a reconnaissance: and that the scheme subsequently adopted, of overpowering the enemy's fire by a superior artillery brought from the fleet, was a wise one. All this may be true; but as we did not succeed in silencing the enemy's batteries, who, on the contrary, put ours to silence, either the project was faulty in its design, or some grievous error was committed in its execution. As far as our position was affected by it, the results were these:—Three days more were lost in making preparations, which ended in nothing; while, by the enemy, these same days were judiciously and indefatigably employed to improve their deficiency and recruit their force.

At last came the idea of digging a canal from the lakes to the river, by means of which a portion of our army might be thrown to the other side; a project which is said to have been suggested by Sir Alexander Cochrane; but which, wheresoever originating, was at once bold and judicious. The canal was accordingly formed; not, however, with sufficient attention to the rules of art in like cases, as was shown by the falling in of the banks, and the consequent impossibility of bringing up boats to transport the whole detachment. Still there it was, and 350 men, instead of 1400, made good their landing on the right bank of the river. It is deeply to be regretted that Sir Edward Pakenham did not delay his own advance with the main body till this fact had been ascertained. His plan of battle was to carry the enemy's works on the right bank, to turn their own guns from that flank against themselves, and to alarm them for their communications, ere he should attack the main position on the left. Nor can it be doubted, that had the detached corps arrived at the hour first named, an easy triumph would have been achieved. But Pakenham was too fiery to restrain his troops, after they had assumed their ground on his own side. Instead, therefore, of causing the columns to fall back out of gun-shot, and wait quietly till the battle began on the left, he hurried them into action as soon as the day dawned; and they became exposed to the whole of that volume of fire which it was one main object of his movement across the Mississippi to destroy. Moreover, from all the moral effects of a partial defeat the enemy were saved; and I need not say how serious such things are to irregular and undisciplined bodies. I do not mean to assert that, in spite of all this, the American lines ought not to have been carried. On the contrary, had every officer and man done his duty, the victory would have been complete, though purchased, beyond a doubt, at a severe cost. Yet it is absurd to deny that, speaking of the movement as an operation of war, the attack on the right ought to have been withheld till that on the left had either failed or succeeded. So far, therefore, the General is liable to censure; and chivalrous and high-minded as he was, it is just that he should receive it. But there were other causes of defeat than this; among which, the gross misconduct of one individual deserves to be especially noticed.

To Lieutenant-Colonel Mullens, with the 44th regiment, of which he was in command, was intrusted the arduous and therefore honourable duty of carrying the fascines and ladders. The orders were given in good time over night; and Colonel Mullens received them as if they had conveyed a sentence of death. He stated, in the hearing of the private soldiers, that his corps was devoted to destruction; and conducted himself, in every respect, like a condemned criminal on the night previous to his execution. When the troops got under arms, instead of bringing his battalion to the redoubt, where he had been instructed to find the ladders, he marched directly past it, and led them into the field without a single ladder or fascine. When the day dawned, and he was sent back for these instruments, he headed his corps in its retrograde movement, but left it to return as it could to the front; and when sought for to guide the attack, he was nowhere to be found. That a regiment thus abused and deserted by its commanding officer should fall into confusion, cannot occasion any surprise; it would have been surprising indeed, had a different result ensued. But the melancholy effect of such confusion was, that other regiments were likewise broken; and before order could be restored, all the Generals were borne dead or wounded from the field. A large share, therefore, of the blame attachable to this failure must rest where fidelity of narration has obliged me to place it.

Again, the recall of the victorious detachment from the left to the right bank of the Mississippi, and the consequent abandonment of that complete command of the river which this partial success had obtained, was a military error of the gravest kind. Great as our numerical loss had been in the principal action of the 8th, the advantages of position were at the close of the day so decidedly with us, that for General Jackson to maintain himself any longer in front of New Orleans was physically impossible. His own dispatch, indeed, addressed to the Secretary-at-War, shows that he felt the truth so forcibly, that he had actually issued orders for a retreat, when the removal of the English from his menaced flank was reported to him; and his battalions, which had begun to get under arms, were directed to resume their places. It is, however, but just to state, that such was the miserable condition of our commissariat, that the fleet contained not provisions enough to feed the people on half rations during a quick passage to Cuba; and General Lambert did not feel that he would be justified in risking the total loss of his army, which, had the campaign been prolonged another fortnight, must under such circumstances have taken place. That he erred in this supposition is certain; but his was probably an error into which most men similarly circumstanced would have fallen.

But the primary cause of all our disasters may be traced to a source even more distant than any yet mentioned; I mean, to the disclosure of our designs to the enemy. How this occurred

I shall not take it upon me to declare, though several rumours bearing at least the guise of probability have been circulated. The attack upon New Orleans was professedly a secret expedition; so secret, indeed, that it was not communicated to the inferior officers and soldiers in the armament till immediately previous to our quitting Jamaica. To the Americans, however, it appears to have been known long before; and hence it was that, instead of taking them unawares, we found them fully prepared for our reception. Nor is this all. It appears difficult to account for the degree of negligence which affected the naval heads of the present expedition, as far as the providing a competent number of boats and small craft to transport the troops is concerned. Throughout the whole fleet, barges enough to carry one-half of the army could not be found; whereas there ought to have been a sufficient quantity to contain not only the entire force, but all its stores and ammunition. To this neglect, indeed, more perhaps than to any other circumstances, is the failure of the attempt to be attributed; since not a doubt can exist that, if General Keane had been enabled to bring the whole of his army to land on the morning of the 23rd, he would have reached New Orleans, without firing a shot, before nightfall. But the opportunity is past, it cannot be recalled, and therefore to point out errors on the part of my countrymen can serve no good end. That the failure is to be lamented no one will deny, since the conquest of New Orleans would have proved beyond all comparison the most valuable acquisition that could be made to the British dominions throughout the whole western hemisphere. In possession of that post we should have kept the entire southern trade of the United States in check, and furnished means of commerce to our own merchants of incalculable value.

The fact, however, is, that when we look back upon the whole series of events produced by the late American war, we shall find little that is likely to flatter our vanity or increase our self-importance. Except a few successes in Canada at its very commencement, and the brilliant inroad upon Washington, it will be found that our arms have been constantly baffled or repulsed on shore; whilst at sea, with the exception of the capture of the Chesapeake and one or two other affairs towards its conclusion, we have been equally unsuccessful. From what cause does this proceed? Not from any inferiority in courage or discipline, because in these particulars British soldiers and sailors will yield to none in the world. There must, then, be some other cause for these misfortunes, and the cause is surely one which has continually baffled all our plans of American warfare.

We have long been habituated to despise the Americans as an enemy unworthy of serious regard. To this alone it is to be attributed that frigates half manned were sent out to cope with ships capable of containing them within their hulls; and to this also the trifling handfuls of troops dispatched to conduct the war by land. Instead of fifteen hundred, had ten thousand men sailed from the Garonne under General Ross, how differently might he have acted! There would have been then no necessity for a re-embarkation after the capture of Washington, and consequently no time given for the defence of Baltimore; but, marching across the country, he might have done to the one city what he did to the other. And it is thus only that a war with America can be successfully carried on. To penetrate up the country amidst pathless forests and boundless deserts, and to aim at permanent conquest, is out of the question. America must be assaulted only on her coasts. Her harbours destroyed, her shipping burned, and her seaport towns laid waste, are the only evils which she has reason to dread; and were a sufficient force embarked with these orders, no American war would be of long continuance.

A melancholy experience has now taught us that such a war must not be entered into, unless it be conducted with spirit; and there is no conducting it with spirit, except with a sufficient numerical force. To the plan proposed of making desert the whole line of coast, it may be objected, that by so doing we should distress individuals, and not the Government. But they who offer this objection, forget the nature both of the people whose cause they plead, and of the Government under which they live. In a democratical Government, the voice of the people must at all times prevail. The members of the House of Representatives are the very persons who, from such proceedings, would suffer most severely, and we all know how far private suffering goes to influence a man's public opinions. Besides, the principle upon which the advocates for the sacredness of private property proceed, is erroneous. Every one will allow that, in absolute monarchies, where war is more properly the pastime of kings than the desire of subjects, non-combatants ought to be dealt with as humanely as possible. Not so, how ever, in States governed by popular assemblies. By compelling the constituents to experience the real hardships and miseries of warfare, you will compel the representatives to a vote of peace; and surely that line of conduct is, upon the whole, most humane, which puts the speediest period to the cruelties of war. There are few men who would not rather endure a raging fever for three days, than a slow and lingering disease for three months. So it is with a democracy at war. Burn their houses, plunder their property, block up their harbours, and destroy their shipping in a few places; and before you have time to proceed to the rest, you will be stopped by entreaties for peace. Whereas, if you do no mischief that can be avoided, if you only fight their fleets and armies wherever you meet them, and suffer the inhabitants to live in undisturbed tranquillity, they will continue their hostilities till they have worn out the means of one party, and greatly weakened those of both.

Should another war break out between Great Britain and America, this is the course to be adopted by the former. Besides which, I humbly conceive that a second attempt might be hazarded upon New Orleans, because the importance of the conquest would authorise almost any sacrifice for its attainment; and once gained, it could easily be defended. The neck of land, upon which it is built, extends in the same form above as below the town; and the same advantages which it holds out to its present defenders would, of course, be afforded to us. A chain of works thrown across from the river to the marsh would render it inaccessible from above; whilst by covering the lakes and the Mississippi with cruisers, all attacks from below would be sufficiently guarded against.

ALSO FROM LEONAUR
AVAILABLE IN SOFTCOVER OR HARDCOVER WITH DUST JACKET

THE COMPLEAT RIFLEMAN HARRIS *by Benjamin Harris as told to & transcribed by Captain Henry Curling*—The adventures of a soldier of the 95th (Rifles) during the Peninsular Campaign of the Napoleonic Wars

WITH WELLINGTON'S LIGHT CAVALRY *by William Tomkinson*—The Experiences of an officer of the 16th Light Dragoons in the Peninsular and Waterloo campaigns of the Napoleonic Wars.

SERGEANT BOURGOGNE *by Adrien Bourgogne*—With Napoleon's Imperial Guard in the Russian Campaign and on the Retreat from Moscow 1812 - 13.

SWORDS OF HONOUR *by Henry Newbolt & Stanley L. Wood*—The Careers of Six Outstanding Officers from the Napoleonic Wars, the Wars for India and the American Civil War, with dozens of illustrations by Stabley L. Wood.

SURTEES OF THE RIFLES *by William Surtees*—A Soldier of the 95th (Rifles) in the Peninsular campaign of the Napoleonic Wars.

ENSIGN BELL IN THE PENINSULAR WAR *by George Bell*—The Experiences of a young British Soldier of the 34th Regiment 'The Cumberland Gentlemen' in the Napoleonic wars.

HUSSAR IN WINTER *by Alexander Gordon*—A British Cavalry Officer during the retreat to Corunna in the Peninsular campaign of the Napoleonic Wars.

NAPOLEONIC WAR STORIES *by Sir Arthur Quiller-Couch*—Tales of soldiers, spies, battles & sieges from the Peninsular & Waterloo campaingns.

JOURNALS OF ROBERT ROGERS OF THE RANGERS *by Robert Rogers*—The exploits of Rogers & the Rangers in his own words during 1755-1761 in the French & Indian War.

KERSHAW'S BRIGADE VOLUME 1 *by D. Augustus Dickert*—Manassas, Seven Pines, Sharpsburg (Antietam), Fredricksburg, Chancellorsville, Gettysburg, Chickamauga, Chattanooga, Fort Sanders & Bean Station..

KERSHAW'S BRIGADE VOLUME 2 *by D. Augustus Dickert*—At the wilderness, Cold Harbour, Petersburg, The Shenandoah Valley and Cedar Creek.

A TIGER ON HORSEBACK *by L. March Phillips*—The Experiences of a Trooper & Officer of Rimington's Guides - The Tigers - during the Anglo-Boer war 1899 - 1902.

AVAILABLE ONLINE AT
www.leonaur.com
AND OTHER GOOD BOOK STORES

ALSO FROM LEONAUR
AVAILABLE IN SOFTCOVER OR HARDCOVER WITH DUST JACKET

CAPTAIN OF THE 95th (Rifles) by *Jonathan Leach*—An officer of Wellington's Sharpshooters during the Peninsular, South of France and Waterloo Campaigns of the Napoleonic Wars.

THE KHAKEE RESSALAH by *Robert Henry Wallace Dunlop*—Service & adventure with the Meerut volunteer horse during the Indian mutiny 1857-1858

BUGLER AND OFFICER OF THE RIFLES by *William Green & Harry Smith* With the 95th (Rifles) during the Peninsular & Waterloo Campaigns of the Napoleonic Wars

BAYONETS, BUGLES AND BONNETS by *James 'Thomas' Todd*—Experiences of hard soldiering with the 71st Foot - the Highland Light Infantry - through many battles of the Napoleonic wars including the Peninsular & Waterloo Campaigns

A NORFOLK SOLDIER IN THE FIRST SIKH WAR by *J W Baldwin*—Experiences of a private of H.M. 9th Regiment of Foot in the battles for the Punjab, India 1845-46

A CAVALRY OFFICER DURING THE SEPOY REVOLT by *A.R.D. Mackenzie*—Experiences with the 3rd Bengal Light Cavalry, the Guides and Sikh Irregular Cavalry from the outbreak to Delhi and Lucknow

THE ADVENTURES OF A LIGHT DRAGOON by *George Farmer & G.R. Gleig*—A cavalryman during the Peninsular & Waterloo Campaigns, in captivity & at the siege of Bhurtpore, India

THE COMPLEAT RIFLEMAN HARRIS by *Benjamin Harris as told to & transcribed by Captain Henry Curling*—The adventures of a soldier of the 95th (Rifles) during the Peninsular Campaign of the Napoleonic Wars

THE RED DRAGOON by *W.J. Adams*—With the 7th Dragoon Guards in the Cape of Good Hope against the Boers & the Kaffir tribes during the 'war of the axe' 1843-48

THE LIFE OF THE REAL BRIGADIER GERARD - Volume 1 - THE YOUNG HUSSAR 1782 - 1807 by *Jean-Baptiste De Marbot*—A French Cavalryman Of the Napoleonic Wars at Marengo, Austerlitz, Jena, Eylau & Friedland

THE LIFE OF THE REAL BRIGADIER GERARD Volume 2 IMPERIAL AIDE-DE-CAMP 1807 - 1811 by *Jean-Baptiste De Marbot*—A French Cavalryman of the Napoleonic Wars at Saragossa, Landshut, Eckmuhl, Ratisbon, Aspern-Essling, Wagram, Busaco & Torres Vedras

AVAILABLE ONLINE AT
www.leonaur.com
AND OTHER GOOD BOOK STORES

Printed in the United Kingdom
by Lightning Source UK Ltd.
121790UK00001B/123/A